Leaving Certificate Examination Papers

English

Higher Level

THE EDUCATIONAL COMPANY OF IRELAND

Leaving Certificate
English Higher Level

Contents

Student Study Essentials

Guide to Better Grades iv

Map your Progress! vii

Online Study Hub – visit **www.edco.ie/onlinestudyhub**

Completed (✓)

2023 – Paper 1 ....(visit www.e-xamit.ie) 1	☐
Paper 2 ....(visit www.e-xamit.ie) 10	☐
2022 – Deferred Paper 1 ....(visit www.e-xamit.ie) 18	☐
Deferred Paper 2 .... (visit www.e-xamit.ie) 27	☐
2022 – Paper 1 ....(visit www.e-xamit.ie) 35	☐
Paper 2 ....(visit www.e-xamit.ie) 44	☐
2021 – Paper 1 ....(visit www.e-xamit.ie) 53	☐
Paper 2 ....(visit www.e-xamit.ie) 62	☐
2020 – Paper 1 ....(visit www.e-xamit.ie) 70	☐
Paper 2 ....(visit www.e-xamit.ie) 79	☐
2019 – Paper 1 ....(visit www.e-xamit.ie) 87	☐
Paper 2 ....(visit www.e-xamit.ie) 96	☐
2018 – Paper 1 104	☐
Paper 2 112	☐

(continued)

			Completed (✓)
2017 –	Paper 1	120	☐
	Paper 2	128	☐
2016 –	Paper 1	135	☐
	Paper 2	143	☐
2015 –	Paper 1	151	☐
	Paper 2	159	☐
2014 –	Paper 1	167	☐
	Paper 2	175	☐
2013 –	Paper 1	183	☐
	Paper 2	191	☐
Sample Paper 1 (A)		198	☐
Sample Paper 2 (A)		206	☐
Sample Paper 3 (B)		213	☐
Sample Paper 4 (B)		220	☐

**Visit www.e-xamit.ie to access Free Online
Tutorials with Sample Answers, Hints and Tips!
(See codes inside)**

Paper 1

Timing the Examination

You have 170 minutes to complete the two sections of the paper: Comprehending and Composing.

Each section carries 100 marks, so it makes sense to allocate your time pretty evenly between the two sections.

A suggested breakdown of your time is:

– 20 minutes for reading and choosing questions.

– 35 minutes on Question A in Section 1, Comprehending.

– 35 minutes on Question B in Section 1, Comprehending.

– 80 minutes on your Composition in Section 2, Composing.

Order in Which to Approach the Paper

The first paper is a thematic paper. Everything on the paper relates to the chosen theme, including the choice of compositions. Think of the paper as a help or resource for yourself.

You can use ideas from the texts in Section 1, Comprehending, in writing your own composition. For this reason it makes sense to do your composition last, after you have looked through the paper and worked on some of the comprehension texts.

Below is a suggested order for approaching the paper:

1. Note the theme of the paper and jot down your initial ideas on this theme.

2. Read the composition assignments. Note both the title and the instruction. Mark the titles that seem inviting.

3. Look at the titles and the introductions to the comprehension texts. Mark the titles that catch your interest.

4. Now read the A and B questions which follow each text. Mark the questions that seem inviting.

By this stage you will have a clearer view of the theme of the paper and the questions you might answer.

5. Now read through the texts quickly, bearing in mind the questions which follow. This will give a clearer focus to your reading.

6. Answer Question A.

7. Answer Question B.

8. Write your Composition.

Comprehending – Question A

Question A is a comprehension question. All Question As are intended to examine how you read – the information you draw from the texts; the inferences you make; the judgements you make on the quality of writing and argumentation.

Keep in mind the idea of critical literacy. Read with an intelligent scepticism in relation to the claims that a writer makes in a text. Bear in mind the context in which the text was written, the audience for whom it was intended and the purpose for which it was written.

Be confident in your own ability to read, to question and to make judgements.

Make sure you answer the question that you are asked and support your answer by reference or quotation.

Be sure to follow any guidelines that you are given.

Comprehending – Question B

In Question B on the comprehension section, you are given the opportunity to demonstrate your understanding of the comprehension text by writing a short piece that arises from the context, content or form of the comprehension text that you have just read.

Read the instructions carefully and make sure that you fulfil the task that is asked of you.

Important considerations for your piece of writing will be:

- Audience.
- Context.
- Form.
- Register.

Write in a way that shows your awareness of how language changes depending on the context in which it is used.

You are not asked for lengthy pieces of writing in Question B, but you are asked to show your awareness of language, as it is used in different settings.

Composing

The composition invites you to engage in a sustained piece of writing related to the theme of the paper. Although there is no recommended length, many students will write between 750 and 1,000 words in the time available.

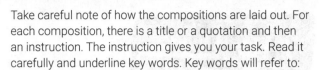

Take careful note of how the compositions are laid out. For each composition, there is a title or a quotation and then an instruction. The instruction gives you your task. Read it carefully and underline key words. Key words will refer to:

Audience or Context – 'school magazine', 'serious newspaper', 'popular magazine'.

Form – 'short story', 'article', 'speech'.

Purpose – 'persuade', 'outline your views', 'encourage readers'.

Register – 'serious, 'humorous'.

Some instructions will be more prescriptive than others. One that contains the words, 'argument' and 'serious magazine' is less open than one which says 'persuasion' and 'magazine'.

An essay founded on argument must have a strong logical thread running through it. An essay that is persuasive may have a strong logical thread, but it may not.

Likewise an instruction that invites you to write a narrative is more open than one which invites you to write a short story.

Some instructions are very open. Take for example an invitation to write an article for a popular magazine, outlining your views on the mobile phone. This article may contain many different strategies and styles of writing. This is perfectly acceptable, as long as you are in control of your writing and stay engaged with the task.

In general the composition is intended to give you an opportunity to show that you can write intelligently, fluently and with a clear sense of purpose, control and enjoyment.

Each year the majority of candidates opt to write a short story. The most important thing to remember is that your writing must be shaped and contain the key elements of the form: a character in a situation; a conflict or dilemma; and a resolution. The writing must create a credible setting and atmosphere. You have to be able to describe; to write convincing dialogue; and reveal the thoughts of the character. Most convincing short stories are based on a single incident.

Many other candidates opt for the Personal Essay. As the name suggests, there are two characteristics of the personal essay. The first is that it is written in essay form – it is not an invitation to write a short story or a speech. The second is that it is personal (without ever becoming too sentimental or cliched) and so it is written in the first person. The Personal Essay often includes personal narrative or anecdote, as well as description, but there must be some reflection there as well.

Paper 2

Timing the Examination

You have 200 minutes to complete the three sections of the paper: The Single Text, The Comparative Study and Poetry.

Section One – The Single Text, carries **60 marks;**

Section Two – The Comparative Study, carries **70 marks;**

Section Three – Poetry, carries **70 marks.**

A suggested breakdown of your time is:

- 15 minutes to read the paper.
- 55 minutes for The Single Text.
- 65 minutes for The Comparative Study.
- 65 Minutes for Poetry (15 minutes for the Unseen Poem, 50 minutes for the question on Prescribed Poetry).

Order in Which to Approach the Paper

This is really a matter of personal choice. The important thing is to give enough time to each question. Don't spend more time on any one question than it is worth in terms of marks.

Section One – Single Text

The Single Text is the text that you need to know inside out. You need to know the story. You need to understand the characters, their relationships and their motivations. You must have a clear appreciation of the world that the characters inhabit. It is important to be clear in your mind about the themes that are explored in the text and the success of failure of the writer in presenting these themes in an interesting way. Finally you must be confident that you have an appreciation of the most important elements in the story telling, elements such as the creation of vivid characters; dramatic moments; the use of symbols or striking patterns of imagery. Knowing the story helps you to provide a context for your answers. However, it is only the focussed retelling of relevant parts of the story that are of interest to the examiner. It is a waste of your time to write unfocused and irrelevant summaries of large parts of the story.

Remember you are asked to show your thoughtful understanding, interpretation and response to the text. Don't be a shrinking violet when it comes to exam time. Express your opinion and do so with forceful honesty, conviction and logic. **A series of short quotation, woven into the fabric of your answer, is better than one or two lengthy quotations,** which interrupt or disrupt your flow. Be sure that you write in a clear and careful manner. Avoid over-elaborate or artificial-sounding language. Avoid cliché and colloquialism. One of the most important exam skills to develop for the single text is the ability to combine a breadth of knowledge with in-depth analysis. The best answers are those which dive down into the text rather than simply skim the surface.

As with all sections of the English examination, read the question on the single text very carefully and make sure you appreciate all the implications in it and address them in your answer. Don't wander off the point. Structure your response, using your knowledge of the language of argument in shaping your answer. The examination invites your personal response. Keep 'I' at the heart of your answer – a thoughtful, engaged and responsive 'I'.

Most students answer on Shakespeare in the Single Text. If you don't, make sure you include Shakespeare in your Comparative Study answer.

Section Two – The Comparative Study

The Comparative Study is not the Single Study multiplied by three. There is no onus on you to know each of the three texts on your comparative study course in the same depth as your single text. The onus is, however, to use the modes of comparison as a means of comparing the three texts from a limited number of perspectives, using key moments from each text to illustrate your argument.

The questions for the comparative study will be general. Your task is to answer the question using the particular texts you have chosen. The use of key moments will ground your answer in the text and help you avoid the temptation to tell the story of the text in your answer.

As with all the questions on your English papers, make sure that you understand the task in the question. Fulfil the task expressing your personal views and opinions. Keep the 'I' at the heart of your answer. Show the examiner that you have engaged with the texts and thought about them. Express your thoughts in a clear style. It is really important to structure your answer into a logical and coherent shape. Write with force and enthusiasm.

Section Three – Poetry

Unseen poem

The Unseen Poem in the poetry section gives you a chance to demonstrate that you can read and answer on a poem in a confident, thoughtful way. The questions will ask you to consider such things as:

– The various patterns in a poem.

– The imagery and its effect.

– The language of the poem.

– The feelings that the poem conveys.

– Your response to the poem.

Be confident in your ability to read a poem. Express your ideas clearly and support them with references or quotations from the poem.

As with all other questions, the examination is testing your response. Be clear, be confident. Be yourself.

Prescribed poetry

The questions on the prescribed poetry offer you a chance to write at length on one of the poets on your course. Questions will address such things as: the poet's themes and concerns; the world of the poems; the poet's life and times; the poetic voice of the poet and his or her style and language. Tackle the task with confidence and show evidence that you have read and responded to the poetry in a thoughtful and engaged manner. As with the single text, use quotations to support your ideas and point-of-view. Make sure that your enthusiasm for the subject is well-managed and controlled. Be sure that your answer has a clear structure.

In no other area of English is personal response so important. So keep the 'I' at the heart of all you write, without, for a moment, losing sight of the task that the question asks you to fulfil.

Tick each question as you complete it and again once you have finished an entire exam paper.

LEAVING CERTIFICATE ENGLISH (HL)	TIME	2023	2022 Deferred Paper	2022	2021	2020	2019	2018	2017	2016	2015	2014	2013	Sample Paper 1 (A)	Sample Paper 2 (A)	Sample Paper 3 (B)	Sample Paper 4 (B)
Paper 1 (200 marks)	**2 hrs 50 mins**																
Read over paper	5 mins																
Section 1 – Comprehending (100 marks) Answer **Two** Questions from this Section. Answer a Question A (50 marks) on one text and a Question B (50 marks) on a different text	35 mins per question																
TEXT 1																	
Question A																	
Question B																	
TEXT 2																	
Question A																	
Question B																	
TEXT 3																	
Question A																	
Question B																	
TEXT 4																	
Question A																	
Question B																	
Section 2 – Composing (100 marks) Answer **One** Question from this Section	80 mins																
Question 1																	
Question 2																	
Question 3																	
Question 4																	
Question 5																	
Question 6																	
Question 7																	

(Continued)

Map Your Progress!

Map Your Progress!

LEAVING CERTIFICATE ENGLISH (HL)	TIME	2023	2022 Deferred Paper	2022	2021	2020	2019	2018	2017	2016	2015	2014	2013	Sample Paper 1 (A)	Sample Paper 2 (A)	Sample Paper 3 (B)	Sample Paper 4 (B)
Paper 2 (200 marks)	**3 hrs 20 mins**																
Read over paper	15 mins																
Section 1 – The Single Text (60 marks) Answer **One** Question from this Section	55 mins																
Question A																	
Question B																	
Question C																	
Question D																	
Question E																	
Section 2 – The Comparative Study (70 marks) Answer **One** Question from this Section	65 mins																
Question A																	
Question B																	

(Continued)

Leaving Cert Grades & CAO Points Calculation Chart

Higher			Ordinary		
% marks	Grade	Points	% marks	Grade	Points
90–100	H1	100			
80 < 90	H2	88			
70 < 80	H3	77			
60 < 70	H4	66			
50 < 60	H5	56	90–100	O1	56
40 < 50	H6	46	80 < 90	O2	46
30 < 40	H7	37	70 < 80	O3	37
0 < 30	H8	0	60 < 70	O4	28
			50 < 60	O5	20
			40 < 50	O6	12
			30 < 40	O7	0
			0 < 30	O8	0

Source: CAO

Progress Tracker Table

LEAVING CERTIFICATE ENGLISH (HL)	TIME	2023	2022 Deferred Paper	2022	2021	2020	2019	2018	2017	2016	2015	2014	2013	Sample Paper 1 (A)	Sample Paper 2 (A)	Sample Paper 3 (B)	Sample Paper 4 (B)
Section 3 – Poetry (70 marks)	65 mins (15 mins – Unseen Poem, 50 mins – Prescribed Poem)																
Question A – Unseen Poem																	
Question B – Prescribed Poetry																	
Exam Complete																	

Study Hub

Your free online guide to smarter study.

Visit

www.edco.ie/onlinestudyhub

Remember

- Paper 1 is a thematic paper, with everything on it relating to the chosen theme. You should familiarise yourself with each of the texts on the paper before beginning your answers. You must attempt both sections of the paper. Answer Three Questions in total from Paper 1. Questions A and B follow each text. Answer a Question A on one text and a Question B on a different text. Note: Questions A and B cannot be answered on the same text. Answer One Question from Section 2. Paper 1, Section 1 has not contained a Text 4 since 2001, however, it is included here to assist you to Map Your Progress!

- In Paper 2, you must attempt one question from Section 1, one question from Section 2, one question on the Unseen Poem from Section 3 A and one question on Prescribed Poetry from Section 3 B.

- In Paper 2, you <u>must</u> answer on Shakespearean Drama. You may do so in either Section 1 (The Single Text) or in Section 2 (The Comparative Study).

Map Your Progress!

Coimisiún na Scrúduithe Stáit
State Examinations Commission

LEAVING CERTIFICATE EXAMINATION, 2023

English - Higher Level - Paper 1

Total Marks: 200

Wednesday, 7 June – Morning, 9.30 – 12.20

- This paper is divided into two sections,
  Section I COMPREHENDING and Section II COMPOSING.
- The paper contains **three** texts on the general theme of **BETWEEN TWO WORLDS.**
- Candidates should familiarise themselves with each of the texts before beginning their answers.
- Both sections of this paper (COMPREHENDING and COMPOSING) must be attempted.
- Each section carries 100 marks.

SECTION I – COMPREHENDING

- Two Questions, A and B, follow each text.
- Candidates must answer a Question A on one text and a Question B on a different text. Candidates must answer only one Question A and only one Question B.

N.B. Candidates may NOT answer a Question A and a Question B on the same text.

SECTION II – COMPOSING

- Candidates must write on **one** of the compositions 1 – 7.

> Do not hand this up.
>
> This document will not be returned to the
> State Examinations Commission.

1

TEXT 1 – BETWEEN TWO WORLDS: VILLAGE AND CITY

This text is based on an edited extract from *Gravel Heart,* **a novel by Abdulrazak Gurnah, 2021 Nobel Prize winner for literature. In this extract Salim, from a small island village in Zanzibar, comes to stay with his uncle in London to further his education. He doesn't know how to belong in this strange city and feels cut off from the world he has left behind.**

When I went to live with Uncle Amir in London, it was his wish that I should study for a career in business. "In your circumstances, it is the perfect option and it will allow you to work anywhere in the world. Make money! Think of the outcomes: accountancy, management, consultancy, and at the end of it all plenty of money in the bank."

It would have sounded cowardly to tell him that I should have preferred to study literature. By the time I left for London, I had worked my way through most of my father's books, had made good progress through the school library shelves, had borrowed and exchanged books with friends, and I thought of myself as someone with proven credentials as a future student of literature. When I came to London I realised how unimpressive my credentials were, how much there was to read, how much there was to work through. Uncle Amir had different plans for me and I did not have the courage to say anything about how I might have preferred to proceed with my life.

I was moved by the pleasure they took in my arrival. They both beamed smiles at me and Auntie Asha spoke to me as if I was a diffident younger brother who needed to be brought out of himself. I was too flustered to take in everything immediately, but I noticed the amplitude of space and the expensive furnishings. Auntie Asha took me upstairs to show me my room which was luxurious: a large bed, a dark wardrobe the depth of a coffin, a wide desk, a chest of drawers, a bookshelf, a comfortable reading chair, and still enough space in the middle for a rug. A whole family lived in a room of this size where I had come from. My suitcase, which I

Gravel Heart by Abdulrazak Gurnah, reproduced by the permission of Bloomsbury.

had bought new just before I left, looked cheap and flimsy and tiny on that rug, like a cardboard box. I sat on the bed when I was left alone, looking around the room, gazing out of the darkened window then at the clean bare desk with its angled lamp, and I smiled. That is the desk where I will sit and write to Mama about the wonders I encounter and I won't allow the thought of my ignorance to discourage me. I allowed this resolution to overcome the slight feeling of panic I sensed at the edge of my mind. What was I doing here?

Dear Mama,
I hope you are well. It is now October and I started college last week. London is full of people from everywhere in the world. I just had not expected to see that, Indians, Arabs, Africans, Chinese, and I don't know where all the European people come from but they are not all English. When a double-decker bus goes by and you see the faces through the window, it is like a glimpse of a page in an illustrated children's encyclopaedia under the title People of the World. Everywhere you go,

you have to push your way through crowds and hold on to your possessions. To be honest, I think I'm scared of that press of people. It gets so crowded on the underground that I feel as if I can't breathe. Trains that travel under the ground! We are so backward! You just cannot imagine how enormous the city is. Love, Salim.

London terrified me so much. The streets confused me. The buses and taxis and cars roared past and churned up my gut. The rush of people and vehicles muddled my sense of direction and panicked me. I felt as if the city despised me, as if I were a tiresome and timorous child who had wandered unwelcome out of the dust and rubble of his puny island shanty into this place where boldness and greed and swagger were required for survival.

Abdulrazak Gurnah
© Mark Pringle

Dear Mama,
I stood on ice today. I woke up in the morning to a deep hush, and went to the window to look out at the back garden, and everything was changed. All the neighbouring roofs were covered with snow and everywhere looked so clean. The pavements were covered too, which was beautiful to walk on at first, crunchy and almost silent, but the snow soon became dirty and perilous from so many feet and from the wash of cars driving by. But that first moment when I stood on ice, I will never forget that. The crisp air made breathing easier. I think today was the happiest day I have had here. Love, Salim.

I learnt to live in London, to avoid being intimidated by crowds and by rudeness, to avoid curiosity, not to feel desolate at hostile stares and to walk purposefully wherever I went. I learnt to live with the cold and the dirt, and to evade the angry students at college with their swagger and their sense of grievance. I learnt to live with the chaotic languages of London which did not speak to each other. I tried but could not join in the city's human carnival. I feared the silent empty streets at night and always hurried home.

From *Gravel Heart* by Abdulrazak Gurnah, reproduced by the permission of Bloomsbury.

N.B. Candidates may NOT answer Question A and Question B on the same text.

QUESTION A – 50 Marks

(i)   Based on your reading of TEXT 1, explain three insights you gain into Salim's character. Support your answer with reference to the text.   (15)

(ii)   To what extent do you agree with Uncle Amir's view that making money is an important consideration when choosing a course to study in college? Develop three points to support your response.   (15)

(iii)   Features of both narrative writing and descriptive writing are used effectively by Abdulrazak Gurnah to capture the world Salim encounters in this passage. Discuss this statement, supporting your response with reference to four language features in the text. You may include features of narrative writing, features of descriptive writing, or both in your discussion.   (20)

QUESTION B – 50 Marks

Imagine you are Salim and you have been in London for over a year. Write a new personal **letter** to your mother in which you: describe a number of experiences you have had that you believe will fascinate your mother, reflect on both the positive and negative insights you have gained into human nature as an outsider in London, and consider some of the ways you believe your experience in this city has altered you as a person.

TEXT 2 – BETWEEN TWO WORLDS: THROUGH WORDS AND PICTURES

Text 2 consists of two elements. The first is an edited text by Henry Eliot entitled, *This Must be the Place* which focuses on literary locations. The second is an iconic photograph, taken in 1907 and published in *Time* magazine's 100 most influential, historical pictures. Both elements illustrate how we can experience different worlds through words and pictures.

As a child I once found a set of old photographs of my home, with unknown people posing. I stood in the exact same spots, imagining a shiver of communication. I have since had the same experience surveying the fields of Waterloo from Napoleon's headquarters, or looking up at the empty sky above Ground Zero. Sharing the same airspace as another, from another time, standing on the same patch of the planet, is a profound feeling. It is similar to the effect of reading a novel: your imagination bridges the gulf between someone else's experience and your own, and expands your understanding in the process.

That's why I get a particular thrill from visiting literary locations. Reading is a creative collaboration, so being in the environment that inspired a novelist enhances both the place and the novel: the setting is overlaid with the events of the book and the book becomes more tangible and memorable as a result. Lyme Regis, in Dorset, for example, is famous for its ancient harbour wall, the Cobb. I am particularly fond of a set of precarious steps on the Cobb, known as "Granny's Teeth".

They recall that dramatic moment at the centre of Jane Austen's *Persuasion*, when Louisa Musgrove runs up them so as to be caught by Captain Wentworth: "He put out his hands; she was too precipitate by half a second, she fell on the pavement on the Lower Cobb, and was taken up lifeless!"

London, where I live, is especially rich in literary associations and sometimes they overlap, creating unexpected contrasts. The top of Primrose Hill, for instance, is the location of both the Twilight Bark in *The Hundred and One Dalmatians* and where the last Martians are torn apart by dogs in HG Wells's *The War of the Worlds.*

Reading certainly enriches the places you know, and it can overpower less familiar settings. I don't know Paris or St Petersburg as well as I know London but since visiting those cities I have read Proust's *In Search of Lost Time* and Dostoevsky's *Crime and Punishment,* and my sense of both places has radically altered. In my mind the streets of Paris now ring with carriages ferrying beautiful people between glittering salons and St Petersburg is sweating in claustrophobic self-recrimination. In many ways the worlds of these books have become more vivid than my own fading memories.

Conversely, I had read Kafka's *The Castle* and Steinbeck's *East of Eden* before I visited Prague or the Salinas valley in California, so from the start both locations were deeply coloured by my experience of those books. Prague was mysterious and impenetrable, with streets and cemeteries huddled around the castle on the hill, whereas Salinas was epic and open, a great canvas on which narratives might play out.

Of course, there are many locations around the world that I have never visited and yet they still form strong impressions in my mind. One of the joys of reading is that it gives us this strong physical sense of a place we may never visit. For example, I know how it feels to walk the dark corridors of Gormenghast Castle; I know the dust of its rooms, its towers and courtyards and its fields of stone in the sky, because Mervyn Peake's prose is so evocative, but I will never visit because it's a pure fantasy.

Often, I select my next book based on where I am. In 2015, on a sailing holiday in Greece, I read the *Argonautica* by Apollonius; it was wonderful to read about Greek heroes, clashing rocks, harpies, monsters and armies sprung from dragon's teeth with the gentle sound of lapping waves and a soft pine-and-salt tang in the air, just as Apollonius would have known.

This photograph, taken in 1907 by Alfred Stieglitz, shows people on board a ship, migrating for work.

'The Steerage' by Alfred Stieglitz

N.B. Candidates may NOT answer Question A and Question B on the same text.

QUESTION A – 50 Marks

(i) Based on your reading of TEXT 2 on page 4, explain three insights you gain, from Henry Eliot, into how reading novels can be an enriching experience. Support your answer with reference to the text. (15)

(ii) Do you think that *Between Two Worlds* (the theme for this paper) would be a good title for Alfred Stieglitz's photograph above? Develop three points to support your response. In your response you should consider the subject matter and visual aspects of the photograph. (15)

(iii) Features of both personal writing and informative writing are used effectively by Henry Eliot (in the written text) to explore the relationship between works of fiction and the worlds in which they are set. Discuss this statement, supporting your response with reference to four language features in the text. You may include features of personal writing, features of informative writing, or both in your discussion. (20)

QUESTION B – 50 Marks

You have been asked to write a **personal reflection** for an educational history magazine. The reflection should recall an experience you had of visiting a place of historic interest. In the reflection you should: outline the expectations you had before your visit to the place of historic interest, describe some of the thoughts and feelings you had in response to this place during the visit and, argue the case for making trips to historic places compulsory for students in Irish schools today.

TEXT 3 – BETWEEN TWO WORLDS: HUMAN AND TECHNOLOGICAL

TEXT 3 consists of two edited articles on the subject of Artificial Intelligence (AI) published in July 2022: an introduction from Patricia Scanlon, Ireland's first Artificial Intelligence Ambassador, published in *The Irish Times* and a feature by Ben Spencer printed in *The Sunday Times* magazine entitled, "I'm better than the Bard."

Patricia Scanlon:

Artificial Intelligence (AI) is driving the fourth Industrial Revolution, building on the impact of steam power, electricity and digital technology.

Every time you speak to Siri, use predictive text or scroll through recommendations on your Netflix or Facebook newsfeed, you are interacting with AI. It is widely used in the world today but many people are still unclear about what AI is and isn't.

One definition of AI is the ability of a machine to perform tasks that require human intelligence. Science fiction is littered with tales of intelligent machines, from *2001: A Space Odyssey* to *Star Trek*. In these storylines the machine has intelligence equal to or surpassing humans; consciousness and the ability to learn, solve problems and plan for the future. This form of AI is known in the scientific community as "generalised".

Some scientists believe it could be decades before generalised AI becomes a reality, while others doubt it ever can. Super AI, where AI surpasses complex human intelligence, is still purely speculative.

AI systems we interact with today are capable of performing a single or limited number of tasks. Within their field, these systems are powerful, can replicate human performance and in many cases even outperform humans. But it is worth noting that once these systems are presented with a situation that falls outside their learned space, they fail.

AI will continue to transform how we live and work into the future. That's why ethical approaches to AI are needed and are in the process of being regulated via the EU Artificial Intelligence Act for the benefit of society and to build trust in AI.

Ben Spencer:

Artificial Intelligence is very good at imitation, but could it one day surpass our abilities as writers, as artists, as journalists? These questions have dominated discussions about AI for decades. George Orwell and Roald Dahl were obsessed with the idea that machines would one day replace them.

In 1949 the neuroscientist Geoffrey Jefferson, in a lecture at Manchester University, said: "Not until a machine can write a sonnet or compose a concerto because of thoughts and emotions felt, and not by the chance fall of symbols, could we agree that machine equals brain." Alan Turing, the renowned codebreaker, said in a published response that the true test of artificial intelligence lies in whether humans can distinguish robot from human.

Does modern AI pass the test?

In the past five years AI has been revolutionised by a series of new machine-learning models – most notably GPT-3, made by OpenAI (founded by Elon Musk and developed with Microsoft investment). I assumed that a Shakespearean sonnet would be the simplest for a computer program to impersonate because it follows strict rules: 14 lines, each of 10 syllables in iambic pentameter; a consistent rhyming pattern.

With kind permission from Patricia Scanlon.

So how did it do?

The words GPT-3 produced were pretty convincing: "Thou art the sun to my day, the stars to my night/The hope to my despair, the faith to my doubt/The love to my heart, the breath to my life." The metaphors make sense and it's quite poetic, but it is 17 lines long, the metre is all wrong and it doesn't rhyme. It is not a sonnet.

GPT-3 is a hugely efficient wordsmith, good at writing the next sentence, but it has no ability to reflect on what it has written as a whole. That means it is very good at producing a short extract of about 200 to 300 words, but beyond that loses track of what it has said and meanders.

I experimented with using GPT-3 to produce a news report on Covid booster vaccines. At first glance the output was fairly convincing, listing the pros and cons of tweaking vaccines to match new variants. It even included a quote from a US health official. Yet the quote was made up.

Mike Sharples, Professor of Educational Technology at the Open University, stresses that this is where the danger lies: "It has no knowledge of ethics (morality), of decency, of the law."

Julian Togelius, an AI researcher at New York University, said of GPT-3: "It performs like a clever student who hasn't done their reading, trying to chance their way through an exam. Some well-known facts, some half-truths and some straight lies are strung together."

Professor Sharples puts it a different way. "You've got this dangerous situation, where you've got machines that can get basic facts wrong, or invent studies to prove their point. They are amoral. To be truly intelligent, truly useful and truly ethical AI needs to merge two functions, it needs to combine the ability to reflect and the ability to perform."

N.B. Candidates may NOT answer Question A and Question B on the same text.

QUESTION A – 50 Marks

(i) Based on your reading of both articles in TEXT 3, explain three insights you gain into the world of Artificial Intelligence. Support your answer with reference to the text. (15)

(ii) Do you find yourself in agreement with the view expressed in both articles in TEXT 3 that an ethical (moral) approach to the development of Artificial Intelligence is needed? Develop three points to support your response. (15)

(iii) Features of both persuasive writing and informative writing are used effectively in TEXT 3 to give a clear and engaging perspective into the world of Artificial Intelligence. Discuss this statement, supporting your response with reference to four language features. You may include features of persuasive language, features of informative language, or both in your discussion. You may refer to either or both of the writers in your response. (20)

QUESTION B – 50 Marks

It is Science Week and you have been asked to write an **article** for your school's website about the increasing role played by technology in schools. In your article you should: describe some of the positive ways technology is utilised in schools today, discuss whether or not, in your view, technology can be a negative influence in schools, and speculate about the role you think technology will play in schools in the future. Your article may be serious or humorous or both.

SECTION II   COMPOSING   (100 marks)

Write a composition on **any one** of the assignments that appear in **bold print** below.

Each composition carries 100 marks.

The composition assignments are intended to reflect language study in the areas of information, argument, persuasion, narration, and the aesthetic use of language.

1.   In TEXT 2, Henry Eliot describes Prague as "mysterious and impenetrable".

   Write a short story which features a confused character in a mysterious setting.

2.   TEXT 1 gives us the protagonist's view of the city of London as he encountered it.

   Write a feature article, for a popular magazine, describing your hometown, city, village or area, in which you consider some of the following: the place, its people, values, atmosphere and general way of life.

3.   In TEXT 1, Salim makes a resolution and refuses to be discouraged.

   Write a personal essay in which you reflect on an occasion or occasions when you made a resolution and refused to be discouraged.

4.   TEXT 3 expresses concern about a world that, "has no knowledge of ethics (morality), of decency, of the law".

   You are taking part in an international debating competition where the motion is: "Society today lacks ethics (morality), decency and respect for the law." Write your speech for or against this motion.

5.   In TEXT 1, Salim tells us that he did not have the courage to challenge his uncle's plans for him.

   Write a short story that features a complex relationship between two characters, where one character disagrees completely with the views of the other.

6.   In TEXT 2, Henry Eliot describes how he gets, "a particular thrill from visiting literary locations".

   Write a personal essay in which you describe and reflect on some of the things that bring excitement and wonder into your life.

7.   TEXT 3 refers to George Orwell and Roald Dahl who were, in different ways, influential writers in the twentieth century.

   **Write a discursive essay about the impact of influential individuals in today's world.
   Your chosen individuals may have positive or negative impacts or a combination of both.**

Acknowledgements

Text 1: Gurnah, Abdulzarak. Gravel Heart. London. Bloomsbury Publishing. 2017. Reproduced by the permission of Bloomsbury.
Images: www.bloomsbury.com/uk/gravel-heart-9781408881309/, reproduced by permission of Bloomsbury; Mark Pringle

Text 2: Eliot, Henry. 'This must be the place'. The Guardian Review. April 2021
Image: https://en.wikipedia.org/wiki/The_Steerage#/media/File:Alfred_Stieglitz_-_The_Steerage_-_Google_Art_Project.jpg

Text 3: Scanlon, Patricia. 'It could be decades before science fiction-inspired tales of intelligent machines become a reality' The Irish Times 2022; Spencer, Ben. 'I'm better than the Bard' The Sunday Times, Culture. 2022
Images: www.technotification.com/2021/06/4-ways-artificial-intelligence-helps-sales-teams.html; https://myhomeworkwriters.com/artificial-intelligence-be-unbiased/

Do not hand this up.
This document will not be returned to the
State Examinations Commission.

Leaving Certificate – Higher Level

English

Wednesday 7 June
Morning 9.30 – 12.20

Coimisiún na Scrúduithe Stáit
State Examinations Commission

LEAVING CERTIFICATE EXAMINATION, 2023

English - Higher Level - Paper 2

Total Marks: 200

Thursday, 8 June – Afternoon, 2.00 – 5.20

Candidates must attempt the following:

- **ONE** question from SECTION I – The Single Text
- **ONE** question from SECTION II – The Comparative Study
- **ONE** question on the Unseen Poem from SECTION III – Poetry
- **ONE** question on Prescribed Poetry from SECTION III – Poetry

N.B. Candidates must answer on Shakespearean Drama.

They may do so in SECTION I, The Single Text (Macbeth) or in Section II, The Comparative Study (Macbeth, Othello).

INDEX OF SINGLE TEXTS

All the Light We Cannot See	Page - 2
A Doll's House	Page - 2
Macbeth	Page - 2
Frankenstein	Page - 3
The Picture of Dorian Gray	Page - 3

> Do not hand this up.
>
> This document will not be returned to the State Examinations Commission.

SECTION I   THE SINGLE TEXT   (60 marks)

Candidates must answer **one** question from this section (**A – E**).

A   ALL THE LIGHT WE CANNOT SEE – Anthony Doerr

(i)   In your opinion, to what extent do innate personal qualities or environmental factors, or both, shape the behaviour of at **least two** characters in *All the Light We Cannot See*?

Develop your discussion with reference to Doerr's novel.

OR

(ii)   "We learn many interesting lessons from Doerr's exploration of resilience and resistance in *All the Light We Cannot See*."

Discuss this statement, developing your response with reference to Doerr's novel.

B   A DOLL'S HOUSE – Henrik Ibsen

(i)   "Torvald Helmer is a complex and tragic character who evokes both disdain and sympathy in the audience."

To what extent do you agree or disagree with this statement? Develop your discussion with reference to Ibsen's play, *A Doll's House*.

OR

(ii)   To what extent does Ibsen's use of dialogue and symbolism in *A Doll's House* increase or diminish the impact of this play on you?

Develop your discussion with reference to Ibsen's play.

C   MACBETH – William Shakespeare

(i)   "Macbeth's unstable and tragic identity is shaped by a variety of ambiguities and complexities in his character."

Discuss this statement, developing your response with reference to Shakespeare's play, *Macbeth*.

OR

(ii)   "Shakespeare makes effective use of Lady Macbeth and the Witches to heighten the dramatic impact of his play *Macbeth* in a variety of ways."

Discuss this statement, developing your response with reference to Shakespeare's play, *Macbeth*.

D   FRANKENSTEIN – Mary Shelley

(i)   In your opinion, to what extent do innate personal qualities or environmental factors, or both, shape the behaviour of at **least two** characters in *Frankenstein?*

Develop your discussion with reference to Shelley's novel.

OR

(ii)   "We learn many interesting lessons from Shelley's exploration of companionship and friendship in *Frankenstein*."

Discuss this statement, developing your response with reference to Shelley's novel.

E   THE PICTURE OF DORIAN GRAY – Oscar Wilde

(i)   In your opinion, to what extent do innate personal qualities or environmental factors, or both, shape the behaviour of at **least two** characters in *The Picture of Dorian Gray*?

Develop your discussion with reference to Wilde's novel.

OR

(ii)   To what extent does Wilde's use of social satire and gothic darkness in *The Picture of Dorian Gray* increase or diminish the impact of this novel on you?

Develop your discussion with reference to Wilde's novel.

SECTION II   THE COMPARATIVE STUDY   (70 marks)

Candidates must answer **one** question from **either A** – General Vision and Viewpoint
or B – Literary Genre **or C** – Theme or Issue.

In your answer you may not use the text you have answered on in **Section I** – The Single Text.

All texts used in this section must be prescribed for comparative study for this year's
examination. Candidates may refer to only one film in the course of their answers.

Please note:
- Questions in this section use the word **text** to refer to all the different kinds of texts
  available for study on this course.
- When used, the word **reader** includes viewers of films and theatre audiences.
- When used, the term **technique** is understood to include techniques employed by all
  writers and directors of films.
- When used, the word **author** is understood to include all writers and directors of films.
- When used, the word **character** is understood to refer to both real people and fictional
  characters in texts.

A   GENERAL VISION AND VIEWPOINT

1. (a)   To what extent does the level of compassion and kindness, evident in **one** text on
   your comparative course, influence your sense of the general vision and viewpoint
   in that text? Develop your response with reference to your chosen text.   (30)

   (b)   Compare the extent to which the levels of compassion and kindness, evident in
   two other texts on your comparative course, influence your sense of the general
   vision and viewpoint in these texts. Develop your response with reference to your
   chosen texts.   (40)

OR

2. Compare how the response of characters to personal or societal crises, in **at least two**
   texts on your comparative course, influence your sense of the general vision and
   viewpoint. Develop your response with reference to your chosen texts. In your response
   you may discuss personal or societal crises, or both.   (70)

B   LITERARY GENRE

1.   (a)   In the case of **one** text on your comparative course, discuss how the author employs a variety of techniques to heighten or lessen your empathy with a central character in that text. Develop your response with reference to your chosen text.   (30)

      (b)   In the case of **two other** texts you studied on your comparative course, compare how each of the authors employ a variety of techniques to heighten or lessen your empathy with a central character in these texts. Develop your response with reference to your chosen texts.
             You may refer to the same or different techniques in relation to each of your chosen texts. You may refer to the same or different techniques to those you referred to in 1. (a) above.   (40)

OR

2.   Compare how the authors, in **at least two** texts on your comparative course, use a a variety of techniques skilfully to produce a riveting climax in each of these texts. You may refer to the same or different techniques in relation to each text. Develop your response with reference to your chosen texts.   (70)

C   THEME OR ISSUE

1.   (a)   In the case of **one** text on your comparative course, discuss how contradictory aspects of human nature emerge from a study of a particular theme or issue. Develop your response with reference to your chosen text.   (30)

      (b)   Compare the extent to which contradictory aspects of human nature emerge from a study of the same theme or issue discussed in 1. (a) above, in **two other** texts on your comparative course. Develop your response with reference to your chosen texts.   (40)

OR

2.   Compare how comprehensively similar or different ethical (moral) questions are explored in the treatment of the same theme or issue, in **at least two** texts on your comparative course. Develop your response with reference to your chosen texts.   (70)

Candidates must answer **A** – Unseen Poem **and** B – Prescribed Poetry.

A   UNSEEN POEM (20 marks)

Read the following poem by Victoria Kennefick and answer **either** Question **1 or** Question **2** which follow.

2023 P2

Guest Room

I change the duvet cover like she showed me,
inside-out, corner-to-corner; lift it over
my head, seams must be flush.
I fold a pyramid of towels jewelled
with tiny soaps, body lotions borrowed
from hotels, the red hot-water-bottle
I'll fill later – her rubber husband.
I *Shake n' Vac* the carpet forest fresh; suck
spiders' webs from each corner, grey
and fuzzy, thick as pelts.

My mother's perfume sniffs out
that I did not iron the sheets.
Her nightdress pressed into a perfect square,
a village of potions on the bedside locker.
My heart sags, an empty hammock
yawning for the cradle of her arms,
the animal comfort of her wolf-fur
coat. I hear her pottering in my kitchen,
tidying. I turn out the light; night
cracks its knuckles.

Victoria Kennefick

Guest Room by Victoria Kennefick (Banshee Lit, 2015).

---

1. (a) What impression do you form of the daughter in this poem?   (10)

     (b) Did the poet's use of language in the above poem add to its impact on you?
         Develop two points with reference to the poem in your response.   (10)

OR

2. *"Guest Room* is a fascinating exploration of the complex relationship between mother
     and daughter." Do you agree or disagree with this statement? Develop your response
     with reference to both the subject matter and style of the poem.   (20)

B   PRESCRIBED POETRY (50 marks)

Candidates must answer **one** of the following questions (1 – 5).

1.   Derek Mahon

"Mahon's evocative imagery conveys thematic concerns that are haunted by suggestions of darkness and anxiety."

Discuss the extent to which you agree or disagree with the above statement, developing your response with reference to the poems by Derek Mahon on your Leaving Certificate English course.

2.   Patrick Kavanagh

How successfully, in your opinion, does Kavanagh employ both a lyrical style and a celebratory tone to elevate the mundane realism of life in his work?

Develop your response with reference to the poetry by Patrick Kavanagh on your Leaving Certificate English course.

3.   Paula Meehan

"Meehan employs vibrant and forceful language skilfully to challenge the often-oppressive forces identified in her poetry."

Discuss the extent to which you agree or disagree with the above statement, developing your response with reference to the poems by Paula Meehan on your Leaving Certificate English course.

4.   John Donne

"Donne makes effective use of inventive and paradoxical language to explore the human condition in his poetry."

Discuss this statement with reference to the poetry by John Donne on your Leaving Certificate English course.

5.   Adrienne Rich

"A powerful sense of sadness is conveyed in Rich's poetry through her exposure of the flawed nature of our existence."

To what extent do you agree or disagree with the above statement? You should refer to both the language and the themes in the poetry by Adrienne Rich on your Leaving Certificate English course.

Do not hand this up.

This document will not be returned to the State Examinations Commission.

Leaving Certificate – Higher Level

English

Thursday 8 June
Afternoon 2.00 – 5.20

Coimisiún na Scrúduithe Stáit
State Examinations Commission

LEAVING CERTIFICATE EXAMINATION

English - Higher Level - Paper 1

Total Marks: 140

Duration: 2 hours 50 minutes

- This paper is divided into two sections,
  Section I COMPREHENDING and Section II COMPOSING.
- The paper contains **three** texts on the general theme of **IRISH WRITERS**.
- Candidates should familiarise themselves with each of the texts before beginning their answers.
- Both sections of this paper (COMPREHENDING and COMPOSING) must be attempted.
- Section I, Comprehending, carries 40 marks.
- Section II, Composing, carries 100 marks.

SECTION I – COMPREHENDING

- Two Questions, A and B, follow each text.
- Candidates must answer **ONE** question in Section I:
  either one Question A **OR one** Question B on **ONE** text.

SECTION II – COMPOSING

- Candidates must write on **one** of the compositions 1 – 7.

Do not hand this up.

This document will not be returned to the State Examinations Commission

TEXT 1 – CIARAN CARTY MEETS PAULA MEEHAN

This edited text is adapted from an interview conducted with poet, Paula Meehan. It appears in Ciaran Carty's collection of interviews entitled, *Writer to Writer, The Republic of Elsewhere*.

It's more than 40 years, and many books, since Paula Meehan emerged from childhood in the inner-city Dublin tenements to give voice to the disenfranchised everywhere. She does this less in anger than with compassion and an intuitive understanding that, through verse, she imbues their lives and memories with mythic dignity. Eavan Boland marvelled at Meehan's "wonderful zest and warmth of tone", noting that her "themes are daring and open up new areas for her own work as well as for contemporary Irish poetry". To English poet Carol Ann Duffy she is "that rare and precious thing – a vocational poet of courage and integrity".

Photo © Dave Meehan, reprinted with permission.

2022 P1 DEFERRED

Born in 1955, she was brought up by her grandparents while her parents were looking for work in England. "We lived on the corner of Sean McDermott Street and Gardiner Street, which is gone now. My childhood city is practically obliterated, the last coherent community in the North inner city. The people had nothing, but they had a sense of sharing. I grew up in an oral tradition. I got my language there. I'm not nostalgic for the poverty, but the attempt to alleviate those terrible living conditions led to much displacement and breaking apart of the community."

Paula lives in Baldoyle with poet and broadcaster Theo Dorgan, whose childhood in Cork in many ways parallels her own. "I'm the eldest from a family of six, he's the eldest of fifteen. He had to take responsibility from an early age. There's something fearless about him. He understands people and sees something in everyone, yet at the same time knows when to remain detached."

Paula's grandfather taught her to read and write. "Without that I don't know how I'd have survived school. Underlying everything was a sense that girls didn't need an education. We were learning the skills for young girls to go into service or factories. So being able to read and write from the start was like a weapon. It gave me independence."

She moved to Finglas as a teenager. "There were bands everywhere. Music was a great unifying culture. We were the first global generation. We felt connected with what was happening in the world. Thanks to O'Malley's free education scheme, we were now allowed to go to secondary school and university."

The nuns at St Michael's Holy Faith Convent didn't know what had hit them. "I was not compliant. So I didn't last long. We were absorbing the language of protest and reading about revolutions. I led a protest. So they threw me out. Looking back, I've a lot of sympathy for them having to put up with us. It must have been a culture shock for them. But for us it was a sense that we had a right to education."

Text reprinted with kind permission from Liliput Press.

After her Leaving Certificate, Paula studied at Trinity College. "I wasn't a good student. I just did the things I wanted to do. The poet Eiléan Ní Chuilleanáin taught me etymology, the history of words and sounds. I'd scribbled poems since I was at school, inspired by music and songs. But I didn't have confidence in my writing. It was a very male milieu. I became a secret writer."

She dropped out for a year, hitching to Crete, "to walk in the landscape that gave rise to the ancient myths". This sense of the past in the present, the living myth embedded in landscape, fed into her poetry. A scholarship brought her to America to study for a master's degree in creative writing. "The North West was a vital place for poetry. Looking back through the stories of the indigenous population gave me a new take on our own early culture, which was also full of stories and songs about hunting and fishing."

Her first collection, *Return and No Blame*, was published in 1984. Although it caught the attention of Eavan Boland, it didn't pay any bills. As the 1980s recession deepened, Paula moved to Leitrim, living on social welfare. Some of her poems were published in a Sunday newspaper. It gave her the confidence to write her long breakthrough poem, "The Statue of the Virgin at Granard Speaks". The playwright, Tom Murphy, wrote her a wonderful letter which she read and read until it was in shreds. "That galvanised me. I thought, I'm going to stand up for the word."

Poetry can be many things to many people. Award-winning English writer, Jeanette Winterson, has called it "a shot of espresso, a rope in a storm, a conversation across time". Paula likens making a poem to a child at a window making a mark with her breath. "It's something we've all done, and I still do."

N.B. Answer only ONE question in Section I, either one Question A OR one Question B on one text.

QUESTION A – 40 Marks

(i) Based on your reading of TEXT 1, explain three insights you gain into the influences that may have helped Paula Meehan to develop as a writer. Support your answer with reference to the text.

(10)

(ii) Jeanette Winterson and Paula Meehan make a variety of observations about poetry in the final paragraph of TEXT 1. To what extent can you relate these writers' observations to your experience of poetry? Explain your response.

(10)

(iii) Identify four elements of the writer's style, evident in the edited interview above, and discuss how these stylistic elements make the piece a positive and revealing portrait of Paula Meehan. Support your answer with reference to the text.

(20)

QUESTION B – 40 Marks

In TEXT 1, Paula Meehan speaks about how her poetry was inspired by music and songs. Write **an open letter**, to be published on a popular social media platform, in which you argue for or against the inclusion of song lyrics in the selection of poetry prescribed for the Leaving Certificate English course. In your open letter you should: explain your position in relation to the inclusion of song lyrics as poetry on the English course, seek to anticipate and refute views that might potentially be offered in opposition to your chosen stance and illustrate your argument with reference to at least one poem and the lyrics of at least one song.

TEXT 2 – BILLY O'CALLAGHAN

This text is adapted from Billy O'Callaghan's essay, *The Nature of Stories*. The essay appears in a collection of essays entitled, *The Danger and the Glory, Irish Authors on the Art of Writing*.

Chinese, Boat with Three Boatmen, 19th century.
Detroit Institute of Arts, Gift of K. T. Keller, 56.147.

In July of 2016, I was in China, travelling by train from Beijing back to Shanghai after a couple of weeks spent exploring some of the northern part of that ridiculously vast country. Still an hour or so out of Shanghai, we crossed a small, dull thread of river. I'd been watching the passing landscape and keeping check on the horizon, hoping that the sea would come into view.

The river had nothing much about it to speak of, except for a little wooden boat, some six or eight feet of scrap lumber nailed to create a high-sided trough, but in the few seconds that it took to pass in and out of my field of vision an entire story fell on me.

I can remember the sensation, the breathlessness of the moment, as if it had been just waiting there for me to pass. I felt at the same time knocked stupid and heightened. I suppose because of the soothing tranquility of the train, I'd been day-dreaming, and thinking a dozen or a thousand thoughts at once; but in that instant, something about the sight of the river, the boat, or maybe the thin yellow-white fall of the light on the water, bound all my strands of thought, conscious and otherwise, together in a particular and specific way, much as how I imagine stars are formed.

I had a notebook in my backpack and struggled to keep up with how fast the story came. I kept getting in the way of it and had to cross out words and whole sentences. At the station in Shanghai, I got off the train and transferred to the subway, hitting the rush hour crowds so that the carriage I boarded was packed almost beyond breathing space. I kept scribbling, stooped down and using the bodies around me for balance. By Heathrow, some fifteen or twenty hours on from that first moment in the train and nearly fit to drop, the story was done, the essential rags of it, anyway, which would be stitched together over the following couple of weeks, the edges trimmed and seams defined.

With neither intent nor expectation, I'd written a new story called, 'The Boatman'. The links within the final text to China, or to that river boat, were almost non-existent, yet something in what I'd seen or felt in that moment on the train helped prompt a deeper and more personal story into being. The finished story, fictional though it was, seemed so much a part of me that I refuse even now to believe it hadn't been smouldering away inside me always, biding its time, waiting to be told. But I also have to wonder, if I'd not been on that particular train in that far corner of the world at that precise second, whether the story would still have been written, or written differently. Would it have been lost to me, and maybe picked up by somebody else, to be slanted the way they needed to see it?

In the manner of its arrival, 'The Boatman' was very much an anomaly, and while my life would be so much easier if all the stories I want to write could drop into the world so complete and with such speed and assurance, it also doesn't matter that the opposite is far closer to my reality. The truth is, I'm not necessarily chasing easy, and I seem to get as much from the actual forging of the work, the struggle of getting it into a shape I want and need it to be, as I do from its completion. Once a story has gone as far as I can take it, there's a feeling of relief and, I suppose of accomplishment. But it doesn't last and probably shouldn't. Because there are so many more stories to tell.

If my stories are at all a reflection of who I am – and I can't help but feel that my better ones are – then it is probably correct that they should come slowly and without certainty, that every sentence needs to be wrestled into place. I am not writing autobiography, except in the sense that what comes out, when it comes out well, speaks of how I see the world, and also my place in it, however peripheral that might be. What I hope for, and strive for, is something that reads as truthful, even if it doesn't always match the facts.

Where the stories themselves come from, is, I'm afraid, imprecise. My starting point generally seems to be with theme. The elements of life that most trouble or haunt me start to coalesce. Some make themselves apparent over a long stretch of time; a few – rootedness and exile, isolation, love and its absence, loneliness, time's passing, guilt and the ability to endure – feel permanent. And it's from this slow fog, largely, that stories emerge, vaguely tormenting, looking to be explained, or made sense of.

Language excites me, the way it can layer meanings into itself, even seemingly in its most simple state, and how it feels 'off' if it should be forced to carry a syllable too many. Words are old magic, and the best stories, poems and novels cast spells and crack eternity and let the light come streaming in. On good days the sentences sing to me in the stillness and I glow with them.

N.B. Answer only ONE question in Section I, either one Question A OR one Question B on one text.

QUESTION A – 40 Marks

(i) Based on your reading of TEXT 2, explain three insights you gain into Billy O'Callaghan's creative writing process. Support your answer with reference to the text. (10)

(ii) In the above essay, Billy O'Callaghan expresses the view that, "the best stories, poems and novels cast spells and crack eternity and let the light come streaming in." To what extent can you relate this observation to your experience of literature? Explain your response. (10)

(iii) Identify four elements of the writer's style, evident in the edited essay above, and discuss how these stylistic elements make the essay an intimate and attractive piece of writing. Support your answer with reference to the text. (20)

QUESTION B – 40 Marks

In TEXT 2, Billy O'Callaghan refers to his travels in China. You have been invited to contribute to a podcast series of travel documentaries. Write **the text for the podcast** in which you: celebrate the many and varied delights of travelling both near and far, reflect on the pleasure you derive from planning possible future trips and explain the reasons why you like to keep a journal when you travel.

TEXT 3 – MAGGIE O'FARRELL

The following text is based on edited extracts from Maggie O'Farrell's novel, *Hamnet*. In this extract, Shakespeare is about to go on stage, playing the role of the ghost in his play, *Hamlet*.

He [Shakespeare] is standing just behind the musicians' gallery, at a small opening that gives out over the whole theatre. The other actors know this habit of his and never store their costumes or props there, never take up the space around that window.

They think he stands there to watch the people as they arrive. They believe he likes to assess how many are coming, how big the audience will be, how much the takings.

But that is not why. To him, it is the best place to be, before a performance: the stage below him, the audience filling the circular hollow in a steady trickle, and the other players behind him, transforming themselves from men to sprites or princes or soldiers or ladies or monsters. It is the only place to be alone in such a crowd. He feels like a bird, above the ground, resting on nothing but air. He is not of this place but above it, apart from it, observing it. It brings to mind, for him, the wind-hovering kestrel his wife used to keep, and the way it would hold itself in high currents, far above the tree tops, wings outstretched, looking down on all around it.

Beneath him, far beneath him, people are gathering. He can hear their calls, their murmurings, the shouts, the greetings, demands for nuts or sweetmeats, arguments that brew up quickly, then die away.

From behind him comes a crash, a curse, a burst of laughter. Someone has tripped on someone else's feet. There is a ribald joke about falling. More laughter. Someone else comes running up the stairs, asking, "Has anyone seen my sword, I've lost my sword, which of you dogs has taken it?".

Soon, he will need to disrobe, to take off

Photographed by John Tramper.

the clothes of daily life, of the street, of ordinariness, and put on his costume. He will need to confront his image in a glass and make it into something else. He will take a paste of chalk and lime and spread it over his cheeks, his nose, his beard. Charcoal to darken the eye sockets and the brows. Armour to strap to his chest, a helmet to slot over his head, a burial sheet to place about his shoulders. And then he will wait, listening, following the lines, until he hears his cue, and then he will step out, into the light, to inhabit the form of another; he will inhale; he will say his words.

He cannot tell, as he stands there, whether or not this new play is good. Sometimes, as he listens to his company speak the lines, he thinks he has come close to what he wanted it to be; other times, he feels he has entirely missed the mark. It is good, it is bad, it is somewhere in between. How does a person ever tell? All he can do is inscribe strokes on a page – for weeks and weeks, this was all he did, barely leaving his room, barely eating, never speaking to anyone else. The play, the complete length of it fills his head. It balances there, like a laden platter on a single fingertip.

The river is casting its frail net of mist. He can scent it on the breeze, its dank and weed-filled fumes wafting towards him. Perhaps it is this fog, this river-heavy air, he doesn't know, but the day feels ill to him. He is filled with an unease, a slight foreboding, as if something is coming for him. Is it the performance? Does he feel something will be amiss with it? He frowns, thinking, running over in his head any moments that might feel un-rehearsed or ill-prepared. There is not one. He knows this because he himself pushed them through it, over and over again.

The playhouse is a round wooden place with a stage jutting out into the gathering crowd, and above them all, a ceiling of sky, a circle containing fast-moving clouds. More and more people are pouring through the doors. Some on the ground are gesturing and shouting to others in the higher balconies. A group in the highest tier is making much of the lowering of a length of rope. There is shouting and laughter. A man selling pies ties to its end a laden basket and the people above begin to haul it up. Several members of the crowd leap to snatch it; the pie-man deals each of them a swift, cracking blow. A coin is thrown down by the people above and the pie-man lunges to catch it. One of the men he has just hit gets to it first and the pie-man grabs him around the throat; the man lands a punch on the pie-man's chin. They go down, hard, swallowed by the crowd amid much cheering and noise.

Trumpets sound, a hush falls over the crowd and two men walk on to the stage. No one speaks. No one moves. Everyone is entirely focused on these actors and what they are saying. Gone is the jostling, whistling, brawling, pie-chewing mass and in its place a silent, awed congregation. It is as if a magician or sorcerer has waved his staff over the place and turned them all to stone.

N.B. Answer only ONE question in Section I, either one Question A OR one Question B on one text.

QUESTION A – 40 Marks

(i) Based on your reading of TEXT 3, explain three insights you gain into the theatrical world at the time in which the novel is set. Support your answer with reference to the text. (10)

(ii) In the final paragraph of TEXT 3, we witness the power of a dramatic performance to transform a raucous crowd into "a silent, awed congregation". To what extent can you relate the experience of the audience in the text to your experience at concerts, matches, dramatic productions or other live performances? Explain your answer. (10)

(iii) Identify four features of the language of narration, evident in TEXT 3, and discuss how effectively these features are employed to craft a dramatic and revealing portrait of Shakespeare prior to the first performance of his new play, *Hamlet*. Support your answer with reference to the text. (20)

QUESTION B – 40 Marks

After a break of several years, your school Principal wants to revive the school's long-established tradition of staging an annual musical production. As a member of the Student Council, you have agreed to give **a talk** at a school assembly in which you: promote the revival of this school tradition, remind the school community of the success of some of the previous productions and encourage members of the school community to become involved in the various roles and tasks associated with the production. Write the text of the talk you would deliver.

SECTION II   COMPOSING   (100 marks)

Write a composition on **any one** of the assignments that appear in **bold print** below.

Each composition carries 100 marks.

The composition assignments are intended to reflect language study in the areas of information, argument, persuasion, narration, and the aesthetic use of language.

1.   TEXT 3 is set in a theatre, a place filled with drama and dramatic characters.

      Write a personal essay in which you reflect on how dull your life would be without those colourful people who occasionally add drama and excitement. In your essay you may refer both to people whom you know and to celebrities.

2.   In TEXT 2, we learn how Billy O'Callaghan was inspired to write his story, 'The Boatman', having seen a little wooden boat on a river in China.

      Write a short story, set in China in the past or in the present, in which a river boatman in a small craft plays an important part.

3.   In TEXT 1, Paula Meehan talks about being part of the first "global generation".

      Write an article to be published in an online journal, on what it means to be part of a "global generation".

4.   In TEXT 3, Shakespeare is filled with a sense of unease and foreboding before the play begins.

      Write a short story, set in Shakespeare's Globe Theatre on the day described in Text 3. Your story should include an event that fulfils Shakespeare's premonition of trouble.

5.   In TEXT 2, the writer states that, "on good days the sentences sing to me in the stillness and I glow with them."

      Write a personal essay in which you reflect on what makes you "glow" with joy or satisfaction.

6.   In TEXT 1, Paula Meehan observes that, "… being able to read and write from the start was like a weapon".

      Write a speech, to be delivered to an international conference on education for young people, about the skills and knowledge that you think young people need to flourish in the twenty-first century.

7.   In TEXT 1, we learn about Paula Meehan's rebellious youth and her independent personality.

      Write a discursive essay on the importance of independent thinking and the role of rebels in society.

Acknowledgements

Images and texts that appear on this examination paper were sourced as follows:

TEXT 1: Carty, C., *Writer to Writer, The Republic of Elsewhere*, The Lilliput Press, Dublin, 2018.
Image: www.irishtimes.con/culture/paula-meehan-the-poet-at-60-1.2115401 photo: Dave Meehan

TEXT 2: Schwall, H. (Ed.), *The Danger and the Glory,* Irish writers on the Art of Writing, Arlen House, Dublin, 2019.
Image: https://upload.wikimedia.org/wikipedia/commons/thumb/a/aa/Unknown_%28Chinese%29_-
_Boat_with_Three_Boatmen_-_56.147_-_Detroit_Institute_of_Arts.jpg/1280px-Unknown_%28Chinese%29_-
_Boat_with_Three_Boatmen_-_56.147_-_Detroit_Institute_of_Arts.jpg

TEXT 3: O'Farrell M., *Hamnet,* Tinder Press, London, 2020.
Image: https://www.shakespearesglobe.com/discover/blogs-and-features/2017/06/12/building-shakespeares-globe/
        Photographer: John Tramper

> # Do not hand this up.
>
> # This document will not be returned to the State Examinations Commission

Leaving Certificate – Higher Level

English

2 hours 50 minutes

Coimisiún na Scrúduithe Stáit
State Examinations Commission

LEAVING CERTIFICATE EXAMINATION, 2022

English - Higher Level - Paper 2

Total Marks: 140

Duration: 3 hours 20 minutes

Candidates must attempt the required number of questions in **any TWO** of the following sections:

- SECTION I – The Single Text
- SECTION II – The Comparative Study
- SECTION III – Poetry, Part A, Unseen Poem and Part B, Prescribed Poetry.
- All sections carry 70 marks.

N.B. Candidates are **NOT** required to answer on Shakespearean Drama.

INDEX OF SINGLE TEXTS

All the Light We Cannot See	Page - 2
A Doll's House	Page - 2
Othello	Page - 2
Frankenstein	Page - 3
The Picture of Dorian Gray	Page - 3

Do not hand this up.

This document will not be returned to the State Examinations Commission

SECTION I   THE SINGLE TEXT   (70 marks)

Candidates must answer **one** question from this section (**A – E**).

A   ALL THE LIGHT WE CANNOT SEE – Anthony Doerr

(i)   "By incorporating elements of history, mystery and legend into the story, Anthony Doerr adds to the narrative power of his novel, *All the Light We Cannot See*."

Discuss the reasons why you do or do not agree with the above statement, developing your discussion with reference to the text.

OR

(ii)   Discuss the insights you gain into the character of Werner Pfennig from his engagement with both Marie-Laure LeBlanc and his sister, Jutta. Develop your discussion with reference to Anthony Doerr's novel, *All the Light We Cannot See*.

cmwrrl
Visit www.e-xamit.ie

B   A DOLL'S HOUSE – Henrik Ibsen

(i)   Discuss how Ibsen skilfully creates moments of heightened dramatic intensity in his play, *A Doll's House*. Develop your discussion with reference to at least three moments of heightened dramatic intensity evident in the text.

OR

(ii)   Discuss the insights we gain into Nora Helmer's character from her engagement with both Christine Linde and Nils Krogstad. Develop your discussion with reference to Ibsen's play, *A Doll's House*.

hbllzf
Visit www.e-xamit.ie

C   OTHELLO – William Shakespeare

(i)   Discuss how Shakespeare skilfully creates moments of heightened dramatic intensity in his play, *Othello*. Develop your discussion with reference to at least three moments of heightened dramatic intensity evident in the text.

OR

(ii)   Discuss the insights we gain into the character of Iago from the relationships he carefully cultivates with both Roderigo and Cassio. Develop your discussion with reference to Shakespeare's play, *Othello*.

D   **FRANKENSTEIN** – Mary Shelley

(i)   "By incorporating elements of science fiction, gothic fiction and horror into the story, Mary Shelley adds to the narrative power of her novel, *Frankenstein*."

Discuss the reasons why you do or do not agree with the above statement, developing your discussion with reference to the text.

OR

(ii)   Discuss the insights you gain into the character of Victor Frankenstein from his relationships with both the monster and Henry Clerval. Develop your discussion with reference to Mary Shelley's novel, *Frankenstein*.

E   **THE PICTURE OF DORIAN GRAY** – Oscar Wilde

(i)   "By incorporating elements of philosophy, melodrama and satiric comedy into the story, Oscar Wilde adds to the narrative power of his novel, *The Picture of Dorian Gray*."

Discuss the reasons why you do or do not agree with the above statement, developing your discussion with reference to the text.

OR

(ii)   Discuss the insights you gain into the character of Dorian Gray from his relationships with both Basil Hallward and Sibyl Vane. Develop your discussion with reference to Oscar Wilde's novel, *The Picture of Dorian Gray*.

SECTION II   THE COMPARATIVE STUDY   (70 marks)

Candidates must answer **one** question from **either A** – Literary Genre **or B** –Cultural Context **or C** – General Vision and Viewpoint.

Candidates who answer a question in **SECTION I** – The Single Text, may not refer to the same text in answer to a question in this section.

All texts used in this section must be prescribed for comparative study for this year's examination. Candidates may refer to only one film in the course of their answers.

Please note:
- Questions in this section use the word **text** to refer to all the different kinds of texts available for study on this course.
- When used, the word **reader** includes viewers of films and theatre audiences.
- When used, the term **technique** is understood to include techniques employed by all writers and directors of films.
- When used, the word **author** is understood to include all writers and directors of films.
- When used, the word **character** is understood to refer to both real people and fictional characters in texts.
- When used, the words **narrative** or **story** are understood to refer to both real life and fictional texts.

A   LITERARY GENRE

1.   (a)   Discuss how effectively two features of storytelling, evident in **one** text on your comparative course, are used to develop one central relationship in this text. Develop your response with reference to the text.   (30)

   (b)   Compare how effectively at least one feature of storytelling, evident in each of **two** other texts from your comparative course, is used to develop one central relationship in each of these texts. You may refer to the same or different feature(s) of storytelling in each of your chosen texts. Develop your response with reference to your chosen texts.   (40)

OR

2.   Compare how the authors create a sense of anticipation for readers in advance of significant developments or dramatic events in each of **at least two** texts on your comparative course. Develop your response with reference to your chosen texts.   (70)

rddcsu
Visit www.e-xamit.ie

B   CULTURAL CONTEXT

1.   (a)   Discuss the extent to which individual rights are respected or threatened in the cultural context established in **one** text on your comparative course. Develop your response with reference to the text.   (30)

      (b)   Compare the extent to which individual rights are respected or threatened in the cultural context established in each of **two other** texts on your comparative course. Develop your response with reference to your chosen texts.   (40)

OR

2.   Compare how democratic you find the society established in **at least two** texts on your comparative course. Develop your response with reference to your chosen texts.   (70)

C   GENERAL VISION AND VIEWPOINT

1.   (a)   Discuss the extent to which your sense of the general vision and viewpoint in **one** text on your comparative course was influenced by your response to the prevailing values evident in this text. Develop your response with reference to the text.   (30)

      (b)   Compare the extent to which your sense of the general vision and viewpoint in **two other** texts on your comparative course was influenced by your response to the prevailing values evident in these texts. Develop your response with reference to your chosen texts.   (40)

OR

2.   Compare the extent to which your sense of the general vision and viewpoint in **at least two** texts on your comparative course was shaped by how successfully a significant conflict or tension was resolved in each of these texts. Develop your response with reference to your chosen texts.   (70)

mbdzcw
Visit www.e-xamit.ie

SECTION III　　　　POETRY　　　　(70 marks)

Candidates must answer **A** – Unseen Poem **and B** – Prescribed Poetry.

A　　UNSEEN POEM (20 marks)

Read the following poem by Simon Armitage and answer **either** Question **1 or** Question **2** which follow.

The English Astronaut

He splashed down in rough seas off Spurn Point.
I watched through a coin-op telescope jammed
with a lollipop stick as a trawler fished him out
of the waves and ferried him back to Mission
Control on a trading estate near the Humber Bridge.
He spoke with a mild voice: yes, it was good to be
home; he'd missed his wife, the kids, couldn't wait
for a shave and a hot bath. 'Are there any more
questions?' No, there were not.

I followed him in his Honda Accord to a Little
Chef on the A1, took the table opposite, watched
him order the all-day breakfast and a pot of tea.
'You need to go outside to do that,' said the
waitress when he lit a cigarette. He read the paper,
started the crossword, poked at the black pudding
with his fork. Then he stared through the window
for long unbroken minutes at a time, but only at the
busy road, never the sky. And his face was not
the moon. And his hands were not the hands of a man
who had held between finger and thumb the blue
planet, and lifted it up to his watchmaker's eye.

Simon Armitage

The English Astronaut by Simon Armitage from Seeing Stars (Faber and Faber, 2011).

1.　(a)　Discuss the portrayal of the English astronaut by Simon Armitage in the above poem.
　　　　　Support your answer with reference to the poem.　　　　　　　　　　(10)

　　(b)　Explain how the meaning of the above poem is enhanced by the observations made
　　　　　by the poet in the last two sentences.　　　　　　　　　　　　　　(10)

OR

2.　　Discuss how effectively, in your opinion, the poet uses language in the above poem to
　　　convey his thoughts and feelings about the astronaut. Support your answer with
　　　reference to the poem.　　　　　　　　　　　　　　　　　　　　(20)

Leaving Certificate – 2022 Deferred Paper
English – Higher Level Paper 2

poxoyh
Visit www.e-xamit.ie

B   PRESCRIBED POETRY (50 marks)

Candidates must answer **one** of the following questions (**1 – 5**).

1.   W.B. Yeats

Discuss how Yeats uses language, including imagery, to convey both passion and frustration in his work. Develop your discussion with reference to the poetry by Yeats on your Leaving Certificate English course.

```
fyubax
Visit www.e-xamit.ie
```

2.   Emily Dickinson

"Dickinson pushes the boundaries of both language and imagination to explore a variety of experiences and emotions in her poetry."

Discuss the extent to which you agree or disagree with the above statement. Develop your discussion with reference to the poetry by Emily Dickinson on your Leaving Certificate English course.

```
szmvnw
Visit www.e-xamit.ie
```

3.   Brendan Kennelly

"Kennelly uses a conversational style to communicate the emotional, imaginative and spiritual aspects of his poetry to readers."

Discuss the extent to which you agree or disagree with the above statement. Develop your discussion with reference to the poetry by Brendan Kennelly on your Leaving Certificate English course.

```
oalvog
Visit www.e-xamit.ie
```

4.   D.H. Lawrence

"Lawrence uses a vivid and evocative style to present a variety of memorable scenes and moments of emotional intensity in his poetry."

Discuss the extent to which you agree or disagree with the above statement. Develop your discussion with reference to the poetry by D.H. Lawrence on your Leaving Certificate English course.

5.   Elizabeth Bishop

"Bishop's precise use of language enables her to effectively convey her reflections on her own life and experiences."

Discuss the extent to which you agree or disagree with the above statement. Develop your discussion with reference to the poetry by Elizabeth Bishop on your Leaving Certificate English course.

```
lldydx
Visit www.e-xamit.ie
```

Do not hand this up.

This document will not be returned to the State Examinations Commission

Leaving Certificate – Higher Level

English

3 hours and 20 minutes

34

Coimisiún na Scrúduithe Stáit
State Examinations Commission

LEAVING CERTIFICATE EXAMINATION, 2022

English - Higher Level - Paper 1

Total Marks: 140

Wednesday, 8 June – Morning, 9.30 – 12.20

- This paper is divided into two sections,
  Section I COMPREHENDING and Section II COMPOSING.
- The paper contains **three** texts on the general theme of **POWERFUL VOICES**.
- Candidates should familiarise themselves with each of the texts before
  beginning their answers.
- Both sections of this paper (COMPREHENDING and COMPOSING) must be
  attempted.
- Section I, Comprehending, carries 40 marks.
- Section II, Composing, carries 100 marks.

SECTION I – COMPREHENDING

- Two Questions, A and B, follow each text.
- Candidates must answer **ONE** question in Section I:
  either one Question A **OR one** Question B on **ONE** text.

SECTION II – COMPOSING

- Candidates must write on **one** of the compositions 1 – 7.

> ## Do not hand this up.
>
> ### This document will not be returned to the
> ### State Examinations Commission

TEXT 1 – A YOUNG POET'S POWERFUL VOICE

This text is adapted from a feature article by Meadhbh McGrath entitled, *Poet. Fashion icon. Future president?*. It originally appeared in the magazine section of a weekend newspaper.

On that chilly inauguration day in January, audiences tuned in to see Joe Biden being sworn in as US president, but it was Amanda Gorman, the youngest inaugural poet in US history, who really stole the show. Dressed in a sunshine yellow coat and scarlet satin headband, the young poet delivered a mesmerising five-minute reading of *The Hill We Climb*. The poem – parts of which Gorman had written on the night of the US Capitol riots – began with the question: "When day comes we ask ourselves, where can we find light in this never-ending shade?". It was about national unity and reconciliation, but Gorman's work also reckoned with the pain of America's past and present, and looked optimistically towards its future, capturing the mood of a country reeling from a deadly pandemic, stark political divisions and domestic terrorism.

The inauguration was a rare moment where a poem made international headlines, showing how poetry, rather than being a solitary occupation or the tiresome homework suffered through at school, can bring people together by interrogating and articulating our shared feelings, fears and insecurities. It was also a moment that catapulted Gorman to global fame. By the following day, she had gained two million new Instagram followers and pre-sales had pushed her two books to numbers 1 and 2 on Amazon's bestseller list, despite not being due for publication until later in the year. Less than three weeks later, she became the first poet to perform at the Super Bowl, reciting a poem honouring frontline workers. Gorman also signed a modelling deal and became the first poet to grace the cover of *American Vogue*.

She has promised to run for president in 2036 – the year in which she will be old enough to run – earning unofficial endorsements from Hillary Clinton and Michelle Obama. She is already working on her second children's book, part of a four-book publishing deal. To top it all off, she co-chaired the Met Gala Ball, the fashion world's biggest night out, alongside Billie Eilish and Timothée Chalamet, an experience Gorman likened to "Cinderella going to the ball".

2021 was an astonishing year for Gorman, who described her background in *The Hill We Climb* as "a skinny Black girl, descended from slaves and raised by a single mother". Born in 1998 in Los Angeles, Gorman was diagnosed with auditory processing disorder as a child which resulted in a speech impediment. She has credited this with enhancing her sensitivity to the sounds of language – she began writing at a young age, she has said, "as a form of self-expression, to get my voice on the page".

Gorman's talent was evident early on, as was her dedication to activism: she and her sister staged a demonstration in school to highlight the lack of diversity in their English class's syllabus and at 16 years of age Gorman founded a non-profit organisation called One Pen One Page, which runs youth literacy programmes. In the same year, she was named youth poet laureate of Los Angeles, and three years later, while studying sociology at Harvard, she became the first national youth poet laureate. Gorman has said she saw her task on inauguration day as "a cleansing by way of words". While acknowledging the "harsh truths" of the country's problems, she has said she wanted "to use my words to envision a way in which our country can still come together and can still heal", offering hope and possibility to those watching. Gorman keenly understands the emotional power of poetry, and how moments of intense feeling call for a heightened form of expression. She also understands that poetry doesn't need to be oblique or formally difficult to make an impact: her writing is clear-eyed and direct, tightly crafted and accessible.

Gorman's vivid recital captivated viewers by drawing on the tradition of spoken-word poetry, which treats poems as performances. The style can be traced back through a long history of Black art forms, including rap, church oratory, religious spirituals and oral folk tales. The activist side of spoken word poetry is rooted in the Black Arts and Black Power movements of the 1960s. Though Gorman's work may be less radical, it relies on the same spontaneity of live performance, using the rhythm and melody of her delivery to temper the uncomfortable message of her words. It turned her poem into an event, a collective experience for the audience and a powerful showcase for what poetry can do. That moment also opened up the world of poetry to people who may have hitherto felt excluded from it. As a young Black woman with a speech impediment, Gorman showed that poetry is a space for everyone.

Gorman's thoughtfulness extends to her styling. She recognises that fashion is itself a storytelling device. The Met Gala confirmed her status as a new kind of style icon. During 2021, she turned down $17 million in brand deals and she is wary of being seen as a model or fashion influencer. She said she won't be posting party photos or pool selfies on her social media, conscious of how they might impact on a future political career. With several decades in public life ahead of her, Gorman's star – already high – will only continue to rise.

N.B. Answer only ONE question in Section I, either one Question A OR one Question B on one text.

QUESTION A – 40 Marks

(i) Based on your reading of TEXT 1, explain three insights you gain into the power of poetry. Support your answer with reference to the text. (10)

(ii) Amanda Gorman's status as a powerful young voice was bolstered by her performance at the US presidential inauguration. Discuss the extent to which you agree or disagree that a diversity of youthful voices should be represented in public debate on all important issues in Irish society. (10)

(iii) Identify four elements of the writer's style, evident in the edited article above, and discuss how these stylistic elements helped to shape your impression of Amanda Gorman both as a poet and as a person. Support your answer with reference to TEXT 1. (20)

QUESTION B – 40 Marks

Some students believe that the study of poetry should be an optional rather than a compulsory element of the Leaving Certificate English course. Write **an open letter**, to be published on a popular social media platform, to encourage discussion on this topic. In your open letter you should: explain what, if any, value you found in the study of poetry as part of your Leaving Certificate English course, explore the reasons why you think the study of poetry should be an optional or a compulsory element of Leaving Certificate English in the future and seek to anticipate and refute views that might potentially be offered in opposition to your chosen stance.

TEXT 2 – THE POWERFUL VOICE OF MUSIC

This text is based on edited extracts from a book compiled by Tom Gatti entitled, *Long Players*. The book is a collection of personal essays in which writers share their thoughts on the albums that helped to shape them. Extract Two features Man Booker prize winner, Nigerian, Ben Okri.

Extract 1: Tom Gatti from the introduction to his book, *Long Players*.

Albums can alter the architecture of our minds. The ones that speak to us, we listen to hundreds of times over decades; we know them far better than any novel or film. They are faithful companions, with us from the first time we lower the needle to the last time we hover a thumb over the screen. They are, truly, long players.

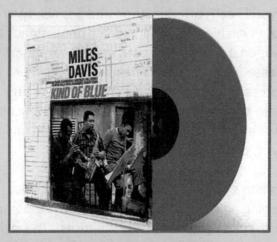

Extract 2: Ben Okri – The Miles Davis album, *Kind of Blue*.

There are some rare albums that seem to lift from their physical condition and become part of the decor and mood of a life. They seem not to be music anymore but one of the things that shape you, like the home you grew up in or your earliest toys. Though music eminently has this capacity, it is often the case that even the greatest music draws attention to itself as music. Very rarely does it become an invisible fact of a life, woven into it like clouds in the sky, or trees along a road.

Miles Davis's *Kind of Blue* first made itself real in my life on a rainy morning in Lagos, in the seventies, when for the first time I was alone in the house. I was around seventeen and the emptiness of the house brought me to something resembling an existential decision: I had to decide what I wanted to do with my life.

All that morning while it rained, I had been thinking. And while I had been thinking, *Kind of Blue* had been playing on the turntable. The music passed into thought, then into the sonic space in which my decision played out in ways unknown to me. That is to say, the music passed into the silence of the mind.

My decision has led, through the turns and revelations of life, to where I am now, and where I will be tomorrow. That day there was Miles and Mozart and the rain and the smells and muted sounds of the ghetto where we had temporarily found ourselves.

Kind of Blue has gone on playing a similar role in my life. Now it is so imprinted on my being that I don't need to listen to it to hear it. In some way it is always playing somewhere inside me, in a constant spirit loop, which is the result of such a saturation of listening. If such a thing as reincarnation exists, I would probably come back in a future life and be convinced of the certainty that I had composed that music. But then I have always been an obsessive listener of music, and would inscribe a piece into my being if it spoke to me that deeply.

Rather than being an urban song of praise, a wild choral hymn for the lost souls that need soothing, rather than being this tender lament, this heartfelt cool breeze on the hot skins of those who walked the narrow paths of the cities, this album was really a moment of memory – a moment of recollection by Miles Davis of a time when he was back in the South and heard music floating over the houses late in the night. That's the story at the plaintive heart of the music. The album was recorded in New York and every track is redolent of the mood of that city, alchemised by a seemingly magical process so that it has in it the essence of cities and their solitudes, their wistful air of stoicism and coiled repose.

What was unique about the recording is that it brought out the best of the classical tradition and the improvisation at the heart of jazz itself. The album, released in my birth year, was created on little rehearsal and with the band having only the sketchiest notion of what they were to play. They had just hints of melodic lines on which to improvise. The result was what is considered one of the greatest albums ever recorded. Its influence transcends music.

It begins with what seems like low-key uncertainty and slides into a call and response that's like limpid poetry, clear and melodious, wreathed with an impressionistic silvery melancholy and muted joy. Something indefinable haunts the music, some sorrow, some calm in the trumpet glissandos – that slide in pitch between the notes – something quiet that pierces the bones. It is that rare thing in all art: the perfect distillation of a spirit, a time and a genius.

I listened to it at the beginning of my writing life and it was one of the pieces of music I listened to all through writing my novel, *The Famished Road*. It helped keep me sane through the long, lonely nights and wild flights of imagination, always bringing me back home.

Now I listen to the silence while I write, because all the music I need is playing in me, in a spiritual, kind of blue way.

N.B. Answer only ONE question in Section I, either one Question A OR one Question B on one text.

QUESTION A – 40 Marks

(i)   Based on your reading of both Extracts 1 and 2 of TEXT 2, explain three insights you gain into the power of music. Support your answer with reference to the text.   (10)

(ii) In Extract 1, Tom Gatti observes that the music we listen to has a greater and a longer lasting impact on us than the books that we read and the films that we watch. Discuss the extent to which you agree or disagree with this observation.   (10)

(iii) Identify four elements of Ben Okri's writing style, evident in Extract 2, and discuss how effectively these stylistic elements are employed to craft a lyrically beautiful and engaging piece of personal writing. Support your answer with reference to Extract 2 of TEXT 2.   (20)

QUESTION B – 40 Marks

You have been invited to contribute to a podcast series entitled, *The Music Playing in Me*. The series will explore the importance of music in the lives of individuals. Write **the text for the podcast** in which you: reflect on the importance of music in your life, discuss some of the particular pieces of music (songs, albums, etc.) that make up the soundtrack to your own life and share the thoughts and feelings this music evokes in you.

TEXT 3 – THE POWERFUL VOICE OF BOOKS

TEXT 3 is based on edited extracts from Hugo Hamilton's novel, *The Pages*. Hamilton uses a book – the novel, *Rebellion*, by Jewish writer Joseph Roth – as the narrator. In these extracts, we witness the book telling its own story, including its rescue from the Nazi book burning in 1933.

BOOKS ARE WEAPONS IN THE WAR OF IDEAS

Here I am, stored inside a piece of hand luggage, being carried through the departure lounge at JFK Airport. The owner of the bag is a young woman by the name of Lena Knecht. She is getting on a flight to Europe. Bringing me home, so to speak. Back to Berlin, the city in which I was written. Where I was first printed by a small publishing house almost a hundred years ago, in 1924. Where I was rescued from the fire on the night of the book-burning. The city from which my author fled on the day Hitler came to power.

It was raining on the night of the fire in May 1933. A last-minute downpour threatened to ruin the event. It was too late to postpone plans that had been underway for weeks. A specialist pyrotechnic company had been hired to oversee the spectacle. On the opera house square, they had set up a dovetailed structure of wooden logs doused with fuel. Underneath, a layer of sand to protect the surface from scorch marks.

At the State Library, next to the site of the proposed fire, students were heard entering with their slogans echoing around corridors, carrying with them a list of unwanted books. My author, Joseph Roth, was on the list. He had already fled to France by then.

A sense of fear ran around the shelves as the titles were called out. Books saying quick goodbyes to each other as they were being tied up in bundles, ready to be carried outside. The students worked diligently, using their considerable learning skills to search the catalogue for titles to be torn from the canon like bad teeth, passing them along in a human chain to the site of the fire outside.

The students had an air of triumph. This was their moment. Their revenge on learning. This was their chance to step outside received wisdom and take part in a glorious act of self-vandalism. Returning to a time before knowledge. The right not to know. Unlearning everything but the spirit of the nation.

As it happened, I was not in the library myself that evening. My author's books were part of the catalogue of the State Library, but I belonged to a professor of German literature by the name of David Glückstein. He had brought me with him in his briefcase to the Humboldt University on the other side of the square because he was unsure how far this cleansing action would go. In his office, the professor had arranged a meeting with one of his trusted students, where I was quietly handed over for safekeeping.

The student's name was Dieter Knecht, Lena's grandfather. He took me in his hands and they spoke about my author for a little while with some fondness. By rescuing this single volume from the fire, he set in motion a quiet wave of resistance. It was a small but significant event taking place behind closed doors, away from the catastrophe outside. It changed the course of people's lives.

Outside on the opera house square, the fire was going strong. Students railed against filth in literature, against sexual freedom, capitalism, Jewish dominance, as they called it. The human chain leading from the library to the site of the fire continued delivering the hated books. Each author was denounced in a summary trial, the name called out, giving a reason why they no longer fitted into the national vision, before their books were committed to the fire. All of this was being broadcast by radio around the nation.

More and more books were being added to the flames. Dieter stood watching the fire with me tucked inside his coat. The faces of the onlookers were lit up in the warm glow of the flames. Their eyes turned jet black. Their lips were green. Their nostrils inhaled the pungent paper-smoke that came from those books, like the smell of burning hair.

It was a bonfire of life stories. The pages were curling and flying over the rooftops. These imagined lives, these human thought roads, were being turned into worthless heat. The words were no longer bound together in sentences. They had been discharged of all meaning. From inside the flames came the sound of voices rising in a collective stream of consciousness, extracted like free prose from the text, a ghostly recital of absurd phrases and detached bits of dialogue dissolving into vapours in one long silent scream of pity that could be heard right around the city.

Just before midnight, Joseph Goebbels [chief propagandist for the Nazi party] came to make a speech. Speaking in a voice that overestimated his stature, he praised the students for their cleansing action. He said it was the end of Jewish supremacy in literature. He spoke about the will of the people.

N.B. Answer only ONE question in Section I, either one Question A OR one Question B on one text.

QUESTION A – 40 Marks

(i) Based on your reading of TEXT 3, explain three insights you gain into the power of books. Support your answer with reference to the text. (10)

(ii) In TEXT 3, we witness an exercise in censorship through the destruction of books. Discuss the extent to which you agree or disagree that censorship, including contemporary cancel culture, should not be used to silence voices of protest or disagreement in society. (10)

(iii) Identify four features of the language of narration, evident in TEXT 3, and discuss how effectively these features are employed to craft a dramatic and disturbing account of the book burning that occurred in Berlin in 1933. Support your answer with reference to TEXT 3. (20)

QUESTION B – 40 Marks

It is 2033 and you are the editor of an internationally distributed newspaper. A book burning event, similar to that described in TEXT 3, has occurred in a major American city. You believe that respect for books of all kinds is vital to democracy and are horrified by this assault on them. Write **an editorial** in which you: give your response to this incident, warn your readers of the dangers inherent in attacking books in this way and urge them to engage in peaceful protest against this and any other form of censorship.

cvkpkw
Visit www.e-xamit.ie

41

Write a composition on **any one** of the assignments that appear in **bold print** below.

Each composition carries 100 marks.

The composition assignments are intended to reflect language study in the areas of information, argument, persuasion, narration, and the aesthetic use of language.

1. ✓   In TEXT 2, Tom Gatti suggests that albums can become "faithful companions" in our lives.

   Write a personal essay in which you identify some of the items or objects that have become "faithful companions" in your life and reflect on the importance of these items or objects to you.

2. ✓   In TEXT 1, we learn that Amanda Gorman may be a candidate in the American presidential election in 2036.

   You are a candidate in the next election for the presidency of Ireland. Write a speech to be delivered during the election campaign, in which you outline the social and cultural values you would promote if elected and explain the perception of Ireland you would cultivate abroad, given the opportunity to do so.

✗   In TEXT 3, a student, Dieter Knecht, undertakes the perilous rescue of Joseph Roth's novel, *Rebellion*, from destruction in the Nazi book burning in Berlin in 1933.

   Write a short story in which the student featured in TEXT 3, Dieter Knecht, has a life changing experience as he attempts to rescue Joseph Roth's denounced novel, *Rebellion*, from the Nazi supporters who wish to see it destroyed.

4. ?   In TEXT 1, we learn that Amanda Gorman recognises that fashion is itself a storytelling device.

   Write a feature article, for the magazine section of a weekend newspaper, in which you reflect on our fascination with all things fashionable and explore the stories we tell about ourselves, intentionally or unintentionally, through our fashion choices.

5.   The theme of this examination paper is "Powerful Voices".

   Write a discursive essay in which you identify some of the powerful voices in modern life and discuss their influence on society.

6. ✓   In TEXT 3, the students in the story are described as "unlearning everything but the spirit of the nation".

   Write a personal essay in which you reflect on the value of engaging in all kinds of learning and the pleasure, satisfaction and personal growth that can be derived from doing so.

✗   In TEXT 2, Ben Okri talks about, "the story at the plaintive heart of the music."

   Write a short story in which a piece of music or the lyrics of a song (or songs) play(s) an important part in the narrative.

Acknowledgements

Images and texts that appear on this examination paper *were* **sourced as follows:**

Text 1: M. McGrath, *Poet. Fashion icon. Future president?* Sunday Independent Life magazine, 19/09/2021
Image: https://www.theguardian.com/us-news/2021/jan/21/amanda-gorman-star-rises-inaugural-poem
Photograph: Alex Wong/Getty Images

Text 2: T. Gatti (Ed.), *Long Players – Writers on the Albums That Shaped Them*, London, Bloomsbury Publishing, 2021
Image: https://www.vinylvinyl.nl/miles-davis-kind-of-blue-blue-180g-vinyl.html

Text 3: H. Hamilton, *The Pages*, London, 4th Estate (An imprint of HarperCollinsPublishers), 2021.
Image: https://lithub.com/during-world-war-ii-literature-reigned-supreme/

Do not hand this up.

This document will not be returned to the
State Examinations Commission

Leaving Certificate – Higher Level

English

Wednesday 8 June
Morning 9.30 – 12.20

Coimisiún na Scrúduithe Stáit
State Examinations Commission

LEAVING CERTIFICATE EXAMINATION, 2022

English - Higher Level - Paper 2

Total Marks: 140

Thursday, 9 June – Afternoon, 2.00 – 5.20

Candidates must attempt the required number of questions in **any TWO** of the following sections:

- SECTION I – The Single Text
- SECTION II – The Comparative Study
- SECTION III – Poetry, Part A, Unseen Poem and Part B, Prescribed Poetry.
- All sections carry 70 marks.

N.B. Candidates are **NOT** required to answer on Shakespearean Drama.

INDEX OF SINGLE TEXTS

All the Light We Cannot See	Page - 2
A Doll's House	Page - 2
Othello	Page - 2
Frankenstein	Page - 3
The Picture of Dorian Gray	Page - 3

Candidates must answer **one** question from this section (**A – E**).

A   ALL THE LIGHT WE CANNOT SEE – Anthony Doerr

(i)   "The consequences of Werner Pfennig's passion for science and technology in Anthony Doerr's novel, *All the Light We Cannot See,* are both fascinating and disturbing."

Discuss the reasons why you agree or disagree with the above statement. Develop your discussion with reference to the text.

OR

(ii)   Discuss the narrative purposes served by Doerr's inclusion of the story of the diamond, the Sea of Flames, in his novel, *All the Light We Cannot See.* Develop your discussion with reference to the text.

B   A DOLL'S HOUSE – Henrik Ibsen

(i)   "Various aspects of Ibsen's exploration of deception and delusion in his play, *A Doll's House*, are both fascinating and disturbing."

Discuss the reasons why you agree or disagree with the above statement. Develop your discussion with reference to the text.

OR

(ii)   Discuss the reasons why our knowledge of Nora Helmer's backstory, involving the loan, enables us to better understand various aspects of Ibsen's play, *A Doll's House*. Develop your discussion with reference to the text.

2022 P2

C   OTHELLO – William Shakespeare

(i)   "Various aspects of the relationship between Iago and Emilia in Shakespeare's play, *Othello*, are both fascinating and disturbing."

Discuss the reasons why you agree or disagree with the above statement. Develop your discussion with reference to the text.

OR

(ii)   Discuss the reasons why our knowledge of Othello's status as an outsider enables us to better understand various aspects of Shakespeare's play, *Othello*. Develop your discussion with reference to the text.

D   FRANKENSTEIN – Mary Shelley

(i)   "The consequences of Victor Frankenstein's passion for scientific knowledge and experimentation in Mary Shelley's novel, *Frankenstein,* are both fascinating and disturbing."

Discuss the reasons why you agree or disagree with the above statement.
Develop your discussion with reference to the text.

OR

(ii)   Discuss the narrative purposes served by Mary Shelley's inclusion of letters between various characters throughout her novel, *Frankenstein.* Develop your discussion with reference to the text.

E   THE PICTURE OF DORIAN GRAY – Oscar Wilde

(i)   "The consequences of Dorian Gray's pursuit of pleasure and a hedonistic lifestyle in Oscar Wilde's novel, *The Picture of Dorian Gray*, are both fascinating and disturbing."

Discuss the reasons why you agree or disagree with the above statement.
Develop your discussion with reference to the text.

OR

(ii)   Discuss the narrative purposes served by Basil Hallward's portrait of Dorian in Wilde's novel, *The Picture of Dorian Gray.* Develop your discussion with reference to the text.

ktbrwt
Visit www.e-xamit.ie

46

SECTION II   THE COMPARATIVE STUDY   (70 marks)

Candidates must answer **one** question from **either A** – Literary Genre **or B** – Cultural Context **or C** – General Vision and Viewpoint.

Candidates who answer a question in **SECTION I** – The Single Text, may not refer to the same text in answer to questions in this section.

All texts used in this section must be prescribed for comparative study for this year's examination. Candidates may refer to only one film in the course of their answers.

Please note:
- Questions in this section use the word **text** to refer to all the different kinds of texts available for study on this course.
- When used, the word **reader** includes viewers of films and theatre audiences.
- When used, the term **technique** is understood to include techniques employed by all writers and directors of films.
- When used, the word **author** is understood to include all writers and directors of films.
- When used, the word **character** is understood to refer to both real people and fictional characters in texts.

A   LITERARY GENRE

1. (a) Identify two techniques used to advance the plot in **one** text on your comparative course and discuss how effectively these techniques are used for this purpose in this text. Develop your answer with reference to the text.
        (30)

    (b) In the case of each of **two other** texts on your comparative course, identify at least one technique used to advance the plot and compare how effectively this technique or these techniques are employed for this purpose in these texts. You may refer to the same technique or different techniques in each text during the course of your response. Develop your answer with reference to your chosen texts.
        (40)

    OR

2. Compare how successfully at least one technique is employed, by the authors of **at least two** texts on your comparative course, to maintain your interest in a central character throughout each of these texts. You may refer to the same technique or different techniques in each text during the course of your response. Develop your answer with reference to your chosen texts.
        (70)

B   CULTURAL CONTEXT

1.   (a)   Discuss how those in power in society maintain their dominant position in **one** text on your comparative course. Develop your response with reference to the text.   (30)

     (b)   Compare how those in power in society maintain their dominant position in each of **two other** texts on your comparative course. Develop your response with reference to your chosen texts.   (40)

OR

2.   Compare the extent to which the expression of individuality or divergence from social or cultural norms is tolerated within the cultural context of each of **at least two texts** on your comparative course. Develop your response with reference to your chosen texts.   (70)

C   GENERAL VISION AND VIEWPOINT

1.   (a)   Discuss how the level of resilience you found displayed by individuals or communities in **one** text on your comparative course helped to shape your sense of the general vision and viewpoint of this text.   (30)

     (b)   Compare how the levels of resilience you found displayed by individuals or communities in each of **two other** texts on your comparative course influenced your sense of the general vision and viewpoint of these texts. Develop your response with reference to your chosen texts.   (40)

OR

2.   Compare the extent to which your response to the treatment of disadvantaged or disempowered characters contributed to your sense of the general vision and viewpoint in each of **at least two** texts on your comparative course. Develop your response with reference to your chosen texts.   (70)

SECTION III   POETRY   (70 marks)

Candidates must answer **A** – Unseen Poem **and B** – Prescribed Poetry.

A   UNSEEN POEM (20 marks)

In his poem, "The Voice You Hear When You Read Silently", Thomas Lux considers the process of silent reading. Read the poem and answer **either** Question **1 or** Question **2** which follow.

The Voice You Hear When You Read Silently

is not silent, it is a speaking –
out-loud voice in your head: it is *spoken*,
a voice is *saying* it
as you read. It's the writer's words,
of course, in a literary sense
his or her 'voice' but the sound
of that voice is the sound of *your* voice.
Not the sound your friends know
or the sound of a tape played back   **(10)**
but your voice
caught in the dark cathedral
of your skull, your voice heard
by an internal ear
informed by internal abstracts
and what you know by feeling,
having felt.
It is your voice saying, for example,
the word 'barn'
that the writer wrote   **(20)**
but the 'barn' you say
is a barn you know or knew.

The voice in your head, speaking as you read
never says anything neutrally – some people
hated the barn they knew,
some people love the barn they know
so you hear the word loaded
and a sensory constellation
is lit: horse-gnawed stalls,
hayloft, black heat tape wrapping   **(30)**
a water pipe, a slippery
spilled chirr* of oats from a split sack,
the bony, filthy haunches of cows ...
And 'barn' is only a noun – no verb
or subject has entered into the sentence
yet!
The voice you hear when you read to
yourself
is the clearest voice: you speak it speaking to
you.   **(40)**

Thomas Lux

*Chirr – a shrill, trilling sound

---

1. (a) How accurately do you think the poet describes the process of silent reading in the first seventeen lines of the above poem? Support your response with reference to the poem.   (10)

   (b) In your opinion, does the poet make effective use of the word 'barn' to explain how our experiences shape our understanding when we read? Explain your response with reference to the poem.   (10)

OR

2. "Thomas Lux makes effective use of simple language and concrete imagery to explore complex, abstract ideas throughout the above poem."

   Discuss the extent to which you agree or disagree with the above statement. Support your discussion with reference to both the content and language of the poem.   (20)

B   PRESCRIBED POETRY (50 marks)

Candidates must answer **one** of the following questions (**1 – 5**).

1.   **Brendan Kennelly**

"Brendan Kennelly effectively employs an appealing descriptive style to reflect on the triumphs, trials and limitations of the human condition."

To what extent do you agree or disagree with the above statement? Develop your response with reference to the poems by Brendan Kennelly on your Leaving Certificate English course.

2.   **Adrienne Rich**

To what extent do you agree or disagree that Adrienne Rich makes effective use of a diverse range of imagery and an engaging style to explore structures and values in society which she considers to be negative or destructive?

Develop your response with reference to the poems by Adrienne Rich on your Leaving Certificate English course.

eulslx
Visit www.e-xamit.ie

3.   **William Wordsworth**

"William Wordsworth's poetry does not have current appeal because his poetic style and use of language are dated and his themes are irrelevant in the twenty-first century."

Discuss the extent to which you agree or disagree with the above statement, developing your response with reference to the poems by William Wordsworth on your Leaving Certificate English course.

wuwnwr
Visit www.e-xamit.ie

4.   **Emily Dickinson**

"Emily Dickinson's effective use of a vivid and energetic style helps to convey her fascination with life and its rich experiences."

Discuss the extent to which you agree or disagree with the above statement, developing your response with reference to the poems by Emily Dickinson on your Leaving Certificate English course.

fhxipo
Visit www.e-xamit.ie

5.   **W.B. Yeats**

"Yeats makes masterful use of aesthetically pleasing language to communicate the insights he draws from history, myth and legend."

To what extent do you agree or disagree with the above statement, developing your response with reference to the poems by W.B. Yeats on your Leaving Certificate English course.

bdmmjv
Visit www.e-xamit.ie

Do not hand this up.

This document will not be returned to the State Examinations Commission

2022 P2

Leaving Certificate – Higher Level

English

Thursday 9 June
Afternoon 2.00 – 5.20

Coimisiún na Scrúduithe Stáit
State Examinations Commission

LEAVING CERTIFICATE EXAMINATION, 2021

English - Higher Level - Paper 1

Total Marks: 140

Wednesday, 9 June – Morning, 9.30 – 12.20

- This paper is divided into two sections,
  Section I COMPREHENDING and Section II COMPOSING.
- The paper contains **three** texts on the general theme of **REFLECTIONS ON TIME.**
- Candidates should familiarise themselves with each of the texts before beginning their answers.
- Both sections of this paper (COMPREHENDING and COMPOSING) must be attempted.
- Section I, Comprehending, carries 40 marks.
- Section II, Composing, carries 100 marks.

SECTION I – COMPREHENDING

- Two Questions, A and B, follow each text.
- Candidates must answer **ONE** question in Section I:
  either one Question A **OR one** Question B on **ONE** text.

SECTION II – COMPOSING

- Candidates must write on **one** of the compositions 1 – 7.

2021 P1

TEXT 1 – TIME PIECES

Text 1 is based on edited extracts from *Time Pieces – A Dublin Memoir* by John Banville. In this text the writer reflects on some childhood memories and shares his thoughts on the past.

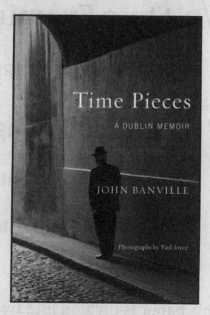

Dublin was never my Dublin, which made it all the more alluring. I was born in Wexford, a small town that was smaller and more remote then, sequestered in its own past. My birthday falls on 8 December. The eighth used to be both a Holy Day and a day when people from the provinces flocked to the capital to do their Christmas shopping and marvel at the Christmas lights. So my birthday treat on successive years in the first half of the 1950s was a trip by train to Dublin, a thing I looked forward to for months beforehand.

We would leave from the town's North Station in the wintry darkness of early morning. I believe there were still steam trains then, although diesel was the coming thing. How thrilling it was to walk through the sombre, deserted streets, my head still fuzzy from sleep, with the long day's adventure all before me. The train would arrive from Rosslare Harbour, carrying blear-eyed passengers off the overnight ferry from Fishguard in Wales. Away we would chug, the window beside me a black glass mirror in which I could study my menacingly shadowed reflection and imagine myself a confidential agent – as spies used to be called in the espionage novels of a previous age – on board the Orient Express and bound on a top-secret mission to the dusky and dangerous East.

We would have been somewhere in the approaches to Arklow when the dawn came up, turning the frost-white fields to a shade of sharply glistening mica-pink. Certain moments in certain places, apparently insignificant, imprint themselves on the memory with improbable vividness and clarity – improbable because, so clear and so vivid are they, the suspicion arises that one must have imagined them. Of those December journeys I recall, or am convinced I recall, a certain spot where the train slowed at a river bend – the Avoca river, it must have been – a spot I can still see clearly in my memory's eye, and which I have returned to repeatedly in my novels.

Dublin, of course, was the opposite of ordinary. Dublin was, for me, a place of magical promise towards which my starved young soul endlessly yearned. That the city itself, the real Dublin, was, in those poverty-stricken 1950s, mostly a grey and graceless place, did not mar my dream of it – and I dreamed of it even when I was present in it, so that mundane reality was being constantly transformed before my eyes into high romance.

When does the past become the past? How much time must elapse before what merely happened begins to give off the mysterious, sacred glow that is the mark of true pastness? After all, the resplendent vision we carry with us in memory was once merely the present, wholly unremarkable, except in those moments when one has just fallen in love or won the lottery. What is the magic that is worked upon experience, when it is consigned to the laboratory of the past, there to be shaped and burnished to a finished radiance? Let us say, the present is where we live, while the past is where we dream. Yet if it is a dream, it is substantial, and sustaining. The past buoys us up, a tethered and ever-expanding hot-air balloon. What transmutation must the present go through in order to become the past? Time's alchemy works in a bright abyss.

Westland Row Station – it did not become Pearse Station until years later – was mostly a vast soot-blackened glass dome, a couple of grim platforms, and a ramp leading down to the street. It seems to me now that on every one of those eighths of December we arrived in rain. This was not the driving, pounding rain of the provinces, but a special urban variety, its drops as fine and as penetrating as neutrinos, those teeming showers of subatomic, indeed sub-subatomic, particles that flash through you and me and all things at every instant. The rain turned the pavements greasy, so that one had to make one's way over them with caution in one's slippery leather soles.

At the station exit we turned left on to Westland Row. At the top of the street, turning left and immediately right, we would come up into Merrion Square, where, at number one, a fine example, at least in its exterior, of a terraced Georgian townhouse, Oscar Wilde was born. I need hardly say I knew none of these things at the time of which I am writing. I doubt I had even heard of poor Oscar, who today is commemorated by a hideous and garishly painted statue, representing him asprawl on a rock at the corner of the square opposite his birthplace. What indignities we consider ourselves free to visit upon the famous dead!

N.B. Answer only **ONE question in Section I**, either **one** Question A OR **one** Question B on **one** text.

QUESTION A – 40 Marks

(i) Based on your reading of TEXT 1, explain three insights you gained into the impact of time on memories. Support your answer with reference to the text. (10)

(ii) In paragraph 5, John Banville observes, "the present is where we live, while the past is where we dream." Give your personal response to this observation by the writer. (10)

(iii) Identify four features of the language of narration, evident in the above text, and discuss how effectively these features are employed by John Banville to tell the story of his childhood trips to Dublin. Support your response with reference to the text. (20)

QUESTION B – 40 Marks

You have been invited to write **a feature article**, entitled *Monumental Matters – The Story of Statues*, to appear in the magazine supplement of a weekend newspaper. In your article you should: reflect on the long-established tradition of erecting statues to celebrate or memorialise people, explore some of the reasons why commemorative statues may be controversial, and give your views on continuing this tradition into the future.

TEXT 2 – DAYDREAMING BACK IN TIME

This text is adapted from poet Doireann Ní Ghríofa's award-winning prose debut, *A Ghost in the Throat*. In this edited extract the writer reflects on how the past and the present come together in her garden.

I love the garden and the garden loves me, but it isn't mine, not really. I will always share it with the woman who began it, who arrived in a sun-dress to a newly built council house and cared for this garden all her life. I don't know where she is now, but her bulbs are buried here. The very first morning that I walked through her garden, her daffodils' buttery hellos were easily translated: they nodded. I nodded back.

To work this soil is to sift an archaeology of a stranger's thought. Each time I find an old bulb or the splinters of a broken cup planted for drainage, I am thankful for her labour. With every month, more of her flowers lift their heads from the soil, waving polite hellos in pinks and yellows and blues. I don't know their names, but I think of her in every small act of weeding and pruning, of watering and fertilising. I pat the earth with gentleness. My nails are always dirty, my palms shovel-blistered, my knees drenched, but I don't care. I am happy here. In mapping my own additions to this small plot, I choose with care, because I hold a specific desire for this place: I want to lure the bees to me.

Plastic seed-trays soon proliferate all along our windowsills, each square of soil brimming with a velvet darkness from which tiny seedlings peek. I love the sprouting of their infant limbs, how they wear their seedcases like jaunty bonnets.

Of the many species of bumblebee in Ireland, I've read that one third may be extinct within a decade. The cat watches from the wall as I set to work, a clumsy gardener who digs not by trowel or spade but by dented soup spoon. Every day, I am digging and grunting and raking, heaving compost from the shed, setting plump armfuls of plants and bulbs, and patting them down. Each new plant I choose is both nectar and pollen-heavy, every clump of colour designed to bloom as a lure. Here will be sunflowers and snowdrops, I tell my husband, holding his hand tight, and over there, lavender and fuchsia. Our peripheries will hold hedges of hawthorn and hazel, I'll lure honeysuckle along the walls, and we'll abandon a fat ribbon of untouched wilderness beyond, in which brambles and dandelions will flourish. It will be so beautiful, I say, and press my smiling lips to his in excitement. I am determined to rewrite the air here until it sings the songs of long ago; I want it rewound and purring with bees.

We may imagine that we can imagine the past, but this is an impossibility. As a child I was so enchanted by history that I would sometimes sit by a stream and try to daydream myself back in time. To the hurry-burble of water, my mind set to work, forgiving first the distant buzz of traffic, and then, through clumsy acts of further deletion, trying to subtract all the other resonances of modernity. This, I told my ears, this soundscape, yes, but minus cars, minus tractors, minus airplanes, minus the sad cow-howl of industrial farming, minus it all, until only stream-lilt and bird-chirp remain. Now, I would tell myself, this, *this* must have been what the past really sounded like. I was wrong. Long ago, the air was never as quiet as I presumed. It was alive, strumming the tune of those sisters so accustomed to drudgery, the background chorus of those who always hum as they work.

As the new plants unfurled into sunlight, the bees began to arrive. I dragged a cobwebbed lawn-chair from the garage and spied on their busy rumps as they browsed the gifts I'd grown for them. I watched the bees and thought of the poet Paula Meehan. I'd heard her describe how cherished bees were in medieval Ireland, when entire tracts of our Brehon laws provided a legal framework for their behaviour. Bees flew through the law and into folklore.

They are only bees, it's true. In the absence of the neurological embellishments that make moral beings of humans, we assume other creatures' lives are somehow lesser by comparison with our own. However, a bee, being a bee, will accept her own death to let her sister bees live, a decision with which any human would surely struggle. The opposite of selfishness; if she stings, it is to protect others from danger, donating her life so that others may survive.

How lonesome I'd be, if the bees left the sweet-shop I've built for them. I've done all I can to hearten them, I have hummed to them, I have fed and sheltered and loved them. I want to keep them here at all costs.

N.B. Answer only **ONE** question in Section I, either **one** Question A OR **one** Question B on **one** text.

QUESTION A – 40 Marks

(i) Based on your reading of TEXT 2, explain three insights you gained into what links the past and the present in the writer's life. Support your answer with reference to the text. (10)

(ii) In paragraph 5, Doireann Ní Ghríofa observes, "We may imagine that we can imagine the past, but this is an impossibility." Give your personal response to this observation by the writer. (10)

(iii) Identify four features of the aesthetic use of language, evident in the above text, and discuss how effectively these features are employed by Doireann Ní Ghríofa to convey her personal experiences, hopes and dreams. Support your response with reference to the text. (20)

QUESTION B – 40 Marks

An assertion that other creatures' lives are somehow lesser than human life has prompted extensive debate on social media. In order to join in this online debate, write **an open letter** to be shared on social media, in which you: state your position in relation to animal rights, explore some of the issues associated with our current engagement with animals and outline what you see as the major challenges we face as we share the planet with animals in the future.

TEXT 3 – THIS IS YOUR TIME

TEXT 3 is based on edited extracts from the transcript of a graduation speech delivered in 2018 by American actor, Chadwick Boseman, at Howard University. In this text Mr Boseman reflects on the time he spent at Howard and how it influenced him.

It is a great privilege, graduates, to address you on your day, a day marking one of the most important accomplishments of your life to date. This is a magical place. I remember walking across this yard on what seemed to be a random day, my head down lost in my own world of issues, like many of you do daily. I raised my head and Muhammad Ali was walking towards me. He raised his fist to a quintessential guard. I was game to play along with him, to act as if I was a worthy opponent. What an honour to be challenged by the greatest of all time for a brief moment. His security let the joke play along for a second before they ushered him away, and I walked away floating like a butterfly, light and ready to take on the world. That is the magic of this place. Almost anything can happen here.

Howard University has many names, the Mecca, the Hilltop. It only takes one tour of the physical campus to understand why we call it the Hilltop. Almost every day I would walk the full length of the hill to Fine Arts where most of my classes were. Throughout ancient times, institutions of learning have been built on top of hills to convey that great struggle is required to achieve degrees of enlightenment.

For some of you, the challenge was actually academics. You worked hard. You did your best, but you didn't make As or Bs, sometimes Cs. That's okay, you are here on top of the hill. Sometimes your grades don't give a real indication of what your greatness might be. For others the challenge was financial. You and your family struggled to make ends meet, but you are here. For a lot of you, your hardest struggle was social. You were never as cool and as popular as you wanted to be and it bothered you, but you are here. Most of you

graduating here today struggled against one or more of the obstacles I mentioned in order to reach this hill-top. I urge you to invest in the importance of this moment and cherish it.

Early in my career I got an audition for a soap-opera on a major network. I was promised more money than I had ever seen before. When I saw the role I was playing – that of a young man in his formative years with a violent streak pulled into the allure of gang involvement – I found myself conflicted. That's somebody's real story. Any role, played honestly, can be empowering, but I was conflicted because this role seemed to be wrapped up in assumptions about us as black folk. Howard had instilled in me a certain amount of pride and for my taste this role didn't live up to those standards.

After filming the first two episodes, I had an opportunity to bring my concerns to the executives of the show. I asked them some questions about the background of my character. Question one: where is my father? The exec answered, "Well, he left when you were younger." Okay. Question two: in this script, it alluded to my mother not being equipped to operate as a good parent, so why exactly did my little brother and I have to go into foster care? Matter-of-factly, he said, "Well, of course she is on heroin." I queried whether some of the assumptions around characterisation were stereotypical. That word lingered. I was let go from that job on the next day. My agents told me it might be a while before I got a job acting on screen again.

But what do you do when the principles and the standards that were instilled in you here at Howard closed the doors in front of you? I thought of Ali in the middle of the yard in his elder years, drawing from his victories and his losses. I realised that he was transferring something to me on that day. He was transferring the spirit of the fighter to me.

Graduating class hear me well this day. This day,

when you have reached the hill top and you are deciding on next jobs, next steps, careers, you should rather find purpose than a job or a career. Purpose is an essential element of you. It is the reason you are on the planet at this particular time in history. Remember, the struggles along the way are only meant to shape you for your purpose.

I don't know what your future is, but if you are willing to take the harder way, the one with more failures at first than successes, the one that is ultimately proven to have more meaning, more victory, more glory, then you will not regret it. Now, this is your time. Howard's legacy is not wrapped up in the money that you will make, but the challenges that you choose to confront. As you commence on your paths, press on with pride and press on with purpose.

N.B. Answer only **ONE** question in **Section I**, either **one** Question A OR **one** Question B on **one** text.

QUESTION A – 40 Marks

(i)   Based on your reading of TEXT 3, explain three insights you gained into how Chadwick Boseman was influenced by his time at Howard University. Support your answer with reference to the text.   (10)

(ii)   In paragraph 7, Chadwick Boseman observes, "Purpose is an essential element of you." Give your personal response to this observation by the writer.   (10)

(iii) Identify four features of the language of persuasion evident in the above text, and discuss how effectively these features are employed by Chadwick Boseman to craft an emotional and inspiring speech. Support your response with reference to the text.   (20)

QUESTION B – 40 Marks

You have decided to apply for the position of editor of your school's Graduation Yearbook. Each year, the Yearbook has a different theme, chosen by the editor. An article by a celebrity contributor is also included annually. To be considered for the post, you must make **a verbal pitch*** to the graduation committee members in which you: promote your preferred theme for the 2021 Graduation Yearbook, impress the committee with your ideas for its content, and nominate your ideal celebrity contributor, explaining your choice to the committee members. Write the text for the verbal pitch that you would make.

*A spoken promotional presentation

SECTION II   COMPOSING   (100 marks)

Write a composition on **any one** of the assignments that appear in **bold print** below.

Each composition carries 100 marks.

The composition assignments are intended to reflect language study in the areas of information, argument, persuasion, narration, and the aesthetic use of language.

1.   In TEXT 1, John Banville tells us of the annual childhood trip to Dublin to celebrate his birthday.

   Write a personal essay in which you reflect on the significance of birthdays, your own and those of others, sharing your thoughts on this annual personal milestone.

2.   Bees, whose lives depend on the community of the hive, feature prominently in Text 2.

   Write a discursive essay in which you consider the meaning and importance of community.

3.   In TEXT 1, John Banville recalls seeing, "blear-eyed passengers off the overnight ferry from Fishguard in Wales" as he waited at the railway station.

   Write a short story, set in a railway station, in which a passenger off the overnight ferry from Fishguard in Wales plays an important role. Your short story may be amusing or menacing in tone.

4.   In TEXT 3, Muhammad Ali's security personnel play along with a joke between the boxer and Chadwick Boseman.

   Write a personal essay in which you reflect on the role of humour, fun and laughter in life.

5.   In TEXT 2, Doireann Ní Ghríofa alludes to the importance of bees in medieval Ireland.

   Write a fable or fairy-tale, set in ancient Ireland, in which a bee or bees feature prominently.

6.   In TEXT 2, Doireann Ní Ghríofa celebrates the colours in her garden, the sounds of the past and the "purring" of bees.

   Write an article, for publication in a popular magazine, about the many and varied colours and sounds that punctuate and surround our daily lives and the impact they have on us.

7.   In TEXT 3, Chadwick Boseman draws attention to the dangers of stereotyping.

   You have been asked to speak, as a representative of a national youth organisation, at the launch of a major campaign against stereotyping. Write the speech you would deliver.

nagjof
Visit www.e-xamit.ie

Acknowledgements

Images and texts that appear on this examination paper were sourced as follows:

Text 1: Time Pieces, A Dublin Memoir, John Banville, Hachette Books Ireland, Dublin, 2016
Image: Cover image – Paul Joyce

Text 2: GHOST IN THE THROAT by Doireann Ní Ghríofa. Copyright © Doireann Ní Ghríofa 2020, used by permission of The Wylie Agency (UK) Limited
Image: https://publicdomainpictures.net/pictures/220000/velka/pollinating-bee-149451888900p.jpg

Text 3: https://washingtonpost.com/education/2020/08/29/chadwick-boseman-praised-student-protesters-2018-commencement-speech-howard-university-watch-video/
Image: Actor Chadwick Boseman attends The 2018 ESPYS at Microsoft Theater in Los Angeles on July 18, 2018 (Axelle / Bauer-Griffin/FilmMagic/Getty Images file) https://www.nbcnews.com/pop-culture/celebrity/hollywood-remembers-chadwick-boseman-superstar-screen-life-n1238779

2021 P1

Leaving Certificate – Higher Level

English

Wednesday 9 June
Morning 9.30 – 12.20

Coimisiún na Scrúduithe Stáit
State Examinations Commission

LEAVING CERTIFICATE EXAMINATION, 2021

English - Higher Level - Paper 2

Total Marks: 140

Thursday, 10 June – Afternoon, 2.00 – 5.20

Candidates must attempt the required number of questions in **any TWO** of the following sections:

- SECTION I – The Single Text
- SECTION II – The Comparative Study
- SECTION III – Poetry, Part A, Unseen Poem and Part B, Prescribed Poetry.
- All sections carry 70 marks.

N.B. Candidates are **NOT** required to answer on Shakespearean Drama.

INDEX OF SINGLE TEXTS

The Handmaid's Tale	Page - 2
Days Without End	Page - 2
Wuthering Heights	Page - 2
King Lear	Page - 3
The Tempest	Page - 3

SECTION I   THE SINGLE TEXT   (70 marks)

Candidates must answer **one** question from this section (**A – E**).

A   THE HANDMAID'S TALE – Margaret Atwood

(i)   Discuss how your knowledge of Offred's life before Gilead, and the insights you gained from her memories and private thoughts, influenced your response to her character. Develop your answer with reference to Margaret Atwood's novel, *The Handmaid's Tale*.

OR

(ii)   Discuss the reasons why, in your opinion, the dystopian aspects of the novel increase or diminish the narrative power of Margaret Atwood's novel, *The Handmaid's Tale*. Develop your response with reference to the text.

B   DAYS WITHOUT END – Sebastian Barry

(i)   Discuss how your knowledge of the challenges Thomas McNulty faced before he met John Cole, and the insights you gained from his relationship with Winona, influenced your response to his character. Develop your answer with reference to Sebastian Barry's novel, *Days Without End*.

OR

(ii)   Discuss the reasons why, in your opinion, the historical aspects of the novel increase or diminish the narrative power of Sebastian Barry's novel, *Days Without End*. Develop your response with reference to the text.

C   WUTHERING HEIGHTS – Emily Brontë

(i)   Discuss how your knowledge of the difficulties Heathcliff experienced as a child, and the insights you gained from his obsessive behaviour throughout the novel, influenced your response to his character. Develop your answer with reference to Emily Brontë's novel, *Wuthering Heights*.

OR

(ii)   Discuss the reasons why, in your opinion, the gothic aspects of the novel increase or diminish the narrative power of Emily Brontë's novel, *Wuthering Heights*. Develop your response with reference to the text.

D   KING LEAR – William Shakespeare

(i)   "Chaos and confusion are used to great effect throughout Shakespeare's play, *King Lear*."

Discuss the above statement, developing your response with reference to the text

OR

(ii)   A production of Shakespeare's play, *King Lear*, in which the characters of Kent and the Fool do not appear has been proposed. Discuss the reasons why, in your opinion, the removal of each of these characters would or would not diminish Shakespeare's play, *King Lear*. Develop your response with reference to the text.

E   THE TEMPEST – William Shakespeare

(i)   "Chaos and confusion are used to great effect throughout Shakespeare's play, *The Tempest*."

Discuss the above statement, developing your response with reference to the text

OR

(ii)   A production of Shakespeare's play, *The Tempest*, in which the characters of Caliban and Miranda do not appear has been proposed. Discuss the reasons why, in your opinion, the removal of each of these characters would or would not diminish Shakespeare's play, *The Tempest*. Develop your response with reference to the text.

SECTION II   THE COMPARATIVE STUDY   (70 marks)

Candidates must answer **one** question from **either A** – Theme or Issue **or B** – Cultural Context **or C** – General Vision and Viewpoint.

Candidates who answer a question in **SECTION I** – The Single Text, may not refer to the same text in answer to questions in this section.

All texts used in this section must be prescribed for comparative study for this year's examination. Candidates may refer to only one film in the course of their answers.

Please note:
- Questions in this section use the word **text** to refer to all the different kinds of texts available for study on this course.
- When used, the word **reader** includes viewers of films and theatre audiences.
- When used, the term **technique** is understood to include techniques employed by all writers and directors of films.
- When used, the word **author** is understood to include all writers and directors of films.
- When used, the word **character** is understood to refer to both real people and fictional characters in texts.

A   THEME OR ISSUE

1.   (a)   Identify a theme or issue you studied on your comparative course. Discuss the various reasons why you did or did not find the exploration of this theme or issue emotionally engaging in **one** text on your comparative course. Support your response with reference to the text.   (30)

    (b)   Compare the reasons why you found the exploration of the same theme or issue discussed above, more, less or equally emotionally engaging in each of **two other** texts you studied on your comparative course. Develop your response with reference to your chosen texts.   (40)

OR

2.   Compare the insights you gained into the same theme or issue through understanding what influences or motivates one central character, from each of **at least two** texts on your comparative course, when making one or more key decisions. Develop your response with reference to your chosen texts.

    The insight or insights you gain into the same theme or issue from different texts may be similar or different.   (70)

B   CULTURAL CONTEXT

1.   (a)   Discuss the extent to which a significant relationship was influenced by at least
one aspect of the cultural context in **one** text on your comparative course.
Develop your response with reference to the text.   (30)

(b)   Compare the extent to which one significant relationship was influenced by
any aspect or aspects of the cultural context in each of **two other** texts on your
comparative course. Develop your response with reference to your chosen
texts.   (40)

OR

2.   Compare the reasons why significant social change does or does not occur within
the cultural context established in each of **at least two** texts on your comparative
course. Develop your response with reference to your chosen texts.   (70)

C   GENERAL VISION AND VIEWPOINT

1.   (a)   Discuss the extent to which a character that you found inspiring in **one**
text on your comparative course influenced your sense of the general vision
and viewpoint of this text. Develop your response with reference to your
chosen text.   (30)

(b)   In relation to **two other** texts on your comparative course, compare the extent
to which a character that you found inspiring influenced your sense of the
general vision and viewpoint of each of these texts. Develop your response with
reference to your chosen texts.   (40)

OR

2.   "The aspects of a text that we find unsettling or disturbing often influence our sense
of the general vision and viewpoint."

In relation to **at least two** texts on your comparative course, compare the extent
to which an aspect or aspects of your chosen texts, that you found unsettling or
disturbing, influenced your sense of the general vision and viewpoint of these texts.
Develop your response with refence to your chosen texts.   (70)

Candidates must answer **A** – Unseen Poem **and B** – Prescribed Poetry.

A   UNSEEN POEM (20 marks)

Read the following poem, in which the poet, Louise Greig, issues instructions for the construction of an Albatross, a seabird noted for its giant wingspan.

Answer **either** Question **1 or** Question **2** which follow.

How to Construct an Albatross

Begin by setting the instructions aside.
Instead tune the mind to flight.
Attach the huge, clunking wings (treat like hangar doors)
– do this by lantern light; now heave them wide.
Next, place the heart inside – adjust to beating;
You may witness a sudden upwards surge
as the chest swells – this will be fleeting –
resist the urge to release;
now, embed the eyes (still asleep – this matters)
and fasten the beak; carry the slumbering bird
to someplace steep, repeating the word wake,
and – this is key – just as the heart (yours) begins to break
and the slow whales blow –
let go

Louise Greig

---

1. (a) Do you find the language used by the poet in the above poem appealing?
   Explain your response with reference to the poem.   (10)

   (b) The poet has not placed a punctuation mark at the end of the above poem. In your opinion, what is the effect of this decision on the poem? Explain your response with reference to the poem.   (10)

   OR

2. Based on your reading of the above poem, explain the reasons why you find it to be serious or amusing or both. Support your response with reference to the poet's use of language and the subject matter of the poem.   (20)

2021 P2

---

nbhvnm
Visit www.e-xamit.ie

B   PRESCRIBED POETRY (50 marks)

Candidates must answer **one** of the following questions (**1 – 5**).

---

1.   Eavan Boland

Discuss how successfully, in your opinion, Eavan Boland employs a range of narrative elements in her poetry to communicate a variety of thematic concerns. Develop your response with reference to the poems by Eavan Boland on your Leaving Certificate English course.

> grgeoy
> Visit www.e-xamit.ie

2.   John Keats

"Our enjoyment of the sensuous beauty of the poetry of John Keats may be diminished by our awareness of the fear or melancholy often evident in his work."

Based on your experience of the poetry by John Keats you have studied for your Leaving Certificate, to what extent do you agree or disagree with the above statement? Develop your response with reference to the poems by John Keats on the Leaving Certificate English course.

> fusiql
> Visit www.e-xamit.ie

3.   Seamus Heaney

"Seamus Heaney transforms the familiar and the mundane through his powerful use of language, thereby enabling us to learn a range of profound lessons from his poetry."

Discuss the above statement, developing your response with reference to your experience of the poems by Seamus Heaney on your Leaving Certificate English course.

4.   Sylvia Plath

Discuss how successfully, in your opinion, Sylvia Plath uses stylistic features in an innovative way to convey both overwhelming wonder and unsettling menace in her work. Develop your response with reference to the poems by Sylvia Plath on your Leaving Certificate English course.

> hoqbqa
> Visit www.e-xamit.ie

5.   Paul Durcan

"Durcan makes effective use of tone or mood to express his emotions, thereby amplifying his various thematic concerns."

Discuss the above statement, developing your response with reference to your experience of the poetry by Paul Durcan on your Leaving Certificate English course.

> kltyrw
> Visit www.e-xamit.ie

2021 P2

Leaving Certificate – Higher Level

English

Thursday 10 June
Afternoon 2.00 – 5.20

Coimisiún na Scrúduithe Stáit
State Examinations Commission

LEAVING CERTIFICATE EXAMINATION, 2020

English - Higher Level - Paper 1

Total Marks: 200

Duration: 2 hours 50 minutes

- This paper is divided into two sections,
  Section I COMPREHENDING and Section II COMPOSING.
- The paper contains **three** texts on the general theme of **EXPLORING GENRE**.
- Candidates should familiarise themselves with each of the texts before beginning their answers.
- Both sections of this paper (COMPREHENDING and COMPOSING) must be attempted.
- Each section carries 100 marks.

SECTION I – COMPREHENDING

- Two Questions, A and B, follow each text.
- Candidates must answer a Question A on one text and a Question B on a different text. Candidates must answer only one Question A and only one Question B.

N.B. Candidates may NOT answer a Question A and a Question B on the same text.

SECTION II – COMPOSING

- Candidates must write on **one** of the compositions 1 – 7.

SECTION I   COMPREHENDING   (100 marks)

TEXT 1 – FROM GENRE to GENRE

This text consists of two elements: firstly, edited extracts adapted from Alan McMonagle's essay, *The Misadventures of a Dithering Writer in Thirteen and A Half Fragments*, in which he discusses writing in different genres. The second element is a genre-related cartoon by Tom Gauld.

I flit anxiously and eagerly from genre to genre. I always have a few stories on the go. Some of them are like eels – they slip away if I do not make a fast grab. Some are like bold children – they pay absolutely no attention to anything I tell them to do. One or two arrive unannounced from the farthest recesses of my imagination and insist on writing themselves with little or no input from myself. I have four novels to write and a couple of plays require open heart surgery. Several poems are threatening to rise up and bite off my fingers if I don't give them immediate attention.

I don't know if my writing is in anyway distinctive. I am an aural learner as opposed to say the more common visual learning that attends so much writing. I can hear things before I see them. My reasons for writing are partly intrinsic, partly spiritual, partly fanatical. Intrinsic because if I do not write I will go mad. Spiritual because I like to hang around with people who do not exist. Fanatical because I like moving as quickly as possible from the everyday world into the world of the imagination. Stretching reality; bending it, distorting it, somehow twisting it out of shape. Watching what characters make of this tilt in their lives – this is what I like to do.

I began writing as a boy. Little stories, plays, poems. My early offering was heavily influenced by an unlikely combination of Agatha Christie and an anthology of Greek myths and legends devoured innumerable times in my local library. By the age of twelve I announced my retirement as a writer. I stopped writing for a long time and was reluctant to resume. Having abandoned it for so long, when I returned to writing as an adult I was so grateful and so relieved upon realising that the realm of the imagination had not abandoned me. Let yourself be led by the child that you were. This is a tendency I adhered to upon my resumption and, indeed, return to when it all threatens to get away from me.

I am, at various times, a reluctant, plodding, instinctive, spontaneous writer. At times I feel that, if I stay awake for long enough, I can reach the end of a considerable narrative arc. At other times I feel that uncapping a pen is a bridge too far. I wake and enter every day with varying combinations of wonder and dread.

I have started several novels. There is the edgy-existential one about the brother-sister assassination squad. There is the comedy-of-desperation one about the office slave finally tipped over the edge by a boss constantly referred to as the highly evolved vegetable. There is the life-weary one about the last day in the working life of a barber terrified beyond measure of the imminent reunion with his poet-activist daughter. There is my novel featuring an as-yet-to-be named antagonist who is more of a genius in dreams than in life. I am all the time hankering to work on the very project I am not currently tangled up inside.

If you know what you want to be you will be it. If you don't know, then you will spend your days reinventing yourself, discovering who you are. I envy the former standpoint in so many ways. But I am an uncertain person and rather than rail against this uncertainty I try to harness it. And so each day becomes the first day; it allows room for discovery, invention, re-invention, wonder, mystery; all of which are manna for the creative urge and time spent dwelling in the imagination. Writing is about taking risks. It is a high wire act. A game you lose almost all the time.

FINISH WRITING YOUR NOVEL AT ONE OF OUR RENTAL PROPERTIES

FOR ROMANCE WRITERS	FOR SCI-FI WRITERS	FOR REALIST WRITERS	FOR HORROR WRITERS
• EXTENSIVE GROUNDS • HORSES AND SERVANTS • BALLROOM	• HERMETICALLY SEALED* • ROBOT BUTLER • HOVER CAR	• CENTRAL HEATING • FITTED KITCHEN • GARAGE	• SINISTER NEIGHBOURS • GRAVEYARD • UNRELIABLE POWER

* Hermetically sealed – sealed with airtight closure   **Cartoon by Tom Gauld**

N.B. Candidates may NOT answer Question A and Question B on the same text.

QUESTION A – 50 Marks

(i) Based on your reading of the written element of TEXT 1, explain three insights you gain into Alan McMonagle's approach to writing. Support your response with reference to the text. (15)

(ii) The edited extract from Alan McMonagle's work that appears on Page 2 is an example of personal writing. Explain why you think genres of personal writing, such as autobiographies, memoirs and diaries, have a wide and enduring appeal. Make three points in your response. (15)

(iii) Based on your reading of the written element of TEXT 1, discuss four stylistic features that make the extract from Alan McMonagle's essay an engaging piece of personal writing. Support your response with reference to four stylistic features evident in the text. (20)

QUESTION B – 50 Marks

You have been asked to write the text for **a promotional article** by the editor of a property magazine called, *Rentals for Writers*. Your article will be illustrated by the cartoon that appears above. In your promotional article you should: advertise the properties featured in the cartoon as inspirational venues in which to finish novels in particular genres, draw attention to previous literary successes associated with some of these properties, and detail any unique terms and conditions which will apply to particular properties. The article may be humorous or serious or both.

vhpmae
Visit www.e-xamit.ie

TEXT 2 – DETECTIVE FICTION

This text is based on edited extracts adapted from *Sherlock Holmes and the Adventure of the Blue Carbuncle*, a short story by Arthur Conan Doyle, originally published in 1892.

I had called upon my friend Sherlock Holmes. He was lounging upon the sofa in a purple dressing gown, a pipe within his reach, and a pile of crumpled morning papers, evidently newly studied, near at hand. Beside the couch was a wooden chair, on which sat a very seedy and disreputable hard-felt hat, much the worse for wear, and cracked in several places. A magnifying glass was lying upon the seat of the chair. I seated myself before his crackling fire, for a sharp frost had set in, and the windows were thick with the ice crystals.

'I suppose,' I remarked, 'that, homely as it looks, that hat has some deadly story linked on to it – that it is the clue which will guide you in the solution of some mystery and the punishment of some crime.'

'No, no, Watson. No crime,' said Sherlock Holmes, laughing. 'Only one of those whimsical little incidents which will happen when you have four million human beings all jostling each other within the space of a few square miles. You know Peterson, the commissionaire*? It is to him this trophy belongs, he found it. Its owner is unknown. I beg that you look upon it as an intellectual problem.'

'The facts are these. About four o'clock in the morning, Peterson was making his way homewards down Tottenham Court Road. In front of him he saw, in the gaslight, a tallish man, walking with a slight stagger. A row broke out between this stranger and a little knot of roughs. One of these knocked off the man's hat. Peterson had rushed forward to protect the stranger from his assailants, but the man, seeing an official looking person in uniform rushing towards him, took to his heels, and vanished amid the labyrinth of small streets. The roughs had also fled.

Peterson was left in possession of the field of battle, and also of the spoils of victory in the shape of this battered hat. He brought the hat to me, knowing that even the smallest problems are of interest to me. Here is my magnifying glass. You know my methods. What can you gather as to the individuality of the man who has worn this article?'

I took the tattered object in my hands and turned it over rather ruefully. It was a very ordinary black hat of the usual round shape, hard, and much the worse for wear. 'I can see nothing,' said I, handing it back to my friend.

'On the contrary, Watson, you can see everything. You fail however, to reason from what you see. You are too timid in drawing your inferences.'

Holmes picked the hat up and gazed at it in the peculiar introspective fashion which was characteristic of him. 'There are a few inferences which are very distinct, and a few others which represent at least a strong balance of probability. That the man was highly intellectual is, of course, obvious. Also, he was fairly well-to-do, although he has now fallen upon harder times. He has grizzled hair, which he has had cut within the last few days. These are the more patent facts that are to be deduced from his hat.'

2020 P1

'You are certainly joking, Holmes. I have no doubt that I am very stupid, but I must confess that I am unable to follow you. How did you deduce that this man was intellectual?'

For answer Holmes clapped the hat upon his head. It came right over the forehead and settled upon the bridge of his nose. 'It is a question of cubic capacity,' said he: 'a man with so large a brain must have something in it.'

'The decline of his fortunes, then?'

'This hat is three years old. These flat brims curled at the edge were fashionable then. It is a hat of the very best quality. Look at the band of ribbed silk and the excellent lining. If this man could afford to buy so expensive a hat three years ago, and has had no hat since, then he has assuredly gone down in the world. The further point, that his hair is grizzled, and that it has been recently cut, are to be gathered from a close examination of the lower part of the lining. The magnifying glass discloses a large number of hair-ends, clean cut by the scissors of the barber.'

'Well, it is very ingenious,' said I, laughing. 'But since, as you said just now, there has been no crime committed, all this seems to be rather a waste of energy.'

Sherlock Holmes had opened his mouth to reply when the door flew open, and Peterson rushed into the apartment with flushed cheeks, dazed with astonishment.

*Commissionaire – a uniformed hotel door attendant.

N.B. Candidates may NOT answer Question A and Question B on the same text.

QUESTION A – 50 Marks

(i)   Based on your reading of the edited extract above, explain three insights you gain into the character of Sherlock Holmes. Support your response with reference to the text.   (15)

(ii) TEXT 2 is an example of writing in the genre, detective fiction. Explain why you think this genre has a wide and enduring appeal. Make three points in your response.   (15)

(iii) Identify four features of good storytelling evident in the extract. Discuss how the features you have identified add to your enjoyment of the extract. Support your response with reference to the extract.   (20)

QUESTION B – 50 Marks

You have been asked to write **the introduction** to a new collection of contemporary detective fiction. In your introduction you should: outline the reasons why you think detective stories have enduring appeal, discuss some of the personal qualities you believe are essential in a memorable fictional detective, and explain why you recommend this particular collection of stories to readers.

TEXT 3 – SCIENCE FICTION (SCI-FI)

Text 3 consists of two elements: edited extracts adapted from Becky Chambers' recent science fiction novella, *To be Taught, if Fortunate*, and a sci-fi magazine cover from the 1950s.

My name is Ariadne O'Neill, and I'm the flight engineer aboard the Open Cluster Astronautics space craft, *Merian*. My crew mates are mission specialists Elena Quesada-Cruz, Jack Vo, and Chikondi Daka. We're part of the Lawki programme, a broad ecological survey of exoplanets – that is, planets that do not orbit our sun – known or suspected to harbour life. Our mission is focused on the habitable worlds in orbit around the red dwarf star Zhenyi (BA-921), including the icy moon, Aecor. In terms of formal training, I'm not a scientist. I'm an engineer. I build the machines that get scientists where they need to go.

We descended into Aecor's atmosphere without a hitch. My heart pounded as I put on my Terrestrial Extra-Vehicular Activity (TEVA) suit. TEVA suits are partially for our own protection, but mostly to protect the world from ourselves. Human skin is laden with bacteria, we exhale bacteria too, and there is no telling what human contaminants could do to an environment. Are we passively poisonous? There's no way of knowing. Plus, *we* could get sick too. Hence, suits.

This was not my first step off Earth. I'd spent a year and a half at the New Millennium Lunar Base. The Moon is incredible. I felt my daily share of reverence. But I felt a similar reverence, a related reverence, when I stood at the rim of the Grand Canyon for the first time, or stood breathless and shivering atop Mount Fuji.

Like any good guests, we carefully checked our surroundings before setting up our temporary home. We scrutinised the ground below us for anything better left alone. We do our best to leave no trace. We try to be mindful tenants and ethical observers, to have as minimal an impact as possible.

Inflatable habitat modules are one of my favourite inventions. The *Merian* comes equipped with two of them – one for the greenhouse, one for the clean lab – each attaching to an airlock on the side of the capsule. You might think that spending years in such a dwelling might start to feel claustrophobic, but consider the fact that ours is the only building at all on any world we travel to. As of yet, we have found no other life forms that build cities or machines.

I was already in my happy place. Landing had worked, the suits worked, the modules worked. In order to do science you need tools, shelter and a means to get where you are going. I was responsible for all of these. I was building a trellis where good work would grow. There was nothing I wanted more than that, nothing that brought me more pride.

We did plenty of work. We catalogued nine hundred and twenty-six species of multi-cellular organisms. We additionally catalogued over three thousand species of bacteria. The *Merian* ran so beautifully on Aecor that I had little to do for her beyond standard maintenance. I spent most of my time in the lab, helping to program image recognition software. Any task that needed an extra pair of hands, I was there for.

I was happy. Content like I could never remember being. I was surrounded by people I loved, safe in a place free of noise and the empty trappings of civilisation. Here, nobody cared about status or money, who was in power, who was kissing or killing whom. The right things mattered on Aecor. I am a secular woman but it felt to me like a sacred place. A monastic world that repaid hard work and patience with the finest of rewards: Quiet. Beauty. Understanding.

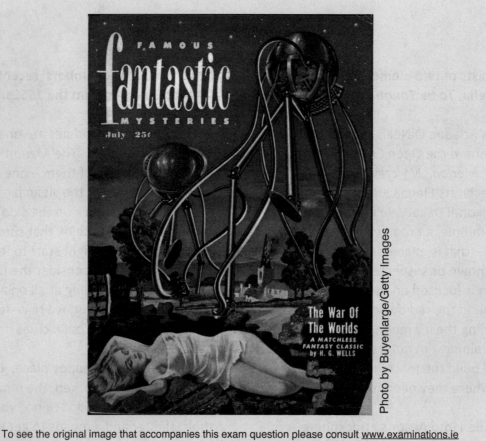

Photo by Buyenlarge/Getty Images

N.B. Candidates may NOT answer Question A and Question B on the same text.

QUESTION A – 50 Marks

(i)   Based on your reading of the written element of TEXT 3, explain three insights you gain into the character of Ariadne O'Neill. Support your response with reference to the text.   (15)

(ii) Both elements of TEXT 3 belong to the genre, science fiction. Explain why you think this genre has a wide and enduring appeal. Make three points in your response.   (15)

(iii) Based on your engagement with TEXT 3, make four points in which you compare the fictional world presented in the written text with that presented in the visual image. Support your answer with reference to both the written and visual elements of TEXT 3.   (20)

QUESTION B – 50 Marks

Enlightened aliens, horrified by the injustice and inequality evident in human society, have decided to eliminate all human beings and recolonise Earth with more deserving inhabitants. You have been chosen to represent humanity and deliver **a speech** to the alien powers in which you try to save us from our fate. In your speech you should: acknowledge some of humanity's failings in relation to justice and inequality, point to evidence of the many admirable qualities of the human race, and explain why the aliens should believe we can be trusted to work together for a better future.

76

SECTION II   COMPOSING   (100 marks)

Write a composition on **any one** of the assignments that appear in **bold print** below.

Each composition carries 100 marks.

The composition assignments are intended to reflect language study in the areas of information, argument, persuasion, narration, and the aesthetic use of language.

---

1. In TEXT 3, flight engineer, Ariadne O'Neill, explains how she takes pride in her work.

    Write a personal essay in which you reflect on what you are proud of in your life.

2. In TEXT 1, Alan McMonagle writes about allowing room for, among other things, discovery, invention and re-invention in life.

    Write a feature article, suitable for publication in a popular magazine, offering some ideas for new inventions and discoveries you think would improve your life or make the world a better place. Your article may be serious or humorous or both.

3. In TEXT 2, the extract from Arthur Conan Doyle's short story ends with a dramatic arrival.

    Write a short story, in which a crime or mystery is solved, that begins with a dramatic arrival. You may set your short story in any era and may choose to include or not include the fictional detective Sherlock Holmes.

4. In TEXT 3, we read about a range of advanced technology such as TEVA suits and inflatable habitat modules.

    Write a discursive essay about our changing relationship with machines and the rise of artificial intelligence.

5. The theme of TEXTS 1, 2 and 3 is "EXPLORING GENRE".

    Write a short story which features the three characters that appear on the magazine cover on Page 7 of this examination paper. You are free to write your story in any genre you choose.

6. In TEXT 3, Ariadne O'Neill observes that on Aecor, "… nobody cared about status or money, who was in power, who was kissing or killing whom."

    Write a speech in which you argue for or against the motion: *Contemporary Irish society is both tolerant and progressive.*

7. In TEXT 2, we see that Sherlock Holmes and his friend, Watson, are very different characters.

    Write a personal essay in which you celebrate friendship, and reflect on how you have been influenced by the unique and diverse personalities of your friends.

zerius

Visit www.e-xamit.ie

2020 P1

Acknowledgements

Images and texts that appear on this examination paper were sourced as follows:

Text 1: H. Schwall (Ed.), *The Danger and the Glory, Irish Authors on the Art of Writing*, Dublin, Arlen House, 2019
Cartoon:https://www.theguardian.com/books/gallery/2015/jul/06/tom-gauld-cultural-cartoons
Text 2: A.C. Doyle, *Sherlock Holmes and the Adventures of the Blue Carbuncle*, London, Daunt Books, 2018
Image: https://www.etsy.com/ie/listing/486168358/vintage-image-bowler-hat-gentleman
TEXT 3: B. Chambers, *To Be Taught, If Fortunate*, London, Hodder & Stroughton Ltd., 2019.
Image: https://briandanacamp.wordpress.com/2018/12/10/science-fiction-art-of-the-1950s-comics-film-tv/

Leaving Certificate – Higher Level

English

2 hours 50 minutes

Coimisiún na Scrúduithe Stáit
State Examinations Commission

LEAVING CERTIFICATE EXAMINATION, 2020

English - Higher Level - Paper 2

Total Marks: 200

Duration: 3 hours 20 minutes

Candidates must attempt the following:
- **ONE** question from SECTION I – The Single Text
- **ONE** question from SECTION II – The Comparative Study
- **ONE** question on the Unseen Poem from SECTION III – Poetry
- **ONE** question on Prescribed Poetry from SECTION III – Poetry

N.B. Candidates must answer on Shakespearean Drama.
They may do so in SECTION I, The Single Text (*Hamlet, The Tempest)* or in
SECTION II, The Comparative Study (*Hamlet, The Tempest*).

INDEX OF SINGLE TEXTS

The Handmaid's Tale	Page - 2
Persuasion	Page - 2
Days Without End	Page - 2
Hamlet	Page - 3
The Tempest	Page - 3

2020 P2

SECTION I   THE SINGLE TEXT   (60 marks)

Candidates must answer **one** question from this section (**A – E**).

A   THE HANDMAID'S TALE – Margaret Atwood

(i)   "Margaret Atwood promotes a feminist message at the expense of constructing a gripping narrative in her novel, *The Handmaid's Tale*."

To what extent do you agree or disagree with this statement? Develop your response with reference to the text.

OR

(ii)   Identify and discuss the various ways in which Margaret Atwood develops the character of Offred throughout her novel, *The Handmaid's Tale*. Develop your response with reference to both the style and content of the text.

> bltvkj
> Visit www.e-xamit.ie

B   PERSUASION – Jane Austen

(i)   "Jane Austen indulges in trivial social comedy at the expense of exploring substantial social issues in her novel, *Persuasion*."

To what extent do you agree or disagree with this statement? Develop your response with reference to the text.

OR

(ii)   Identify and discuss the various ways in which Jane Austen develops the character of Anne Elliot throughout her novel, *Persuasion*. Develop your response with reference to both the style and content of the text.

> grofuy
> Visit www.e-xamit.ie

C   DAYS WITHOUT END – Sebastian Barry

(i)   "Sebastian Barry sacrifices realism for a romanticised view of history in his novel, *Days Without End*."

To what extent do you agree or disagree with this statement? Develop your response with reference to the text.

OR

(ii)   Identify and discuss the various ways in which Sebastian Barry develops the character of Thomas McNulty throughout his novel, *Days Without End*. Develop your response with reference to both the style and content of the text.

D   HAMLET – William Shakespeare

(i)   "Uncertainty, which features constantly in Shakespeare's play, *Hamlet*, adds significantly to the dramatic impact of the play."

Discuss the above statement, developing your response with reference to the text.

OR

(ii)   Discuss how Shakespeare makes effective use, for a variety of purposes, of the contradictions and inconsistencies evident in Hamlet's character. Develop your discussion with reference to Shakespeare's play, *Hamlet*.

E   THE TEMPEST – William Shakespeare

(i)   "The various magical and fantastical elements that feature throughout Shakespeare's play, *The Tempest*, add significantly to the dramatic impact of the play."

Discuss the above statement, developing your response with reference to the text.

OR

(ii)   Discuss how Shakespeare makes effective use, for a variety of purposes, of Prospero's less attractive traits and also of his admirable qualities. Develop your discussion with reference to Shakespeare's play, *The Tempest*.

SECTION II   THE COMPARATIVE STUDY   (70 marks)

Candidates must answer **one** question from **either A** – Cultural Context **or B** – Literary Genre.

In your answer you may not use the text you have answered on in **SECTION I** – The Single Text. All texts used in this section must be prescribed for comparative study for this year's examination. Candidates may refer to only one film in the course of their answers.

Please note:

- Questions in this section use the word **text** to refer to all the different kinds of texts available for study on this course.
- When used, the word **reader** includes viewers of films and theatre audiences.
- When used, the term **technique** is understood to include techniques employed by all writers and directors of films.
- When used, the word **author** is understood to include all writers and directors of films.
- When used, the word **character** is understood to refer to both real people and fictional characters in texts.
- When used, the words **narrative** or **story** are understood to refer to both real life and fictional texts.

A   CULTURAL CONTEXT

1. (a)   Identify and discuss two aspects of cultural context which you believe make a significant contribution to the level of social division or the level of social unity evident in **one** text on your comparative course. Develop your response with reference to the text.   (30)

    (b)   Compare the extent to which social division is evident in each of **two other** comparative texts you have studied. Develop your response with reference to the aspect or aspects of cultural context that you believe contribute(s) to the level of social division evident in these texts.

    In your answer you may refer to the same aspect or different aspects of cultural context in each of the texts that you have studied.   (40)

OR

2.   Choose one central character from each of **three** texts on your comparative course. Compare the factors, related to cultural context, that affect the extent to which these characters are accepted or rejected as members of their societies. Develop your response with reference to your chosen texts.

    In your answer you should refer to at least one relevant factor related to cultural context in each of your three comparative texts. You may refer to the same factor or different factors in each of your chosen texts.   (70)

B LITERARY GENRE

1. (a) Discuss how effectively the author employs imagery to convey or enhance the narrative in **one** text on your comparative course. Develop your answer with reference to the text. (30)

   (b) Compare how effectively the authors of **two other** texts on your comparative course employ imagery to convey or enhance the narrative in these texts. Develop your answer with reference to your chosen texts. (40)

   OR

2. Compare the extent to which the authors of **three** texts on your comparative course use setting or aspects of setting to help define and develop characters. Develop your answer with reference to at least one character in each of your chosen texts. (70)

SECTION III   POETRY   (70 marks)

Candidates must answer **A** – Unseen Poem **and B** – Prescribed Poetry.

A   **UNSEEN POEM** (20 marks)

Read the following poem by Maurice Riordan and answer **either** Question **1**
or Question **2** which follow.

Badb*

I was walking where the woods begin
with an almost sheer drop to the river
– so that I was eye level with the tops
of nearby trees and higher than the branch
when I came upon the crow sitting there,
so close I could have touched her with a stick.
She was creaturely and unwary, as the wind
bore her away and brought her back.
We shared the same tangy woodland smells,
the same malt-pale October sunlight.
Then I must have made a sound,
for she came alert and looked at me.
And, in that interval before the legs
could lift her weight from the branch,
as the beak sprang open to deliver
its single rough vowel, she held me off
with a look, with a sudden realignment
of the eyes above the gorping mouth.
It is the look known to legend and folk belief
– though also an attribute useful for a bird
without talons or guile to defend it.
Then she was gone, in a few wing beats
indistinguishable from her fellows wheeling
above the trees, carrying on their business,
neighbourly and otherworldly.

Maurice Riordan

Badb* - is the name of a Celtic war goddess, known for taking the form of a crow.

1.   (a)   Based on your reading of the above poem, discuss the impact and suitability
of its title. Develop your response with reference to the poem.   (10)

         (b)   Discuss how the poet brings the above poem to life by appealing to the senses.
Develop your response with reference to the poem.   (10)

OR

2.   Discuss the poet's use of language in the above poem to convey various aspects of his
experience with the crow. Develop your response with reference to the poem.   (20)

B   PRESCRIBED POETRY (50 marks)

Candidates must answer **one** of the following questions (**1 – 4**).

---

1.   **Eavan Boland**

Based on your reading of Boland's poetry, to what extent is your emotional response to her work heightened by her use of both provocative and evocative imagery? Develop your response with reference to the poems by Eavan Boland on your course.

> **lliwqs**
> Visit www.e-xamit.ie

2.   **Emily Dickinson**

Discuss how Dickinson's unique approach to language, and the balance between beauty and horror in her imagery, help to relieve some of the darker aspects of her poetry. Develop your response with reference to the poems by Emily Dickinson on your course.

> **qblbqe**
> Visit www.e-xamit.ie

3.   **Adrienne Rich**

Discuss how Rich makes effective use of a variety of characters, often in dramatic settings, to probe both personal issues and wider social concerns in her poems. Develop your response with reference to the poetry by Adrienne Rich on your course.

> **xdptjr**
> Visit www.e-xamit.ie

4.   **William Wordsworth**

Discuss Wordsworth's use of natural imagery, often in specific settings, to convey insights into the power of memory and the value of reflection. Develop your response with reference to the poetry by William Wordsworth on your course.

> **exifeh**
> Visit www.e-xamit.ie

Leaving Certificate – Higher Level

English

3 hours 20 minutes

Coimisiún na Scrúduithe Stáit
State Examinations Commission

LEAVING CERTIFICATE EXAMINATION, 2019

English - Higher Level - Paper 1

Total Marks: 200

Wednesday, 5 June – Morning, 9.30 – 12.20

- This paper is divided into two sections,
  Section I COMPREHENDING and Section II COMPOSING.
- The paper contains **three** texts on the general theme of **FEEDING OUR IMAGINATIONS**.
- Candidates should familiarise themselves with each of the texts before beginning their answers.
- Both sections of this paper (COMPREHENDING and COMPOSING) must be attempted.
- Each section carries 100 marks.

SECTION I – COMPREHENDING

- Two Questions, A and B, follow each text.
- Candidates must answer a Question A on one text and a Question B on a different text. Candidates must answer only one Question A and only one Question B.

N.B. Candidates may NOT answer a Question A and a Question B on the same text.

SECTION II – COMPOSING

- Candidates must write on **one** of the compositions 1 – 7.

TEXT 1 – WHAT IS ART FOR?

**This edited piece is based on an article by Jeanette Winterson entitled, "What is Art for?"
The writer uses the term "art" to include all artistic forms, e.g. painting, writing, music, etc.
The original article appears on the writer's website, jeanettewinterson.com.**

An American lady travelling to Paris in 1913 asked the poet Ezra Pound what he thought art was for. Pound replied, 'Ask me what a rose bush is for.' I know there is a sneaking feeling, even among art lovers, that art is a luxury. The endless rows over funding centre on an insecurity about the role of art in society. Nobody doubts that hospitals and schools must be paid for by all of us. Mention art, and the answer seems to be that it should rely on the market place; let those who want it pay for it. Art is being treated as a commodity. Dead artists – whether authors or painters or musicians – belong to the Heritage industry. Live artists belong to the PR industry.

Art is a different value system, it leaves us with footprints of beauty. We sense there is more to life than the material world can provide, and art is a clue, an intimation, at its best, a transformation. We can experience it. The experience suggests that the monolith of corporate culture is only a partial reality. This is important information, and art provides it. When you take time to read a book or listen to music or look at a picture, the first thing you are doing is turning your attention inwards. The outside world, with all of its demands, has to wait. As you withdraw your energy from the world, the artwork begins to reach you with energies of its own – very different energies to the getting and spending going on all around. When I read Heaney or Hughes, I'm not just reading a poet's take on the world, I am entering into a different world – a world built from the beginning on other principles.

'It's hard to get the news from poems, but men die miserably every day for lack of what is found there' (William Carlos Williams).

Art's counter-culture, however diverse, holds in plain sight what the material world denies – love and imagination. Art is made out of both – a passionate reckless love of the work in its own right, as though nothing else exists, and an imaginative force that creates something new out of disparate material

Art's experiments are not funded by huge state programmes, venture capital, or junk bonds, they are done when someone picks up a pen or a brush, or sits down at the piano, or takes a piece of clay and changes it forever. A money culture wants the figures, the bottom line, the sales, the response, it wants a return on its investment, it wants more money. Art can offer no obvious return. There is only the experience. Art can't change your life. It can waken us to truths about ourselves and our lives, but the responsibility to act on what we find, is ours.

I know of a man who volunteered as an ambulance driver in World War II. While other men had pictures of their sweethearts in their breast pockets, he carried a photo of a Queen Anne chair. In his despair at where human folly had brought him, he needed to remember the glory of the human spirit.

He believed that art affirms and sustains life at its highest level. It is the reason why art is timeless. It is the reason why art does not date. We don't go to Shakespeare to find out about life in Elizabethan England; we go to Shakespeare to find out about ourselves now.

Mass production is about cloned objects. Art is about individual vision. It has a way of forcing us to concentrate on the thing in itself as it really is. Capitalism doesn't want you to concentrate – you might notice that much is amiss. A blurred, out of focus consuming is what suits the market place best. Somebody has to buy all that overproduction of useless dead objects. In contrast, all art is live theatre. The dialogue continues between object, maker, owner, viewer, listener, reader.

Art is proof of a living spirit that defies the orthodoxy of materialism Yes, art becomes a collector's item, or a rich man's trophy. Yes, art is traded for large sums of money, but this is not art's purpose, nor its nature. If money ceased to exist, art would continue. Why did the Taliban bullet-down the Buddhas? Why did Hitler burn books? Why was Ulysses banned? Why did Franco refuse to show Picasso's masterpiece, Guernica?

Art is potent, confrontational, difficult. It challenges what we are. We can muzzle the power of art in all sorts of ways – destroying it or banning it is too obvious. Don't be fooled by the way capitalism co-opts art. It pretends to do it for money, but underneath money is terror. Terror that there might be a different way to live. There is a different way, it's a celebration of the human spirit. Art reminds us of all the possibilities we are persuaded to forget.

N.B. Candidates may NOT answer Question A and Question B on the same text.

QUESTION A – 50 Marks

(i)   Based on your reading of TEXT 1, explain three points Jeanette Winterson makes about the value and importance of the arts. Support your response with reference to the text.   (15)

(ii) In TEXT 1, Jeanette Winterson claims that, "We go to Shakespeare to find out about ourselves now." With reference to a Shakespearean play you have studied for your 2019 Leaving Certificate course, identify an image, moment or episode that revealed something to you about "ourselves now". Explain the insight(s) you gained about "ourselves now" from engaging with this image, moment or episode.   (15)

(iii) Identify four elements of argumentative or persuasive language, evident in TEXT 1, and explain why their use might encourage readers to agree with the views expressed by the writer in the article. You may include any combination of elements of the language of argument or the language of persuasion in your response. Support your answer with reference to the text.   (20)

QUESTION B – 50 Marks

In TEXT 1, Jeanette Winterson extols the virtues of the arts, arguing that artistic activities are beneficial both for individuals and for society in general. She also gives her views on the relationship between art and money. Write **an opinion piece**, suitable for publication in a broadsheet newspaper, in which you extol the varied virtues of sport, put forward a reasoned argument to persuade readers that sport benefits both individuals and society, and give your views on the appropriate relationship between sport and money.

TEXT 2 – A PHOTOGRAPHER'S PERSPECTIVE

This text is composed of two elements. The first consists of a series of edited extracts from David Park's novel, *Travelling in a Strange Land*. We meet the character Tom, a photographer, who is in a reflective mood as he undertakes a journey. The second is a photograph, taken from the Apollo 17 spacecraft in 1972, that provided us with a startling new perspective on our world.

The wake of the boat tumbles and froths in a V-shape almost like we're churning snow, but the sea itself as it stretches out beyond seems almost stalled in a grey torpor. There isn't a feature that would make a photograph even if I had my camera; however there are lots of people taking selfies, either on their own or as a couple. The camera phone and the unrelenting progress of technology and everything coming after it are what will kill off the jobs of people like me. Soon all social photography will be self-done in this way. It sometimes makes me feel like the last of a dying breed. Last of the Mohicans, taking pictures with an actual camera, and it makes it worse to know that however good the technology employed, these pictures of self are in my mind mostly worthless, devoid of whatever it is that makes a proper photograph – one that springs from thoughtful creative decisions and a particular way of seeing. So in my eyes they're not much more than an indulgence, expressions of human vanity and devoid of the dignity that the right photograph can bestow. But if [my daughter] Lilly's right, maybe I really am the "fun sponge" she's called me and I'm railing against something that's just a bit of harmless pleasure.

I had an exhibition once in our local library but it wasn't a great success if I think only in commercial terms. Hardly anything sold and then only to people who knew me and wanted to be supportive. Maybe it's just an excuse for failure but I think where I live most people want pictures of sunsets over Dunseverick Castle, the snowy peaks of the Mournes or right now the Dark Hedges, preferably also with sunset, rainbow or some similar piece of extra-visual drama. So what do I want to take photographs of? It's hard to put it into words but I suppose the moment that lies just below the surface of things, or a glimpse of the familiar from a different angle. Maybe I don't even know.

As a languid drift of snow starts to fall I am mindful of the right image's power to impact on our consciousness. So I think of the little boy lying in the surf on a Turkish beach, drowned trying to reach a Greek island in a plastic dinghy. And even though I forget his name I do remember the feeling that it produced and I know that somehow for a time, however short it proved, it changed things. Changed more than any reporter's words or politician could do because in a photograph there's nothing between you and the subject, nothing to sanitise or mitigate – it's just you there in that moment as close as the camera places you and held still and silent.

I have come to understand the truth of what Ansel Adams said: that you don't make a photograph just with a camera, but that you bring to the act all the pictures you have seen, the books you have read, the music you have heard, the people you have loved.

People don't understand photographs. They think they always freeze the moment in time but the truth is that they set the moment free from it and what the camera has caught steps forever outside its onward roll. So it will always exist, always live just as it was in that precise second, with the same smile or scowl, the same colour of sky, the same fall of light and shade, the very same thought or pulse of the heart. It's the most perfect thing that sets free the eternal in the sudden stillness of the camera's click. I find a comfort in that and I'll take comfort anywhere it offers itself.

N.B. Candidates may NOT answer Question A and Question B on the same text.

QUESTION A – 50 Marks

(i) Based on your reading of page 4 of TEXT 2, explain three points the character, Tom, makes about the value and power of "proper" photographs. Support your response with reference to the text.

(15)

(ii) Exploring texts can provide opportunities for "a glimpse of the familiar from a different angle". With reference to any text on your Leaving Certificate English course*, identify an image, moment or episode that enabled you to see something familiar from a different perspective. Explain the insight(s) you gained into something familiar from engaging with this image, moment or episode.

*Texts specified for study for Leaving Certificate English in 2019, including poetry, single texts and texts (including films) prescribed for comparative study.

(15)

(iii) Identify and discuss four elements of the language of narration, evident on page 4 of TEXT 2, that contribute to making Tom a real and convincing character. Support your answer with reference to the text.

(20)

QUESTION B – 50 Marks

Look at the photograph on page 5 and imagine you are fleeing Earth on the last spaceship evacuating the planet after human actions have made our world uninhabitable. Write **a reflective journal entry**, which you hope will be preserved for future generations. In it you should criticise humanity's folly which resulted in the loss of our earthly home, share your personal memories of the planet, and celebrate some of Earth's former glories.

ywratp
Visit www.e-xamit.ie

TEXT 3 – LIBRARIES: CATHEDRALS OF OUR SOULS

The following text is adapted from Caitlin Moran's essay, *Libraries: Cathedrals of Our Souls*. The essay appears in a collection of her work entitled, *Moranthology*, and is also anthologised in *The Library Book*, a series of essays by well-known writers in support of public libraries.

Home educated and, by seventeen, writing for a living, the only alma mater I ever had is Warstones Library, Pinfold Grove, Wolverhampton.

A low, red-brick box on grass that verged on wasteland, I would be there twice a day – rocking up with all the ardour of a clubber turning up to a rave. I read every book in there – not *really*, of course, but as good as: when I'd read all the funny books, I moved on to the sexy ones, then the dreamy ones, the mad ones; the ones that described distant mountains, idiots, plagues, experiments. I sat at the big table and read all the papers: on a council estate in Wolverhampton, the broadsheets as incongruous and illuminating as an Eames lamp.

Warstones Library

The shelves were supposed to be loaded with books – but they were of course, really doors: each book-lid opened as exciting as Alice in Wonderland putting her gold key in the lock. I spent days running in and out of other worlds like a time bandit, or a spy. I was as excited as I've ever been in my life, in that library; scoring new books the minute they came in: ordering books I'd heard of – then waiting, fevered, for them to arrive, like they were Word Christmas. I had to wait nearly a year for *Les Fleurs de Mal* by Baudelaire to come: I was still too young for it and abandoned it twenty pages in for Jilly Cooper. But *Fleurs de Mal*, man! In a building overlooked by a Kwiksave supermarket where the fags and alcohol were kept in a locked, metal cage, lest they be stolen! Simply knowing I could have it in my hand was a comfort, in this place so very far from anything extraordinary or exultant.

Everything I am is based on this ugly building on its lonely lawn which allowed a girl so poor she didn't even own a purse to come in twice a day and experience actual magic: travelling through time, making contact with the dead – Dorothy Parker, Stella Gibbons, Charlotte Brontë, Spike Milligan.

A library in the middle of a community is a cross between an emergency exit, a life-raft and a festival. They are cathedrals of the mind; hospitals of the soul; theme parks of the imagination. On a cold, rainy island, they are the only sheltered public spaces where you are not a consumer, but a citizen instead. A human with a brain and a heart and a desire to be uplifted, rather than a customer with a credit card and a 'need' for 'stuff'. A mall – the shops – are places where your money makes the wealthy wealthier. But a library is where the wealthy's taxes pay for you to become a little more extraordinary, instead. A satisfying reversal. A balancing of the power.

Last month, after protest, an injunction was granted to postpone library closures in Somerset. In September, both Somerset and Gloucestershire councils will be the subject of a full judicial review over their closure plans. As the cuts kick in, protesters and lawyers are fighting for individual libraries like villagers pushing stranded whales back into the sea. A library is such a potent symbol of a town's values: each one closed down might as well be 6,000 stickers plastered over every available surface, reading 'WE CHOOSE TO BECOME MORE STUPID AND DULL'.

What happens when the economy gets back to 'normal' again? Do we then – prosperous once more – go round and re-open all these centres, clinics and libraries, which have sat, dark and unused, for nearly half a decade? It's hard to see how – it costs millions of pounds to re-open deserted buildings, and cash-strapped councils will have looked at billions of square feet of prime real estate with a coldly realistic eye. Unless the government *has* developed an exit strategy for the cuts, and insisted councils not sell closed properties, by the time we get back to 'normal'

again, our Victorian and post-war and 1960s red-brick boxy libraries will be coffee shops, supermarkets and pubs. No new libraries will be built to replace them. These libraries will be lost forever.

And, in their place, we will have a thousand more public spaces where you are simply the money in your pocket, rather than the hunger in your heart. Kids – poor kids – will never know the fabulous, benign quirk of self-esteem of walking into 'their' library and thinking, 'I have read 60 per cent of the books in here. I am awesome'. Libraries that stayed open during the World War II Blitz will be closed by budgets. A trillion small doors closing.

N.B. Candidates may NOT answer Question A and Question B on the same text.

QUESTION A – 50 Marks

(i) Based on your reading of TEXT 3, explain three points Caitlin Moran makes about the social benefits of public libraries. Support your response with reference to the text. (15)

(ii) Exploring texts can open metaphorical doors into other worlds. With reference to any text on your Leaving Certificate English course*, identify an image, moment or episode that opened a door into another world for you. Explain the insight(s) you gained about the value of imaginatively entering another world by engaging with this image, moment or episode.

*Texts specified for study for Leaving Certificate English in 2019, including poetry, single texts and texts (including films) prescribed for comparative study. (15)

(iii) Identify and discuss four elements of the writer's style, evident in TEXT 3, that contribute to making this a good example of a personal essay. Support your answer with reference to the text. (20)

QUESTION B – 50 Marks

The expansion of online shopping has had a devastating effect on all types of real shops and department stores. Write **an introduction to a collection of essays** in support of real shops, in which you celebrate the joys of 'real' shopping, explain what the presence of shops and shoppers brings to communities, and discuss some of the implications for us all of the ever-increasing popularity of online shopping.

SECTION II   COMPOSING   (100 marks)

Write a composition on **any one** of the assignments that appear in **bold print** below.

Each composition carries 100 marks.

The composition assignments are intended to reflect language study in the areas of information, argument, persuasion, narration, and the aesthetic use of language.

1. In TEXT 2, Tom expresses the view that people favour photographs that feature sunsets.

    Write a descriptive essay which captures a sense of the difference between dawn and dusk and celebrates both the beginning and the end of the day.

2. In TEXT 3, Caitlin Moran describes herself like a time bandit or spy in her local library.

    Write a short story, suitable for publication in a collection of spy stories, in which a librarian, a photograph and a chair are central to the narrative.

3. The theme of TEXTS 1, 2 and 3 is "Feeding Our Imaginations".

    Write a personal essay in which you reflect on what feeds your imagination.

4. TEXT 2 is based on a series of edited extracts from the novel, *Travelling in a Strange Land*.

    Write a short story which captures the evolving relationship between two characters – one young and one old – as they travel in a strange land.

5. In TEXT 1, we are told that "Art is a different value system".

    Write a discursive essay about some of the items you think symbolise the values held by people of your age in Ireland in 2019.

6. In TEXT 3, Caitlin Moran writes about a place that helped to shape and define her.

    Write a personal essay in which you reflect on some of the places that have helped to shape and define you, and the significance of these places in your life.

7. Tom, the character in David Park's novel featured in TEXT 2, is critical of selfies.

    Write a speech, to be broadcast online, for or against the motion: *We are a self-obsessed generation.*

Acknowledgements

Images and texts that appear on this examination paper were sourced as follows:

Text 1: http://www.jeanettewinterson.com/journalism/what-is-art-for/
Image: banksyeditions.com/project/barcode-leopard-signed
Text 2: *Travelling in a Strange Land*, David Park, Bloomsbury Publishing, 2018
Image: https://www.nasa.gov/image-feature/apollo-17-blue-marble
Text 3: *Moranthology*, Caitlin Moran, Ebury Press, 2013
Image: Photo Richard Law https://www.geograph.org.uk/photo/1949627

Leaving Certificate – Higher Level

English

Wednesday 5 June
Morning 9.30 – 12.20

Coimisiún na Scrúduithe Stáit
State Examinations Commission

LEAVING CERTIFICATE EXAMINATION, 2019

English - Higher Level - Paper 2

Total Marks: 200

Thursday, 6 June – Afternoon, 2.00 – 5.20

Candidates must attempt the following:
- **ONE** question from SECTION I – The Single Text
- **ONE** question from SECTION II – The Comparative Study
- **ONE** question on the Unseen Poem from SECTION III – Poetry
- **ONE** question on Prescribed Poetry from SECTION III – Poetry

N.B. Candidates must answer on Shakespearean Drama.

They may do so in SECTION I, The Single Text (*Macbeth*) or in SECTION II,
The Comparative Study (*Macbeth, The Tempest*).

INDEX OF SINGLE TEXTS

Americanah	Page - 2
The Handmaid's Tale	Page - 2
Persuasion	Page - 2
By the Bog of Cats	Page - 3
Macbeth	Page - 3

SECTION I   THE SINGLE TEXT   (60 marks)

Candidates must answer **one** question from this section (**A – E**).

A   AMERICANAH – Chimamanda Ngozi Adichie

(i)   Identify and discuss a variety of insights you gained into the subject of identity through your engagement with Adichie's novel, *Americanah*. Develop your answer with reference to the text.

OR

(ii)   "The female characters in Adichie's novel, *Americanah,* fail each other."

Based on your reading of the novel, to what extent do you agree or disagree with the above statement? Explain your answer, giving reasons for your response. Develop your answer with reference to Adichie's novel, *Americanah*.

B   THE HANDMAID'S TALE – Margaret Atwood

(i)   Identify and discuss a variety of insights you gained into the subject of identity through your engagement with Atwood's novel, *The Handmaid's Tale*. Develop your answer with reference to the text.

OR

(ii)   "The female characters in Atwood's novel, *The Handmaid's Tale,* fail each other."

Based on your reading of the novel, to what extent do you agree or disagree with the above statement? Explain your answer, giving reasons for your response. Develop your answer with reference to Atwood's novel, *The Handmaid's Tale*.

C   PERSUASION – Jane Austen

(i)   Identify and discuss a variety of insights you gained into the subject of identity through your engagement with Austen's novel, *Persuasion*. Develop your answer with reference to the text.

OR

(ii)   "The female characters in Austen's novel, *Persuasion,* fail each other."

Based on your reading of the novel, to what extent do you agree or disagree with the above statement? Explain your answer, giving reasons for your response. Develop your answer with reference to Austen's novel, *Persuasion*.

D   **BY THE BOG OF CATS** – Marina Carr

(i)   Discuss the reasons why, in your opinion, Marina Carr's use of a variety of horrific, bizarre and unbelievable elements does or does not heighten the tragic intensity of her play, *By the Bog of Cats*. Develop your answer with reference to the text.

OR

(ii)   Discuss how Marina Carr uses language to create dark comedy and add a poetic quality to her play, *By the Bog of Cats*. Develop your answer with reference to the text.

E   **MACBETH** – William Shakespeare

(i)   Discuss the reasons why, in your opinion, Shakespeare's use of a variety of horrific, bizarre and unbelievable elements does or does not heighten the tragic intensity of his play, *Macbeth*. Develop your answer with reference to the text.

OR

(ii)   Discuss how Shakespeare's use of language, including imagery, plays an important part in developing our understanding of **one** of the following aspects of his play, *Macbeth*: themes; characterisation; setting and atmosphere. Develop your answer with reference to the text.

SECTION II   THE COMPARATIVE STUDY   (70 marks)

Candidates must answer **one** question from **either A** – General Vision and Viewpoint **or** **B** – Literary Genre.

In your answer you may not use the text you have answered on in **SECTION I** – The Single Text. All texts used in this section must be prescribed for comparative study for this year's examination. Candidates may refer to only one film in the course of their answers.

Please note:

- Questions in this section use the word **text** to refer to all the different kinds of texts available for study on this course.
- When used, the word **reader** includes viewers of films and theatre audiences.
- When used, the term **technique** is understood to include techniques employed by all writers and directors of films.
- When used, the word **author** is understood to include all writers and directors of films.
- When used, the word **character** is understood to refer to both real people and fictional characters in texts.

A   GENERAL VISION AND VIEWPOINT

1. "Our personal beliefs – our views and values – can influence our sense of the general vision and viewpoint of a text."

   (a) With reference to **one** text on your comparative course, explain how your sense of the general vision and viewpoint was influenced by at least one of your personal beliefs. Develop your response with reference to the text. (30)

   (b) Compare how your sense of the general vision and viewpoint in each of **two other** comparative texts was influenced by at least one of your personal beliefs. Develop your response with reference to your chosen texts.

   In response to 1. (b) you may refer to the same or different personal belief(s) that you referred to in 1. (a) above. You may refer to the same personal belief or different personal beliefs in relation to each of your two other comparative texts. (40)

   ### OR

2. "Our view of the personal integrity of a central character can help to shape our impression of the general vision and viewpoint of a text."

   Compare the extent to which your view of the personal integrity of one central character, in each of **three** texts on your comparative course, helped to shape your impression of the general vision and viewpoint of your chosen texts. Develop your answer with reference to the texts. (70)

B   LITERARY GENRE

1.   (a)   Discuss how effectively two techniques are used to provide insight(s) into the mindset of a central character in **one** text on your comparative course. Develop your answer with reference to the text.   (30)

(b)   Compare how effectively at least one technique is used to provide insight(s) into the mindset of a central character in each of **two other** texts on your comparative course. Develop your answer with reference to your chosen texts.

In response to 1. (b) you may refer to the same technique or different techniques in relation to each of your chosen texts. You may refer to the same or different techniques to those you referred to in 1. (a) above.   (40)

OR

2.   Compare how mood or atmosphere is created in each of **three** texts on your comparative course. Refer to at least one technique used to create mood or atmosphere in each of your chosen texts. Develop your answer with reference to your chosen texts.

You may refer to the same technique or different techniques in each of your chosen texts.   (70)

Candidates must answer **A** – Unseen Poem **and B** – Prescribed Poetry.

A   UNSEEN POEM (20 marks)

Read the following poem, written by Carol Ann Duffy to mark the 100th anniversary of the end of World War One.

Answer **either** Question **1** or Question **2** which follow.

The Wound in Time

It is the wound in Time. The century's tides,
chanting their bitter psalms, cannot heal it.
Not the war to end all wars; death's birthing place;
the earth nursing its ticking metal eggs, hatching
new carnage. But how could you know, brave
as belief as you boarded the boats, singing?
The end of God in the poisonous, shrapneled air.
Poetry gargling its own blood. We sense it was love
you gave your world for; the town squares silent,
awaiting their cenotaphs*. What happened next?
War. And after that? War. And now? War. War.
History might as well be water, chastising this shore;
for we learn nothing from your endless sacrifice.
Your faces drowning in the pages of the sea.

                                                            Carol Ann Duffy

* Cenotaph – war memorial

---

1.   (a)   Discuss the appropriateness of the title, "The Wound in Time". In your response, make detailed reference to the words chosen by the poet for the title. Develop your answer with reference to the poem as a whole.   (10)

      (b)   Choose two images from the poem that you find particularly effective in capturing the horror of war and explain why you find these images particularly effective for this purpose.   (10)

                                        OR

2.   Explain how language is used effectively to maximise the emotional impact of this poem. Make detailed reference to the use of language for this purpose in the poem.   (20)

B   PRESCRIBED POETRY (50 marks)

Candidates must answer **one** of the following questions (**1 – 4**).

1.   Brendan Kennelly

Discuss how Kennelly's sensitive exploration of a range of emotions, and his imaginative use of a variety of characters, help to reveal the humanity intrinsic to his work. Develop your response with reference to the poems by Brendan Kennelly on your course.

yxmapr
Visit www.e-xamit.ie

2.   Elizabeth Bishop

"Bishop makes skillful use of a variety of poetic techniques to produce poems that are often analytical but rarely emotional."

Discuss the extent to which you agree or disagree with the above statement. Develop your response with reference to the poems by Elizabeth Bishop on your course.

wbcyzs
Visit www.e-xamit.ie

3.   W.B. Yeats

"Yeats's poetry is both intellectually stimulating and emotionally charged."

Discuss the extent to which you agree or disagree with the above statement. Develop your response with reference to the themes and language evident in the poems by W. B. Yeats on your course.

nyfmso
Visit www.e-xamit.ie

4.   Sylvia Plath

Discuss how effectively Plath uses a range of images to develop her themes and add drama to her poetry. Develop your response with reference to the poems by Sylvia Plath on your course.

adrezb
Visit www.e-xamit.ie

Leaving Certificate – Higher Level

English

Thursday 6 June
Afternoon 2.00 – 5.20

Coimisiún na Scrúduithe Stáit
State Examinations Commission

LEAVING CERTIFICATE EXAMINATION, 2018

English - Higher Level - Paper 1

Total Marks: 200

Wednesday, 6th June – Morning, 9.30 – 12.20

- This paper is divided into two sections,
  Section I COMPREHENDING and Section II COMPOSING.
- The paper contains **three** texts on the general theme of YOUNG WRITERS.
- Candidates should familiarise themselves with each of the texts before beginning their answers.

- Both sections of this paper (COMPREHENDING and COMPOSING) must be attempted.
- Each section carries 100 marks.

SECTION I – COMPREHENDING

- Two Questions, A and B, follow each text.
- Candidates must answer a Question A on one text and a Question B on a different text. Candidates must answer only one Question A and only one Question B.
- **N.B.** Candidates may NOT answer a Question A and a Question B on the same text.

SECTION II – COMPOSING

- Candidates must write on **one** of the compositions 1 – 7.

TEXT 1 – ADVICE TO YOUNG WRITERS

Award-winning writer, Colum McCann, teaches creative writing in Hunter College, New York. This text is based on edited extracts from Colum McCann's book, *Letters to a Young Writer*.

Why do we tell stories? Why do we need to lean across the table, or the fireside, or the fabulously intertwined wires of the Internet and whisper "Listen"? We do it because we're sick of reality and we need to create what isn't yet there. Literature proposes possibilities and then makes truth of them. Literature can be a stay, or a foothold against despair. Of course it's not enough, but it's all we've got.

A first line should open up your rib cage. It should reach in and twist your heart backward. It should suggest that the world will never be the same again. Guide your reader into your story. Your duty is to make the reader see and hear. With the right word, you will find the balance of imaginative richness and form. You have to drag the moment reluctantly from silence. As a writer, you are alive to every sentence. Your imagination is creating a reality. It is as if you are unpeeling time.

One of the great joys of fiction writing is discovering who your character truly is. There is little better than creating someone from the dust of your imagination. Your characters must be intricate, complicated, flawed. They need to step up and bear the weight of reality. They need to be a heart-breaking mess of flesh and bone.

For the purposes of good storytelling you must know your character in the most exact detail. The story will be nothing if the character is not part of a great human stew. We have to make them so utterly real that the reader can never forget them. Writing a character into being is like meeting someone you want to fall in love with. You don't care (yet) about the facts of his or her life.

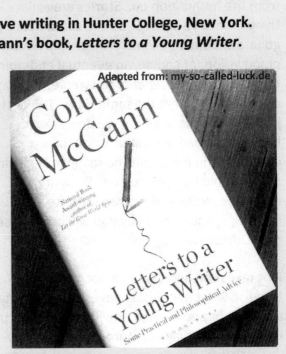

Adapted from: my-so-called-luck.de

Don't overload us with too much information. Allow that to seep out later. We are attracted by a moment in time – a singular moment of flux or change or collapse – not by grand résumés or curricula vitae. So don't generalise. Be specific.

Carry a notebook. Write in it when you get a chance. Images, ideas, snatches of street dialogue, addresses, descriptions, whatever might eventually make its way into a sentence.

Be a camera. Make us feel as if we are there. Colours, sounds, sights. Bring us to the pulse of the moment. See the whole landscape at first, then focus in on a detail, and bring that detail to life. There is no harm in trying all angles. Try first person, second person, third person. Try from the viewpoint of your main character, then try it from the perspective of the outsider. Sometimes the outsider is the one who makes absolute sense. Eventually – if you persevere – you will hear the right voice, and you will see the right form, and you will uncover the right structure, and it will unfold from there.

Our stories rely on the human instinct for architecture. Structure is, essentially, a container for content. The shape into which your story gets placed is a house slowly built from the foundation up. Stories are agile things. They're elusive. So the containers they go into should be pliable. You should have a grand vision, of course, an eventual end-point, but you must be prepared to swerve, chop and change direction at the same time. The best journeys are those where we don't exactly know what road we will take: we have a destination in mind, but the manner of getting there should be open to flux. So, write and rearrange, write and rearrange, write and rearrange, and eventually you will begin to see the structure emerge.

Plot takes the backseat in a good story because what happens is never as interesting as *how* it happens. And how it happens occurs in the way language captures it and the way our imaginations transfer that language into action. Listen for the quiet line. Anyone can tell a big story but not everyone can whisper something beautiful in your ear. In the end, what plot must do is twist our hearts in some way. It must change us. It must make us realise that we are alive. One thing leads to the next. And the issues of the human heart unfold in front of us. Such, then, is plot. Anything can happen, even nothing at all. And even if nothing happens, the world still changes, second by second, word by word. Perhaps this is the most astounding plot of all.

In the end it is only the well-chosen word that is capable of dealing with truth. Only that language which is capable of reaching the poetic will be able to stand in opposition to that which is wrong. In other words, nothing short of your best work will do. Language is a great weapon. You do owe allegiance to that elusive notion of truth. You should write so as not to fall silent.

N.B. Candidates may NOT answer Question A and Question B on the same text.

QUESTION A – 50 Marks

(i) Based on your reading of TEXT 1 above, what skills or qualities do you think a young writer would need in order to follow the advice offered by Colum McCann? Refer to three skills or qualities in your answer, supporting your response with reference to the text.   (15)

(ii) Colum McCann tells us that sometimes in writing, "The issues of the human heart unfold in front of us." From the texts you have studied for your Leaving Certificate course*, identify a moment in a text where you feel an issue of the human heart unfolded in front of you. Explain in detail what this moment revealed to you about the human heart.

 * Texts specified for study for Leaving Certificate English in 2018, including poetry, single texts and texts (including films) prescribed for comparative study.   (15)

(iii) Based on your reading of TEXT 1, do you find Colum McCann's approach to advising young writers appealing or unappealing? Discuss the elements of Colum McCann's writing style that make his approach to advising young writers appealing or unappealing. Support your answer with reference to the text.
                    (20)

QUESTION B – 50 Marks

Young people are often the recipients of unwanted advice. Write **an open letter*** to all those who have ever offered you unwanted advice. In your letter you should identify some nuggets of unwanted advice you have received, describe your response to receiving such advice, and share your opinion on how and when advice could be appropriately offered. Your letter may be amusing or serious or both.

* A letter intended for a wide audience often published online or in the print media.

TEXT 2 – A SUCCESSFUL YOUNG WRITER

This text is based on edited extracts from Fiona Mozley's debut novel, *Elmet*. Fiona Mozley was the youngest writer nominated for the Man Booker Prize in 2017.

We arrived in summer when the landscape was in full bloom and the days were long and hot and the light was soft. I roamed shirtless and sweated cleanly and enjoyed the hug of the thick air. The sun set slowly and the evenings were pewter before they were black, before the mornings seeped through again.

Adapted from:thetimes.co.uk

Now pocked with clutches of trees, once the whole county had been woodland and the ghosts of the ancient forest could be marked when the wind blew. The soil was alive with ruptured stories that cascaded and rotted then found form once more and pushed up through the undergrowth and back into our lives. Tales of green men peering from thickets with foliate faces and legs of gnarled timber. The calls of half-starved hounds rushing and panting as they snatched at charging quarry. Robyn Hode and his pack of scrawny vagrants, whistling and wrestling and feasting as freely as the birds whose plumes they stole. An ancient forest ran in a grand strip from north to south. Boars and bears and wolves. Does, harts, stags. Miles of underground fungi. Snowdrops, bluebells, primroses. The trees had long since given way to crops and pasture and roads and houses and railway tracks and little wooded copses were all that was left.

Daddy and Cathy and I lived in a small house that Daddy built with materials from the land here about. He chose for us a small ash copse two fields from the east coast main line, far enough not to be seen, close enough to know the trains well. We heard them often enough: the hum and ring of the passenger trains, the choke and gulp of the freight, passing by with their cargo tucked behind in painted metal tanks. They had timetables and intervals of their own, drawing growth rings around our house with each journey, ringing past us like prayer chimes.

On the day we arrived an old squaddy [soldier] drove up the hill in an articulated lorry filled with cracked and discarded stone from an abandoned builders' yard. The squaddy let Daddy do most of the unloading while he sat on a freshly cut log and smoked cigarette after cigarette. He talked all afternoon about the army and the fighting he had done in Iraq and in Bosnia and how he had seen boys as young as me slashed open with knives. There was little darkness in him when he told us this. Daddy worked on the house during the day and in the evening the two grown men went down the hill to drink some of the cider the squaddy had brought in a plastic pop bottle. Daddy did not stay long. He did not like drinking much and he did not like company save for me and my sister.

When Daddy came back he told us that he had an argument with the squaddy. He had clouted the squaddy about the head with his left fist and now had a bloody nick in his skin just by the thumb knuckle.

Our house was laid out like any bungalow on the outskirts of any smallish city where old people and poor families live. Our house was stronger than others of its type though. It was built with better bricks, better mortar, better stones and timber. I knew it would last many dozen seasons longer than those houses we saw on the roads into town. And it was more beautiful. The green mosses and ivies from the wood were more eager to grip at its sides, more ready to pull it back into the landscape.

On the clearest evenings we stayed out until morning. Years ago, Daddy had bought me a wooden recorder and Cathy a violin. We had had free lessons when we were still at school. We were not experts but made a decent sound because of the instruments we played. Daddy had chosen well. He knew nothing of music but a great deal about fine objects.

Before the house was built, in those few hot, dry months when we camped and sang, Daddy talked to us properly. He used few words but we heard much more. He spoke of the men he had fought and the men he had killed, in the peat fields of Ireland or that black mud of Lincolnshire that clings to the hands and feet like forensic ink. Daddy boxed for money with bare knuckles

far from gymnasiums or auditoriums but the money could be big and men whose cash came from nowhere arrived from across the country to lay their bets on him to win. Anyone was a fool not to back my Daddy.

Yes, it was during this summer in the woods that Daddy told us these stories, confided in us, and Cathy and I listened like we were receiving precious heirlooms. Daddy's eyes became wide when he spoke to us, flecked, light blue, like worn denim, and he would lean in and open them generously then pinch them closed ever so slightly when he reached for a memory that was not quite clear. He sat forward in his chair with his long, thick legs apart, his elbows resting above his knees and his cavernous chest bearing broad, weighted shoulders.

N.B. Candidates may NOT answer Question A and Question B on the same text.

QUESTION A – 50 Marks

(i) Based on your reading of TEXT 2 above, what do you learn about Daddy's character? Refer to three aspects of Daddy's character in your answer, supporting your response with reference to the text. (15)

(ii) In the above text, Fiona Mozley has created a place that grips the reader's imagination. From the texts you have studied for your Leaving Certificate course*, identify a place that gripped your imagination. Explain in detail why this place gripped your imagination.

* Texts specified for study for Leaving Certificate English in 2018, including poetry, single texts and texts (including films) prescribed for comparative study. (15)

(iii) Based on your reading of TEXT 2, do you agree that Fiona Mozley displays superb narrative skills, including the effective use of aesthetic language, which enable her to craft an atmospheric and occasionally disturbing story? Support your answer with reference to the text. (20)

QUESTION B – 50 Marks

The children in TEXT 2 experience an unconventional education. Based on your experience of second level education, write **an opinion piece, suitable for publication in a national newspaper**, in which you acknowledge what you see as the strengths of the education you have received, criticise what you see as its weaknesses and make suggestions for its improvement.

TEXT 3 – A TRAGIC YOUNG POET

TEXT 3 is adapted from *Above the Dreamless Dead*, a collection of illustrated songs and poems from World War 1. The poetic extract which forms part of the text is from "Dead Man's Dump", a poem by Isaac Rosenberg, a young poet killed in action in 1918.

PANEL 1

The air is loud with death,
The dark air spurts with fire,
The explosions ceaseless are.
Timelessly now, some minutes past,
These dead strode time with vigorous life,
Till the shrapnel called 'an end!'

PANEL 2

Original material created by Pat Mills, David Hitchcock and Todd Klein

N.B. Candidates may NOT answer Question A and Question B on the same text.

QUESTION A – 50 Marks

(i)   Compare and contrast the pictures in PANEL 1 and PANEL 2 that appear on Page 6. Support your answer with reference only to the visual elements of the text.   (15)

(ii)   TEXT 3 presents a poetic extract in a visual format. From the poems you have studied for your Leaving Certificate course*, identify a poem, or an extract from a poem, which you think is particularly suited to presentation in a visual format. Specify the type of visual format in which you would choose to present it (e.g. painting, photographic image, video clip, etc.) and explain in detail why you think this poem, or poetic extract, would be suitable for presentation in this way.

       * Poems specified for study for Leaving Certificate English in 2018.   (15)

(iii)   Based on your reading of the material on Page 6 of TEXT 3, do you agree that the combination of poetry and illustration, found in the text, is extremely effective in amplifying and extending the meaning of the poem and adding to the overall impact of the text? In your answer you should make detailed reference to the combination of poetry and illustration found in the text and consider the overall impact the text makes on you.   (20)

QUESTION B – 50 Marks

Write **an article for your school website**, in which you consider the experience of reading a text and watching a film adaptation of the same text. In your article you should identify at least one written text which has been adapted as a film. Consider the advantages and disadvantages of each of these formats, and explain which format you would recommend as the way in which to experience the text(s) for the first time. You may refer to any text(s) of your choice in your answer.

Write a composition on **any one** of the assignments that appear in **bold print** below.

Each composition carries 100 marks.

The composition assignments are intended to reflect language study in the areas of information, argument, persuasion, narration, and the aesthetic use of language.

1. In TEXT 2 Fiona Mozley writes "it was during this summer in the woods, that Daddy told us these stories".

    Write a descriptive essay in which you capture how the landscape reflects the transition of the seasons. You may choose to include some or all of the seasons in your essay.

2. Fiona Mozley's characters in TEXT 2 are outsiders who "arrived in summer".

    Write a short story in which the central character's status as an outsider has a direct influence on the plot.

3. TEXTS 1, 2, and 3 relate to young writers.

    Write a personal essay reflecting on what you perceive to be the pleasures particular to youth.

4. TEXT 3 offers a thought-provoking depiction of soldiers and their leaders.

    Write a discursive essay in which you consider the subject of leaders and leadership.

5. In TEXT 1, Colum McCann tells us that "Literature proposes possibilities".

    Write a short story, for inclusion in a collection of detective fiction, about a character who explores various possibilities in order to solve a crime.

6. In TEXT 1, Colum McCann tells young writers to "Listen for the quiet line".

    Write a personal essay in which you reflect on the value of personal space and quietness in the modern world.

7. TEXT 1 contains the statement: "Language is a great weapon".

    You are competing in the final of a national public speaking competition. The topic to be addressed is: *Language is a great weapon*. You are free to agree or disagree. Write the speech you would deliver.

Coimisiún na Scrúduithe Stáit
State Examinations Commission

LEAVING CERTIFICATE EXAMINATION, 2018

English - Higher Level - Paper 2

Total Marks: 200

Thursday, 7th June – Afternoon, 2.00 – 5.20

Candidates must attempt the following:
- **ONE** question from SECTION I – The Single Text
- **ONE** question from SECTION II – The Comparative Study
- **ONE** question on the Unseen Poem from SECTION III – Poetry
- **ONE** question on Prescribed Poetry from SECTION III – Poetry

N.B. Candidates must answer on Shakespearean Drama.
They may do so in SECTION I, The Single Text (*King Lear*) or in SECTION II,
The Comparative Study (*King Lear, Macbeth*).

INDEX OF SINGLE TEXTS

Wuthering Heights	Page - 2
The Great Gatsby	Page - 2
All My Sons	Page - 3
Americanah	Page - 3
King Lear	Page - 3

SECTION I THE SINGLE TEXT (60 marks)

Candidates must answer **one** question from this section (**A – E**).

A WUTHERING HEIGHTS – Emily Brontë

(i) "Emily Brontë's portrayal of love and marriage in her novel, *Wuthering Heights*, is entirely negative."

To what extent do you agree or disagree with the above statement? Support your response with reference to the text.

OR

(ii) "The development of characters is influenced by a variety of personal, social and cultural factors in texts."

Discuss the factors in the novel, *Wuthering Heights*, that you think are most influential in the development of Heathcliff's character. Support your answer with reference to the text.

B THE GREAT GATSBY – F. Scott Fitzgerald

(i) "Fitzgerald's portrayal of love and marriage in his novel, *The Great Gatsby,* is entirely negative."

To what extent do you agree or disagree with the above statement? Support your response with reference to the text.

OR

(ii) "The development of characters is influenced by a variety of personal, social and cultural factors in texts."

Discuss the factors in the novel, *The Great Gatsby*, that you think are most influential in the development of Jay Gatsby's character. Support your answer with reference to the text.

C   ALL MY SONS – Arthur Miller

(i)   "Miller's play, *All My Sons*, provides moments of riveting drama that offer thought-provoking insights into the human condition."

Identify three moments of riveting drama in the play that, in your opinion, provide thought-provoking insights into the human condition. Give reasons why you find these moments dramatically riveting and discuss the thought-provoking insights they provide. Support your response with reference to the play.

OR

(ii)   "Kate Keller plays a more significant role than her husband, Joe, in the play, *All My Sons*."

To what extent do you agree or disagree with the above statement? In your response you should consider the roles played by both characters. Support your answer with reference to the text.

D   AMERICANAH – Chimamanda Ngozi Adichie

(i)   "Adichie's portrayal of love and marriage in her novel, *Americanah*, is entirely negative."

To what extent do you agree or disagree with the above statement? Support your response with reference to the text.

OR

(ii)   "The development of characters is influenced by a variety of personal, social and cultural factors in texts."

Discuss the factors in the novel, *Americanah*, that you think are most influential in the development of Ifemelu's character. Support your answer with reference to the text.

E   KING LEAR – William Shakespeare

(i)   "Shakespeare's play, *King Lear*, provides moments of riveting drama that offer thought-provoking insights into the human condition."

Identify three moments of riveting drama in the play that, in your opinion, provide thought-provoking insights into the human condition. Give reasons why you find these moments dramatically riveting and discuss the thought-provoking insights they provide. Support your response with reference to the play.

OR

(ii)   "Cordelia plays a more significant role than Goneril or Regan in the play, *King Lear*."

To what extent do you agree or disagree with the above statement? In your response you should consider the roles played by all three sisters. Support your answer with reference to the text.

SECTION II   THE COMPARATIVE STUDY   (70 marks)

Candidates must answer **one** question from **either A** – The Cultural Context **or B** – Literary Genre.

In your answer you may not use the text you have answered on in **SECTION I** – The Single Text. All texts used in this section must be prescribed for comparative study for this year's examination. Candidates may refer to only one film in the course of their answers.

Please note:

- Questions in this section use the word **text** to refer to all the different kinds of texts available for study on this course.
- When used, the word **reader** includes viewers of films and theatre audiences.
- When used, the term **technique** is understood to include techniques employed by all writers and directors of films.
- When used, the word **author** is understood to include all writers and directors of films.
- When used, the word **character** is understood to refer to both real people and fictional characters in texts.

A   THE CULTURAL CONTEXT

1.   (a)   Identify at least one type of behaviour considered to be unacceptable within the world of **one** text on your comparative course. Explain why such behaviour is considered unacceptable in this cultural context and discuss the response or responses of society to such behaviour. Support your answer with reference to the text.   (30)

(b)   With reference to **two other** texts on your comparative course, identify at least one type of behaviour considered to be unacceptable in the world of each of these texts. Compare why such behaviour is considered unacceptable in these cultural contexts and the response or responses of society to such unacceptable behaviour. Support your answer with reference to the texts.

In response to 1. (b) you may refer to the same or different types of behaviour in each of your chosen texts. You may refer to the same or different type(s) of behaviour as those referred to in 1. (a) above.   (40)

OR

2.   "Aspects of cultural context affect the extent to which a character can be happy or successful within the world of a text."

Identify a central character in each of **three** texts on your comparative course. Compare the aspect of the cultural context in each of these texts that, in your opinion, most affects the extent to which your chosen characters are happy or successful. You may refer to the same or different aspects of cultural context in each of your chosen texts. Support your answer with reference to the texts.   (70)

B   LITERARY GENRE

1.   "The effective use of a variety of techniques can influence how we respond to characters."

   (a)   Identify two techniques which influenced how you responded to a central character in **one** text on your comparative course. Explain how your response to this character was influenced by the effective use of these techniques. Support your answer with reference to the text.   (30)

   (b)   Identify at least one technique which influenced how you responded to a central character in each of **two other** texts on your comparative course. Compare how your response to your chosen characters was influenced by the effective use of your chosen technique(s). Support your answer with reference to the texts.

   In response to 1. (b) you may refer to the same technique or different techniques in relation to each of your chosen texts. You may refer to the same or different techniques to those you referred to in 1. (a) above.   (40)

OR

2.   "Our interest and attention can be captured at the beginning of a text by the effective use of various techniques."

   With reference to **three texts** on your comparative course, compare how effectively at least one technique was used to capture your interest and attention at the beginning of each of these texts. You may refer to the same technique or different techniques in each of your chosen texts. Support your answer with reference to your chosen texts.
                                                                                                                   (70)

SECTION III POETRY (70 marks)

Candidates must answer **A** – Unseen Poem **and** B – Prescribed Poetry.

A   UNSEEN POEM (20 marks)

Read the following poem by Moya Cannon and answer **either** Question **1 or** Question **2** which follow.

> ### Two ivory swans
>
> fly across a display case
> as they flew across Siberian tundra
> twenty thousand years ago,
> heralding thaw on an inland sea –
> their wings, their necks, stretched,
> vulnerable, magnificent.
>
> Their whooping set off a harmonic
> in someone who looked up,
> registered the image
> of the journeying birds
> and, with a hunter-gather's hand,
> carved tiny white likenesses
> from the tip of the tusk
> of the great land-mammal,
> wore them for a while,
> traded or gifted them
> before they were dropped
> down time's echoing chute,
> to emerge, strong-winged,
> whooping
> to fly across our time.
>
> (British Museum, April 2013)
>
> *Moya Cannon*

1.   (a)   What do you think the poet is saying about time in the above poem?
            Support your answer with reference to the poem.   (10)

      (b)   Identify two images from the poem that make an impact on you and give
            reasons for your choice.   (10)

OR

2.   Discuss the language, including the imagery, used by the poet throughout this poem.
      Make detailed reference to the poem in support of your answer.   (20)

B   PRESCRIBED POETRY (50 marks)

Candidates must answer **one** of the following questions (**1 – 4**).

1.   <u>Robert Frost</u>

From your study of the poetry of Robert Frost on your course, select the poems that, in your opinion, best demonstrate how the poet helps us to understand the darker aspects of his poetic vision through his effective use of poetic narrative and dramatic scenes.

Justify your selection by demonstrating how Robert Frost helps you to understand the darker aspects of his poetic vision through his effective use of poetic narrative and dramatic scenes in the poems you have selected.

2.   <u>Eiléan Ní Chuilleanáin</u>

"Eiléan Ní Chuilleanáin tells fascinating stories, often examining themes that are relevant to contemporary Ireland, in a style that is both beautiful and mysterious."

To what extent do you agree or disagree with this statement? Support your answer with reference to the poetry of Eiléan Ní Chuilleanáin on your course.

3.   <u>John Montague</u>

From your study of the poetry of John Montague on your course, select the poems that, in your opinion, best demonstrate his effective use of place, both literal and metaphorical, to explore elements of his personal and cultural identity.

Justify your selection by demonstrating Montague's effective use of place, both literal and metaphorical, to explore elements of his personal and cultural identity in the poems you have selected.

4.   <u>Philip Larkin</u>

Philip Larkin wanted his poetry to appeal to "the common reader", not just academics and professional literary critics.

Based on your experience of his poetry, do you think Larkin's poems hold appeal for "the common reader"? Justify your response by discussing Larkin's thematic concerns and elements of his poetic style that you think make his work appealing or unappealing to "the common reader". Support your answer with reference to the poetry by Philip Larkin on your course.

Leaving Certificate – Higher Level

English

Thursday 7 June
Afternoon 2.00 – 5.20

Coimisiún na Scrúduithe Stáit
State Examinations Commission

LEAVING CERTIFICATE EXAMINATION, 2017

English - Higher Level - Paper 1

Total Marks: 200

Wednesday, 7th June – Morning, 9.30 – 12.20

- This paper is divided into two sections,
  Section I COMPREHENDING and Section II COMPOSING.
- The paper contains **three** texts on the general theme of DIFFERENT WORLDS.
- Candidates should familiarise themselves with each of the texts before beginning their answers.

- Both sections of this paper (COMPREHENDING and COMPOSING) must be attempted.
- Each section carries 100 marks.

SECTION I – COMPREHENDING

- Two Questions, A and B, follow each text.
- Candidates must answer a Question A on one text and a Question B on a different text. Candidates must answer only one Question A and only one Question B.
- **N.B.** Candidates may NOT answer a Question A and a Question B on the same text.

SECTION II – COMPOSING

- Candidates must write on **one** of the compositions 1 – 7.

TEXT 1 – THE WORLD OF POETRY

This text is based on two images that incorporate work by the poet Robert Montgomery, and *The Medium is the Message – The Power of Public Poetry*, an edited article from *The Guardian* newspaper, written by Marta Bausells. The images are from the website robertmontgomery.org.

IMAGE 1   Montgomery's work, lit with recycled sunlight, in Bexhill-on-Sea

© Robert Montgomery

2017 P1

IMAGE 2   Montgomery's work used in an anti-war protest in Trafalgar Square, London

© Robert Montgomery

The Medium is the Message – The Power of Public Poetry by Marta Bausells

He has been called a vandal, a street artist, a punk artist. Scottish poet Robert Montgomery has consciously made an "awkward space" for himself in between artistic categories – and he thoroughly enjoys it. His work puts poetry in front of people in eye-catching visual formats, from advertising billboards he has covered with poems, to words he has set on fire or lit with recycled sunlight in public spaces. The texts tend to be lyrical, dreamy and almost optimistic. "I feel it's a kind of responsibility to critique things that you think are bad – but I also feel an almost moral obligation to propagate hope," he says.

A new global crisis has propelled him to focus his work on climate change. "I think the ecological crisis we are facing is the major historical crisis of our time and our generation will be judged on it." By putting poetry in our faces, Montgomery hopes to bring it into the public discourse. "I'm interested in Roland Barthes's idea that speech defines a culture. Poetry can define the dominant languages we have in culture."

Montgomery approves of another kind of page leaping phenomenon: the proliferation of new "Instagram poets" who also mix the written word with careful visual presentations. "The internet is a wonderful medium for poetry," he says. He celebrates the fact that poets can garner audiences that "bring their work alive" before they get a chance to get published.

His work seems to have developed into the realm of inspirational quotes for fans, with his poems popping up on selfies, clothes, walls and bodies. "Getting institutional recognition is great, but someone getting tattooed is such a personal compliment. After all, the goal of art, for me, is to communicate our innermost feelings to strangers."

Montgomery's work on London billboards has, on occasion, provoked run-ins with the law. He was put into the back of a police van after he pasted his poem for William Blake on a billboard in Bethnal Green. "But I got into a conversation about literature and one of the police officers was really engaged with it. I guess it was a lucky experience. I think most people wouldn't be averse to having a poem at the end of the street instead of another Diet Coke ad."

These texts have been adapted, for the purpose of assessment, without the authors' prior consent.

**N.B. Candidates may NOT answer Question A and Question B on the same text.
Questions A and B carry 50 marks each.**

QUESTION A

(i) Based on your reading of TEXT 1 (images and written text), what do you learn about Robert Montgomery's approach to poetry? Support your answer with reference to TEXT 1. (15)

(ii) Robert Montgomery believes that poetry can be of benefit to society. In your opinion, have you benefitted from engaging with poetry during your time at school? Give reasons for your answer. (15)

(iii) Compare the two images featuring Robert Montgomery's work that appear on Page 2. You should address the following in the course of your answer: setting and atmosphere, the poems, the visual impact of the images. Support your answer with reference to both images. (20)

QUESTION B

Your school Principal has agreed to your suggestion to display three poems, or extracts from three poems, on the 2017 Leaving Certificate Higher Level English poetry course, in your school. You have been asked to choose the poetry and decide how and where it will be displayed. Write **an article for your school's website** in which you explain your choice of poetry, your ideas for its display and the impact you hope this project will have on the school community. (50)

TEXT 2 – A CONNECTED WORLD

This text is based on edited extracts from *Free Speech – Ten Principles for a Connected World* by Oxford Professor, Timothy Garton Ash. Professor Garton Ash writes about free speech, also termed "freedom of expression", in the digital global city or "virtual cosmopolis" which we all now inhabit.

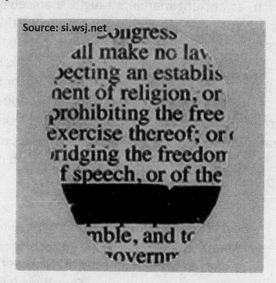

Source: si.wsj.net

We are all neighbours now. There are more phones than there are human beings and close to half of humankind has access to the internet. In our cities, we rub shoulders with strangers from every country, culture and faith. The world is a global city, a virtual cosmopolis. We can post our thoughts and photos online, where in theory any one of billions of other people might encounter them. Never in human history was there such a chance for freedom of expression as this. And never have the evils of unlimited free expression – death threats, paedophile images, sewage-tides of abuse – flowed so easily across frontiers.

As of 2015, there are already somewhere around three billion internet users. The digital age brings both acceleration and convergence of two previously distinct lines of communication: one-to-one and one-to-many. Key advances in the history of one individual communicating with another include the development of postal services, the telegraph, the telephone, the mobile phone, email and the smartphone. The smartphone has given access to the 'mobile internet', where one-to-one converges with one-to-many and all other variants, including many-to-many and many-to-one.

The internet subverts the traditional unities of time and space. It telescopes space, making us virtual neighbours, but it also concertinas time. Once something is up there online, it is usually there forever. Whether an ill-advised remark was made this morning or twenty years ago if it comes up on an online search it is still part of the here and now.

The transformed context in which the question of free speech is posed today is the result of more recent developments in communication. New technologies afford possibilities that were not there before, or not in the same degree. If someone gives you a wheel, you can lay the wheel on its side and sit on it, but the new possibility it affords is the ability to travel further, faster and carrying a heavier load than you could before. What are the most characteristic "affordances" of the internet? Put most simply, it is easier to make things public and more difficult to keep things private. The first affordance has a great liberating potential; the second harbours an oppressive potential, including a threat to free speech.

Free speech has never meant unlimited speech – everyone spouting whatever comes into his or her head. It entails discussing where the limits to freedom of expression and information should lie in important areas such as privacy, religion, national security and the ways we talk about human difference. I contend that the way to live together well in this world-as-city is to have more and better free speech.

An English judge wrote in a late twentieth-century judgement that 'freedom of speech is the lifeblood of democracy'. A right to say something does not mean that it is right to say it. A right to offend does not entail a duty to offend. What social, journalistic, artistic, educational and other ways are there of making free speech fruitful, enabling creative provocation without tearing lives and societies apart? How can we treat each other like grown-ups, exploring and navigating our difficulties with the aid of this defining human gift of self-expression?

The ancient philosopher, Philodemus, argued that the use of free speech should be taught as a skill like medicine or navigation. This seems to me to be a vital thought for our time. In this crowded world, we must learn to navigate by speech, as ancient mariners taught themselves to sail across the Aegean Sea. The goal of this journey is not to eliminate conflict between human aspirations, values and ideologies. This is not just unachievable but also undesirable, for it would result in a sterile world, monotonous, uncreative and unfree. Rather, we should work towards a framework of civilised and peaceful conflict, suited to and sustainable in this world of neighbours.

Over the last half century, human enterprise and innovation from the jet plane to the smartphone have created a world in which we are all becoming neighbours, but nowhere is it written that we will become good neighbours. That requires a transcultural effort of reason and imagination. Central to this endeavour is free speech. Only with freedom of expression can I understand what it is to be you. Only with freedom of information can we control both public and private powers. Only by articulating our differences can we see clearly what they are and why they are what they are. We will never all agree, nor should we. But we must strive to create conditions in which we agree on how we disagree.

This text has been adapted, for the purpose of assessment, without the author's prior consent.

N.B. Candidates may NOT answer Question A and Question B on the same text.
Questions A and B carry 50 marks each.

QUESTION A

(i) Based on your reading of TEXT 2, what do you learn about the impact of developments in technology on modern communication? Support your answer with reference to the text. (15)

(ii) In your opinion, what should schools do to promote the appropriate use of free speech in society? Give reasons for your answer. (15)

(iii) "Professor Garton Ash makes effective use of the languages of argument and persuasion to convince readers that today's society needs more and better free speech."

Do you agree with the above statement? Support your answer with reference to Professor Garton Ash's use of the languages of argument and persuasion in the above text to convince readers that today's society needs more and better free speech. (20)

QUESTION B

The views people hold today are often influenced by the news and information they receive from the online world of the internet and social media. Write **an opinion piece,** for publication in a national newspaper, in which you give your views on the extent to which people today rely on the online world as a source of news and information, the reliability of these sources and the impact of this development on society. (50)

TEXT 3 – THE WORLD OF CHILDHOOD

This edited text is adapted from a memoir entitled *Report from the Interior* by American writer Paul Auster. In this extract he focuses on the world of childhood.

In the beginning everything was alive. The smallest objects were endowed with beating hearts, and even the clouds had names. Scissors could walk, telephones and teapots were first cousins, eyes and eyeglasses were brothers. The face of the clock was a human face, each pea in your bowl had a different personality, and the grille on the front of your parents' car was a grinning mouth with many teeth. Pens were airships. Coins were flying saucers.

Your earliest thoughts, remnants of how you lived inside yourself as a small boy. You can remember only some of it, brief flashes of recognition that surge up in you unexpectedly at random moments – brought on by the smell of something, or the touch of something, or the way the light falls on something in the here and now of adulthood. You still occasionally fall into old ways of thinking. Each summer as you lie on your back in the grass, you look up at the drifting clouds and watch them turn into faces, into birds and animals, into states and countries and imaginary kingdoms.

The world was of course flat. When someone tried to explain to you that the earth was a sphere, a planet orbiting the sun with eight other planets in something called a solar system, you couldn't grasp what the older boy was saying. If the earth was round, then everyone below the equator would fall off, since it was inconceivable that a person could live his life upside down. The older boy tried to explain the concept of gravity to you, but that was beyond your grasp as well. You imagined millions of people plunging headlong through the darkness of an infinite, all-devouring night. If the earth was indeed round, you said to yourself, then the only safe place to be was the North Pole.

Stars, on the other hand, were inexplicable. Not holes in the sky, not candles, not electric lights, not anything that resembled what you knew. The immensity of the black air overhead, the vastness of the space that stood between you and those small luminosities, was something that resisted all understanding. Benign and beautiful presences

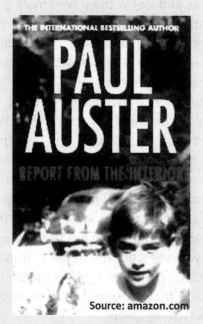

Source: amazon.com

hovering in the night, there because they were there and for no other reason.

You were five and a half when your family left the cramped garden apartment in Union and installed itself in the old white house on Irving Avenue in South Orange. Not a big house, but the first house your parents had ever lived in, which made it your first house as well. Even though the interior was not spacious, the yard behind the house seemed vast to you. In fact it was two yards, the first one a small grassy area directly behind the house, bordered by your mother's crescent-shaped flower garden, and the back yard which was wilder and bigger, a secluded realm in which you conducted your most intense investigations into the flora and fauna of your new kingdom.

Robins, finches, blue jays, scarlet tanagers, crows, sparrows, wrens, cardinals, blackbirds and an occasional bluebird. Birds were no less strange to you than stars, and because their true home was in the air, you felt that birds and stars belonged to the same family. The incomprehensible gift of being able to fly, a fit subject for study and observation. What intrigued you most about them were the sounds they made, a different language spoken by each kind of bird, whether tuneful songs or harsh, abrasive cries, and early on you were convinced they were talking to one another.

Six years old. Standing in your room one Saturday morning, having just dressed yourself and tied your shoes, all ready for action, about to go downstairs and begin the day, and as you stood there in the light of the early spring morning, you were engulfed by a feeling of happiness, an ecstatic, unbridled sense of well-being and joy, and an instant later you said to yourself: There is nothing better than being six years old, six is far and away the best age anyone can be. What had happened to cause such an overpowering feeling? Impossible to know, but you suspect it had something to do with the birth of self-consciousness, that thing that happens to children around the age of six, when the inner voice awakens and the ability to think a thought and tell yourself you are thinking that thought begins. Our lives enter a new dimension at that point. Until that morning, you just were. Now you knew that you were.

At some point during the year you turned six, you were taken by someone to a film that was shown at night. You remember the immensity of the crowded theatre, the spookiness of sitting in the dark when the lights went out, a feeling of anticipation and unease. The film was *The War of the Worlds*, based on the novel by H. G. Wells. Stone-round metal spaceships landed out of the night sky, one by one the lids of these flying machines would open, and slowly a Martian would emerge from within, an unnaturally tall insect-like figure with stick arms and eerily long fingers. The Martian would fix his gaze on an earthling, zero in on him with his grotesque, bulbous eyes, and an instant later there would be a flash of light. Seconds after that, the earthling would be gone. Transfixed is probably the word that best captures what was happening to you.

This text has been adapted, for the purpose of assessment, without the author's prior consent.

N.B. Candidates may NOT answer Question A and Question B on the same text.
Questions A and B carry 50 marks each.

QUESTION A

(i)   What characteristics of a child's world does Paul Auster convey in the above extract? Support your answer with reference to the text.   (15)

(ii) In the extract above Paul Auster states that "six is far and away the best age anyone can be". In your opinion, is there a "best age" to be? Give reasons for your answer.   (15)

(iii) "Paul Auster makes effective use of aesthetic language to create a charming and reflective memoir."

      Based on your reading of the above extract, do you agree with this statement? Support your answer with reference to Paul Auster's use of aesthetic language in the above text to create a charming and reflective memoir.   (20)

QUESTION B

You have been asked to participate in a radio programme entitled *Reflections on the World of Childhood*. Write **the text to be broadcast on radio,** in which you reflect on the world of your childhood, discuss what captured your childish imagination, and recall a selection of the songs or sounds or stories that live on in your memory.   (50)

SECTION II   COMPOSING   (100 marks)

Write a composition on **any one** of the assignments that appear in **bold print** below.

Each composition carries 100 marks.

The composition assignments are intended to reflect language study in the areas of information, argument, persuasion, narration, and the aesthetic use of language.

1. Robert Montgomery, whose work features in TEXT 1, sometimes uses advertising billboards to display his work.

    Write a discursive essay in which you explore the positive and negative aspects of different types of advertising.

2. In TEXT 3, Paul Auster describes the stars as, "benign and beautiful presences hovering in the night."

    Write a descriptive essay entitled *Night Scene*.

3. In TEXT 2, Timothy Garton Ash quotes an English judge, "freedom of speech is the lifeblood of democracy".

    Write a speech, to be delivered to a World Youth Conference, in which you give your views on how democracy can be supported in the world today.

4. We learn in Text 1 that fans have been tattooed with Robert Montgomery's poetic words.

    Write a short story in which a tattoo plays an important part in the narrative.

5. Timothy Garton Ash alludes to the invention of the wheel in TEXT 2.

    Imagine it is the Stone Age and you have just invented the wheel. Write a dialogue in dramatic form, in which you introduce and promote your new invention to your sceptical friends and neighbours. Your drama may be humorous or serious or both.

6. In TEXT 3, Paul Auster describes a moment of revelation he experienced one Saturday morning when he was six years old.

    Write a personal essay in which you reflect on moments of insight and revelation you have experienced.

7. TEXT 1 and TEXT 3 feature the work of a poet and a novelist.

    Write an article for a serious publication in which you consider whether scientists or writers and artists have made, and continue to make, the greater contribution to society.

Coimisiún na Scrúduithe Stáit
State Examinations Commission

LEAVING CERTIFICATE EXAMINATION, 2017

English - Higher Level - Paper 2

Total Marks: 200

Thursday, 8ᵗʰ June – Afternoon, 2.00 – 5.20

Candidates must attempt the following:
- **ONE** question from SECTION I – The Single Text
- **ONE** question from SECTION II – The Comparative Study
- **ONE** question on the Unseen Poem from SECTION III – Poetry
- **ONE** question on Prescribed Poetry from SECTION III – Poetry

N.B. Candidates must answer on Shakespearean Drama.
They may do so in SECTION I, The Single Text (*Hamlet*) or in SECTION II,
The Comparative Study (*Hamlet, Othello*).

INDEX OF SINGLE TEXTS

Emma	Page - 2
The Great Gatsby	Page - 2
A Doll's House	Page - 3
Death and Nightingales	Page - 3
Hamlet	Page - 3

SECTION I   THE SINGLE TEXT   (60 marks)

Candidates must answer **one** question from this section (**A – E**).

A   EMMA – Jane Austen

(i)   Jane Austen's novel, *Emma*, has been described as "a frivolous romance of limited appeal."

To what extent do you agree or disagree with this description of the novel?
In your response you should deal with all aspects of the statement, supporting your answer with reference to the text.

OR

(ii)   "For a variety of reasons, all the female characters in Jane Austen's novel, *Emma*, are equally powerless."

To what extent do you agree or disagree with the above statement?
Support your answer with reference to at least two female characters in the text.

B   THE GREAT GATSBY – F. Scott Fitzgerald

(i)   *The Great Gatsby* has been described as "a study of selfish individuals which fails to offer a critical examination of society."

To what extent do you agree or disagree with this description of the novel?
In your response you should deal with all aspects of the statement, supporting your answer with reference to the text.

OR

(ii)   "For a variety of reasons, all the female characters in Fitzgerald's novel, *The Great Gatsby*, are equally powerless."

To what extent do you agree or disagree with the above statement?
Support your answer with reference to at least two female characters in the text.

C   A DOLL'S HOUSE – Henrik Ibsen

(i)   Ibsen's play, *A Doll's House*, has been described as "a domestic drama which fails to address significant social issues."

To what extent do you agree or disagree with this description of the play?
In your response you should deal with all aspects of the statement, supporting your answer with reference to the text.

OR

(ii)   "Ibsen makes effective use of both Dr Rank and Nils Krogstad to fulfil a variety of dramatic functions in his play, *A Doll's House*."

Discuss this statement, supporting your answer with reference to the text.

D   DEATH AND NIGHTINGALES – Eugene McCabe

(i)   *Death and Nightingales* has been described as "a far-fetched tale of violence and deceit."

To what extent do you agree or disagree with this description of the novel?
In your response you should deal with all aspects of the statement, supporting your answer with reference to the text.

OR

(ii)   "For a variety of reasons, all the female characters in McCabe's novel, *Death and Nightingales*, are equally powerless."

To what extent do you agree or disagree with the above statement?
Support your answer with reference to at least two female characters in the text.

E   HAMLET – William Shakespeare

(i)   Shakespeare's play *Hamlet* has been described as "a disturbing psychological thriller."

To what extent do you agree or disagree with this description of the play?
In your response you should deal with all aspects of the statement, supporting your answer with reference to the text.

OR

(ii)   Shakespeare makes effective use of both Laertes and Horatio to fulfil a variety of dramatic functions in his play, *Hamlet*."

Discuss this statement, supporting your answer with reference to the text.

SECTION II   THE COMPARATIVE STUDY   (70 marks)

Candidates must answer **one** question from **either A** – The General Vision and Viewpoint **or B** – Theme or Issue.

In your answer you may not use the text you have answered on in **SECTION I** – The Single Text. All texts used in this section must be prescribed for comparative study for this year's examination. Candidates may refer to only one film in the course of their answers.

Please note:

- Questions in this section use the word **text** to refer to all the different kinds of texts available for study on this course, i.e. novel, play, short story, autobiography, biography, travel writing and film.
- When used, the word **reader** includes viewers of films and theatre audiences.
- When used, the term **technique** is understood to include techniques employed by all writers and directors of films.
- When used, the word **author** is understood to include all writers and directors of films.

A   THE GENERAL VISION AND VIEWPOINT

1. "Relationships between characters can influence our sense of the general vision and viewpoint of texts."

    (a) Discuss the extent to which your sense of the general vision and viewpoint of **one** text on your comparative course is influenced by one (or more) relationship(s) in the text. Support your answer with reference to the text.   (30)

    (b) Compare the extent to which your sense of the general vision and viewpoint of **two other** texts on your comparative course is influenced by at least one relationship in each of these texts. Support your answer with reference to your chosen texts.   (40)

OR

2. "A variety of factors in texts can change or reinforce our initial impression of the general vision and viewpoint."

    Compare the main factor or factors in **three** texts on your comparative course that changed or reinforced your initial impression of the general vision and viewpoint in these texts.   (70)

131

B   THEME OR ISSUE

1.   "The same theme or issue can appear more relevant to life today in some texts than in others."

    (a)   In relation to **one** text on your comparative course, discuss the aspects of the text that, in your opinion, make your chosen theme or issue appear more or less relevant to life today. Support your answer with reference to the text.   (30)

    (b)   In relation to **two other** texts on your comparative course, compare the aspects of those texts that, in your opinion, make your chosen theme or issue appear more or less relevant to life today. Support your answer with reference to your chosen texts.   (40)

OR

2.   "There are many reasons why the exploration of the same theme or issue can be more entertaining in some texts than in others."

Compare the reasons why you found the exploration of the same theme or issue more entertaining in some texts than in others. Support your answer with reference to **three** texts on your comparative course.   (70)

Candidates must answer **A** – Unseen Poem **and B** – Prescribed Poetry.

A   UNSEEN POEM (20 marks)

Read the following poem by Robyn Sarah and answer **either** Question **1 or** Question **2** which follow.

Bounty

Make much of something small.
The pouring-out of tea,
a drying flower's shadow on the wall
from last week's sad bouquet.
A fact: it isn't summer any more.

Say that December sun
is pitiless, but crystalline
and strikes like a bell.
Say it plays colours like a glockenspiel*.
It shows the dust as well,

the elemental sediment
your broom has missed,
and lights each grain of sugar spilled
upon the tabletop, beside
pistachio shells, peel of a clementine.

Slippers and morning papers on the floor,
and wafts of iron heat from rumbling rads,
can this be all? No, look – here comes the cat,
with one ear inside out.
Make much of something small.

Robyn Sarah

*Glockenspiel – a type of musical instrument.
* Rads – radiators

'Bounty' is reprinted from *A Day's Grace* by Robyn Sarah by permission of the Porcupine's Quill. Copyright Robyn Sarah, 2003.

2017 P2

1.   (a)   What do you learn about the poet's approach to life from reading this poem?
              Explain your answer with reference to the poem.   (10)

      (b)   Identify a mood or feeling evoked in the above poem and explain how the poet creates
              this mood or feeling. Support your answer with reference to the poem.   (10)

OR

2.   Discuss the appeal of this poem with reference to its theme, tone and the poet's use of
      language and imagery. Refer closely to the text in support of your answer.   (20)

B   PRESCRIBED POETRY (50 marks)

Candidates must answer **one** of the following questions (**1 – 4**).

1. **Eavan Boland**

   "Boland makes effective use of symbols and metaphors to explore personal experiences and deliver penetrating truths about society."

   To what extent do you agree or disagree with this statement? Support your answer with reference to the poetry of Eavan Boland on your course.

2. **John Donne**

   "Donne's poetry can be simultaneously playful and challenging both in style and content."

   To what extent do you agree or disagree with this statement? Support your answer with reference to the poetry of John Donne on your course.

3. **John Keats**

   "Keats uses sensuous language and vivid imagery to express a range of profound tensions."

   To what extent do you agree or disagree with this statement? Support your answer with reference to the poetry of John Keats on your course.

4. **Elizabeth Bishop**

   From the poetry of Elizabeth Bishop that you have studied, select the poems that, in your opinion, best demonstrate her skilful use of language and imagery to confront life's harsh realities.

   Justify your selection by demonstrating Bishop's skilful use of language and imagery to confront life's harsh realities in the poems you have chosen.

134

Coimisiún na Scrúduithe Stáit
State Examinations Commission

LEAVING CERTIFICATE EXAMINATION, 2016

English – Higher Level – Paper I

Total Marks: 200

Wednesday, 8ᵗʰ June – Morning, 9.30 – 12.20

- This paper is divided into two sections,
  Section I COMPREHENDING and Section II COMPOSING.
- The paper contains **three** texts on the general theme of JOURNEYS.
- Candidates should familiarise themselves with each of the texts before beginning their answers.

- Both sections of this paper (COMPREHENDING and COMPOSING) must be attempted.
- Each section carries 100 marks.

SECTION I – COMPREHENDING

- Two Questions, A and B, follow each text.
- Candidates must answer a Question A on one text and a Question B on a different text. Candidates must answer only one Question A and only one Question B.
- **N.B.** Candidates may NOT answer a Question A and a Question B on the same text.

SECTION II – COMPOSING

- Candidates must write on **one** of the compositions 1 – 7.

TEXT 1 – A DRAMATIC JOURNEY

This text consists of both visual images and an edited written extract. The written text is adapted from Andrew Dickson's book, *Worlds Elsewhere – Journeys Around Shakespeare's Globe.*

It was June 2012, and I had come to the Globe Theatre in London. The company was called Rah-e-Sabz ('Path to Hope'), and they were from Afghanistan; they were about to perform a version of *The Comedy of Errors* translated into Persian as part of a festival of global Shakespeare. This play was a brave choice as the text is a notoriously tall order. Two sets of identical twins (two masters, two servants) find themselves separated by a shipwreck. One pair end up in Ephesus (in present-day Turkey) – set up home, settle down. Little do they know that their brothers have set off from Syracuse (present-day Sicily) in search of them and have just arrived in town. For the Sicilian twins all hell breaks loose: people they have never met keep recognising them, mysterious women sidle up, claiming to share intimate histories. For the Turkish ones, it's nearly as bad: everyone in town suddenly seems to have gone crazy. Not realising they are constantly being mistaken for their twins, all four fear they are bewitched.

For most of its history on stage in the west, *The Comedy of Errors* has been dismissed as a creaky and mechanistic farce with its rampant improbabilities, Elizabethan wordplay, its corny sight gags. But as I watched the performance, set in contemporary Kabul, I saw something quite new. The word "comedy" was in the title but it had escaped me how much it dwelt on exile and separation. I'd forgotten altogether the character of Egeon, father to two of the twins, who prior to the action has been searching the world for five years, frantic to find his absent sons. He also arrives in Ephesus/Kabul and is brusquely arrested for being an illegal immigrant and then placed on death row. There was farce aplenty, a joyous amount of yelling and chasing around with brooms, but much else seemed fraught. The visiting twins were required to swap clothes – something that produced hoots in the audience but also had the sinister implication that it was too dangerous to stay as they were. It was an example of how Shakespeare's plays could take root in places geographically and ideologically remote from those of sixteenth-century England.

As we worked towards the conclusion of the play, as father and brothers separated for so long hugged each other disbelievingly, it occurred to me that there was something else, too. This story of journeys, mistakes, confusions, misplaced identities – being in a strange land, trying to know and comprehend its culture, finding both less and more than you ever imagined – asked a question that lay at the root of global Shakespeare. What does it really feel like to travel?

These texts have been adapted, for the purpose of assessment, without the copyright holders' prior consent.

N.B. Candidates may NOT answer Question A and Question B on the same text.

Questions A and B carry 50 marks each.

QUESTION A

(i) Outline, in your own words, the insights Andrew Dickson shares about Shakespeare's play *The Comedy of Errors* in the written text above. (15)

(ii) From the four posters in the above text, choose the poster that you think is most effective in advertising a production of the play, *The Comedy of Errors*. Explain your choice with reference to the written text and the content and visual appeal of the poster. (15)

(iii) The writer suggests that Shakespeare's plays have timeless and global qualities. Do you agree with this view? Support your answer with reference to the above text (written and visual) and your own experience of at least one Shakespearean drama, other than *The Comedy of Errors*. You may refer to written texts, stage productions or films. (20)

QUESTION B

Imagine that you are the adjudicator for a poster competition; entries must promote a production of Shakespeare's play, *The Comedy of Errors* to a contemporary audience. The entries on Page 2 represent the finalists in the competition. Write a **speech** in which you announce the first and second prize winners. In your speech you should explain your judgement, commenting on the visual appeal of the first and second prize winning entries and their effectiveness in promoting a production of this Shakespearean play to a contemporary audience. (50)

TEXT 2 – A PERSONAL JOURNEY

The following edited extract is adapted from Sara Baume's award-winning debut novel, *spill simmer falter wither*. Ray, the middle-aged, reclusive narrator and his beloved dog, One Eye, are on the run from the authorities. One Eye attacked another dog and its owner and Ray fears his dog may be impounded. In the extract below, Ray is talking to One Eye.

We are driving, driving, driving.
Over hillslopes and humpback bridges, through loose chippings and potholes wide as children's paddling pools and deep as old people's graves. Past lavender hedges, betting shops, sports grounds. Past countless closed doors behind which are countless uncaring strangers. We are heading inland, keeping to the back roads as much as possible. You are looking out the rear window where the view is best, or perching on the passenger seat with your maggot nose pressed to the air vents. What do you smell? Fox spray and honeysuckle, pine martens and seven different kinds of sap? Riding in the car is like watching a neverending reel at a wraparound cinema, complete with the surround-sound of engine putter, the piped scent of petrol fumes and passing countryside.

We are driving, driving, driving.
And every time the engine stops, you expect we've reached the end. But each stop is never an arrival, just another pause along the way. A snack, a walk, a smoke, a sleep, and off again. The car wavers onto the white lines and the cat's eyes bonk beneath our wheels. BONKbonk, BONKbonk, BONKbonk, and I wake to the red twigs of the dogwood shrubs clawing our paintwork. I expected it would be exciting; I expected that the freedom from routine was somehow greater than the freedom to determine your own routine. I wanted to get up in the morning and not know exactly what I was going to do that day. But now that I don't, it's terrifying. Now nothing can be assumed, now everything's ill-considered, and if I spend too long thinking it makes my eyes smart and molars throb. I tense myself into a stone and forget how to breathe. I list aloud all the things that are good and all the reasons I must go on. Glass pebbles are good, games of football on deserted strands, oil refineries by night, jumble shop windows, gingernuts, broken buoys, nicotine, fields of flowering rape. And I must go on because of you. Now it's okay; I can breathe again. And on we go. Is this how people cope, I wonder. Is this how everybody copes?

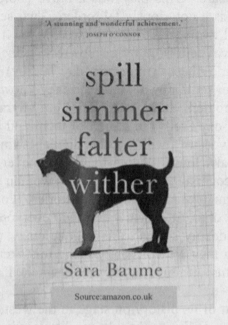

'A stunning and wonderful achievement.'
JOSEPH O'CONNOR

spill
simmer
falter
wither

Sara Baume

Source:amazon.co.uk

We are driving, driving, driving.
And the wraparound car screen is reeling off fields and fields and fields, of wheat and oats and barley which have all died now, and in death, turned to gold. Torn filaments of their gold blows to the ditches, sticks in the prickles, dangles and glitters like premature tinsel.

We are driving, driving, driving.
And the car is our house now, home. The boot is our attic. The loose chippings are our floorboards. The sunroof is our balcony. The back roads and hinterlands are our ceaselessly surging view.

The car bounces, rolls and jitters like a steel orb in a pinball machine, with no right way to go and no particular destination. We round an everlasting succession of hairpin bends, bump through ten thousand bottomless ruts. Every day we see abandoned traffic cones and signposts heralding road works which never materialise. Now the ditches are distended by blackberry brambles, ferns, nettles, fuchsia, knapweed, elderberries and rose hips, so overgrown they narrow the road to a single lane for travelling both directions. See how the hedge trimming tractor has left a trail of massacred vegetation in its wake. Flowers with their throats slit and berries chopped, popped.

Every dawn, we leave the car to walk, to follow your directionless route of indecipherable landmarks. Over a drumlin and a bog, past a saltwater lake and a shooting sanctuary, through a patch of magic mushrooms and a fairy circle. Now here's an alien thing which might be a lizard and might be a stranded newt. You lick its dead belly. What does it feel like? Like boiled, cooled leather, like licking your own tongue back again? You learn each new stopping spot detail by detail, by its symphony of smell, and never by its signpost. BUNRAFFY, the signposts say, DOWRASH, CREGGISH, LISFINNY.

They are mostly villages, the signposted places, some hardly even that. After several villages we stop at the sight of a post office. "Back in a minute," I tell you. I slide my savings book and driver's licence beneath the safety glass to a girl with an armload of copper bangles. I ask her how much I'm allowed to withdraw at once. She says "what?" three times before she hears me properly, and each time I repeat myself, I feel smaller and smaller and smaller. I drive from the village until we are between cow fields again.

A village becomes a town when somebody builds a supermarket, a library, a secondary school, a third or fourth or fifth pub, a retirement home.

And we are avoiding them, the towns. Here come the featureless bungalows, each with a couple of garden ornaments distributed about their neatly trimmed lawns. Now here's an electronic gate with a keypad mounted to a post. At the far end of the extensive driveway, see the unfinished palace. Naked plaster and a lake of mud where grass-seeds ought to have sprouted. Count the front-facing windows. There are no fewer than twelve, plus three dormers and a skylight.

In almost every village there's a shop, and almost every village shop is attached to a pub with a sign over the door bearing the full name of the original proprietor: JAMES O'SHEA, they say, JOHN T. MURPHY. The shelves are dusty. The merchandise is bizarrely organised. A box of powdered custard sits next to a can of engine oil, which sits next to a tin of marrowfat peas, which sits next to a tub of nappy powder. Now these are the only places we stop to shop. They never stock exactly what I think we want, but there's always something close enough to compromise.

And I like the cramped proportions. I like the cold and clammy air, the surplus of useless clutter; it puts me in mind of my father's house.

This text has been adapted, for the purpose of assessment, without the copyright holder's prior consent.

N.B. Candidates may NOT answer Question A and Question B on the same text.

Questions A and B carry 50 marks each.

QUESTION A

(i) Outline, in your own words, what is revealed about Ray's mental and emotional state in the above extract. (15)

(ii) In your opinion, to what extent is the portrayal of contemporary Ireland in the above extract accurate or inaccurate? Give reasons for your answer. (15)

(iii) Do you agree that elements of narrative and aesthetic language are used effectively to engage the reader in the above passage? Give reasons for your answer, supporting your views with reference to the elements of narrative and aesthetic language evident in the text. (20)

QUESTION B

Your Transition Year class has decided to enter a film-making competition. Entries must be based on an extract from a novel and portray aspects of contemporary Irish life. Your class's entry is based on the above extract from Sara Baume's novel, *spill simmer falter wither*. Write the text for your class's **competition entry** in which you identity the elements in the above extract that you think make it suitable for filming, and outline the aspects of contemporary Irish life the passage portrays that you would like to capture in your film. (50)

TEXT 3 – JOURNEY INTO SPACE

This edited text is adapted from a speech delivered by President Barack Obama at the National Aeronautics and Space Administration (NASA), Kennedy Space Centre in Florida. In this extract he acknowledges the history, and outlines the future, of American space exploration.

Source: exploringnation.com

Little more than half a century ago in a remote and desolate region of what is now called Kazakhstan the Soviet Union launched Sputnik, the first artificial satellite to orbit the Earth. The Soviets, it was perceived, had taken the lead in a race for which we were not yet fully prepared. But we caught up very quickly. In the years that have followed, the space race inspired a generation of scientists and innovators. It has contributed to immeasurable technological advances that have improved our health and well-being, from satellite navigation to water purification, from aerospace manufacturing to medical imaging. On a personal note, I have been part of that generation so inspired by the space programme. One of my earliest memories is sitting on my grandfather's shoulders, waving a flag as astronauts arrived in Hawaii.

So today, I'd like to talk about the next chapter in this story. The challenges facing our space programme are different, and our imperatives for this programme are different, than in decades past. We're no longer racing against an adversary. We're no longer competing to achieve a singular goal like reaching the Moon. In fact, what was once a global competition has long since become a global collaboration. I am one hundred percent committed to the mission of NASA and its future. Because broadening our capabilities in space will continue to serve our society in ways that we can scarcely imagine. Because exploration will once more inspire wonder in a new generation – sparking passions and launching careers. And because, ultimately, if we fail to press forward in the pursuit of discovery, we are ceding our future and we are ceding that essential element of the American character.

We will start by increasing NASA's budget by $6 billion over the next five years. We will ramp up robotic exploration of the solar system, including a probe of the Sun's atmosphere; new scouting missions to Mars and other destinations and an advanced telescope to follow Hubble, allowing us to peer deeper into the universe than ever before.

We will increase Earth-based observation to improve our understanding of our climate and our world – science that will garner tangible benefits, helping us to protect our environment for future generations. And we will extend the life of the International Space Station, while actually using it for its intended purpose: conducting advanced research that can help improve the daily lives of people here on Earth, as well as testing and improving upon our capabilities in space.

After decades of neglect, we will increase investment – right away – in other ground-breaking technologies that will allow astronauts to reach space sooner and more often, to travel farther and faster for less cost, and to live and work in space for longer periods more safely. That means tackling major scientific and technological challenges. How do we shield astronauts from radiation on longer missions? How do we harness resources on distant worlds? How do we supply spacecraft with energy needed for these far-reaching journeys? These are questions that we can answer and will answer. And these are the questions whose answers no doubt will reap untold benefits right here on Earth. We're not looking just to continue on the same path – we want to leap into the future; we want major breakthroughs; a transformative agenda for NASA.

Through our plan, we'll be sending many more astronauts to space over the next decade. By 2025, we expect new spacecraft designed for long journeys to allow us to begin the first ever crewed missions beyond the Moon into deep space. We'll start by sending astronauts to an asteroid for the first time in history. By the mid-2030s, I believe we can send humans to orbit

Mars and return them safely to Earth. And a landing on Mars will follow. And I expect to be around to see it.

Now, I understand that some believe that we should attempt a return to the surface of the Moon first, as previously planned. But I just have to say pretty bluntly here: we've been there before. There's a lot more of space to explore, and a lot more to learn when we do. I believe it's more important to ramp up our capabilities to reach a series of increasingly demanding targets and that's what this strategy does.

So this is the next chapter that we can write together here at NASA. We will partner with industry. We will invest in cutting-edge research and technology. We will set far-reaching milestones and provide the resources to reach those milestones. I know that some Americans have asked the question: why spend money on NASA at all? Why spend money solving problems in space when we don't lack for problems to solve here on the ground? And obviously our country is still reeling from the worst economic turmoil we've known in generations. But you and I know this is a false choice. We have to fix our economy. But the space programme has fuelled jobs and entire industries. The space programme has improved our lives, advanced our society, strengthened our economy, and inspired generations of Americans. I have no doubt that NASA can continue to fulfil this role. This is exactly why it's so essential that we pursue a new course and that we revitalize NASA and its mission – not just with dollars, but with clear aims and a larger purpose.

Now, little more than forty years ago, astronauts descended the nine-rung ladder of the lunar module and allowed their feet to touch the dusty surface of Earth's only Moon. This was the culmination of a daring and perilous gambit – of an endeavour that pushed the boundaries of our knowledge, of our technological prowess, of our very capacity as human beings to solve problems. It wasn't just the greatest achievement in NASA's history – it was one of the greatest achievements in human history.

The question for us now is whether that was the beginning of something or the end of something. I choose to believe it was only the beginning.

This text has been adapted, for the purpose of assessment, without the copyright holder's prior consent.

N.B. Candidates may NOT answer Question A and Question B on the same text.

Questions A and B carry 50 marks each.

QUESTION A

(i) Outline, in your own words, what President Obama reveals about the changing focus of America's space programme in the above speech. (15)

(ii) In your opinion, what possible disadvantages could be associated with the ambitious space programme envisaged in the extract above? Give reasons for your answer. (15)

(iii) Do you agree that elements of informative and persuasive language are used effectively in the above speech to win support for the envisaged space programme? Give reasons for your answer, supporting your views with reference to the elements of informative and persuasive language evident in the text. (20)

QUESTION B

Imagine that you are an American citizen and you have just listened to President Obama's speech above. You are opposed to the amount of public money committed by the President for space exploration and decide to mount an online campaign against this expenditure. Write a **post for your blog** in which you give your reasons for opposing the spending of so much public money in this way, and propose how you think these public funds could be better spent. (50)

SECTION II   COMPOSING   (100 marks)

Write a composition on **any one** of the assignments that appear in **bold print** below.

Each composition carries 100 marks.

The composition assignments are intended to reflect language study in the areas of information, argument, persuasion, narration, and the aesthetic use of language.

1.   In TEXT 3, President Obama reflects on the NASA Moon landing, describing it as one of "the greatest achievements in human history".

          Write a persuasive essay entitled, "The Three Greatest Achievements in Human History".

2.   Mistaken identity is a feature of Shakespeare's play, *The Comedy of Errors* in TEXT 1.

          Write a short story in which mistaken identity is central to the plot.

3.   Sara Baume takes her readers on a journey through the countryside in her novel, *spill simmer falter wither*, featured in TEXT 2.

          Write a descriptive essay in which you take your readers on an urban journey.

4.   The village shops in Sara Baume's novel contain a "surplus of useless clutter".   (TEXT 2)

          Write a personal essay in which you reflect on the "useless clutter" that is a feature of many aspects of our lives.

5.   In TEXT 1, Shakespeare's characters encounter many adventures on their travels.

          Write a speech, for a class debate for or against the motion: *"Young people should travel and see the world before joining the workforce or furthering their education."*

6.   Much of the action in TEXT 2 takes place within the confines of Ray's car.

          Write a short story that centres on two characters and a car journey.

7.   In TEXT 3, President Obama refers to "the pursuit of discovery" as an essential element of the American character.

          You are participating in a public speaking competition for second-level students. Write a speech, that can be serious or amusing or both, in which you describe what you see as the essential elements of the Irish character.

Coimisiún na Scrúduithe Stáit
State Examinations Commission

LEAVING CERTIFICATE EXAMINATION, 2016

English - Higher Level - Paper 2

Total Marks: 200

Thursday, 9th June – Afternoon, 2.00 – 5.20

Candidates must attempt the following :
- **ONE** question from SECTION I – The Single Text
- **ONE** question from SECTION II – The Comparative Study
- **ONE** question on the Unseen Poem from SECTION III – Poetry
- **ONE** question on Prescribed Poetry from SECTION III – Poetry

N.B. Candidates must answer on Shakespearean Drama.
They may do so in SECTION I, the Single Text (*King Lear)* or in SECTION II, The Comparative Study (*King Lear*, *Othello*).

INDEX OF SINGLE TEXTS

Wuthering Heights	– *Page 2*
The Great Gatsby	– *Page 2*
Translations	– *Page 2*
Death and Nightingales	– *Page 3*
King Lear	– *Page 3*

2016 P2

SECTION I   THE SINGLE TEXT   (60 marks)

Candidates must answer **one** question from this section (**A – E**).

A   **WUTHERING HEIGHTS** – Emily Brontë

    (i)   "Catherine Earnshaw and Heathcliff share a variety of character traits that contribute to the dramatic and tragic aspects of the story."

          To what extent do you agree or disagree with this statement? Support your answer with reference to the novel, *Wuthering Heights*.

OR

    (ii)   "Brontë's effective use of a range of contrasts helps to create a darkly fascinating world in the course of her novel, *Wuthering Heights*."

          Discuss this statement, supporting your answer with reference to the novel.

B   **THE GREAT GATSBY** – F. Scott Fitzgerald

    (i)   "Daisy Buchanan and Jay Gatsby possess a variety of character traits that contribute to the dramatic and tragic aspects of the story."

          To what extent do you agree or disagree with this statement? Support your answer with reference to the novel, *The Great Gatsby*.

OR

    (ii)   "Fitzgerald's effective use of a range of contrasts helps to create a clearly unequal world in the course of his novel, *The Great Gatsby*."

          Discuss this statement, supporting your answer with reference to the novel.

C   **TRANSLATIONS** – Brian Friel

    (i)   "The central characters in Friel's play, *Translations*, are tragic but not heroic."

          To what extent do you agree or disagree with this statement? Support your answer with reference to at least two of the play's central characters.

OR

    (ii)   "Friel explores the theme of identity in a variety of ways throughout the play, *Translations*."

          Discuss this statement, supporting your answer with reference to the play.

D   DEATH AND NIGHTINGALES – Eugene McCabe

(i)   "Billy and Beth Winters share a variety of character traits that contribute to the dramatic and tragic aspects of the story."

To what extent do you agree or disagree with this statement? Support your answer with reference to the novel, *Death and Nightingales*.

OR

(ii)   "McCabe makes effective use of a range of conflicts to create a deeply disturbing world in the course of his novel, *Death and Nightingales*."

Discuss this statement, supporting your answer with reference to the novel.

E   KING LEAR – William Shakespeare

(i)   "Throughout the course of the play, both Lear and Gloucester are tragic characters, but Lear develops into the more heroic figure."

To what extent do you agree or disagree with this statement? Support your answer with reference to the play, *King Lear*.

OR

(ii)   "Shakespeare explores both the destructive and the redemptive power of love throughout the play, *King Lear*."

Discuss this statement, supporting your answer with reference to the play.

SECTION II   THE COMPARATIVE STUDY   (70 marks)

Candidates must answer **one** question from **either A** – The Cultural Context **or B** – Literary Genre.

In your answer you may not use the text you have answered on in **SECTION I** – The Single Text. All texts used in this section must be prescribed for comparative study for this year's examination. Candidates may refer to only one film in the course of their answers.

Please note:
- Questions in this section use the word **text** to refer to all the different kinds of texts available for study on this course, i.e. novel, play, short story, autobiography, biography travel writing and film.
- When used, the word **reader** includes viewers of films and theatre audiences.
- When used, the term **technique** is taken to include techniques employed by all writers and directors of films.
- When used, the word **author** is taken to include all writers and directors of films.

A   THE CULTURAL CONTEXT

1. "Understanding who holds power and who is powerless helps to reveal the cultural context in texts."

   Compare how the distribution of power within each of **three** texts on your comparative course helps to reveal the cultural contexts in these texts. Support your answer with reference to your chosen texts.   (70)

OR

2. "Central characters can be successful or unsuccessful in challenging aspects of the cultural context in texts."

   (a) Discuss the extent to which at least one central character is successful or unsuccessful in challenging at least one aspect of the cultural context in **one** text on your comparative course. Support your answer with reference to the text.   (30)

   (b) Compare the extent to which at least one central character, from each of **two other** comparative texts, is either successful or unsuccessful in challenging at least one aspect of the cultural context in these texts. Support your answer with reference to your chosen texts.

   You may refer to the same aspect or different aspects of the cultural contexts in your answers.   (40)

B   LITERARY GENRE

1.   "Authors can use various techniques to make settings real and engaging."

Compare how the authors of **three** of the texts on your comparative course make the settings in these texts real and engaging. Support your answer with reference to your chosen texts.   (70)

OR

2.   "Different techniques may be used to heighten the impact of moments of crisis in texts."

(a) Discuss the technique(s) used to heighten the impact of at least one moment of crisis in **one** of the texts you have studied for your comparative course. Support your answer with reference to the text.   (30)

(b) With reference to **two other** comparative texts, compare the technique(s) used to heighten the impact of at least one moment of crisis in each of these texts. Support your answer with reference to your chosen texts.   (40)

Candidates must answer **A** – Unseen Poem **and B** – Prescribed Poetry.

A   **UNSEEN POEM** (20 marks)

Read the following poem by Czesław Miłosz and answer **either** Question **1 or** Question **2** which follow.

And Yet the Books

And yet the books will be there on the shelves, separate beings,
That appeared once, still wet
As shining chestnuts under a tree in autumn,
And, touched, coddled, began to live
In spite of fires on the horizon, castles blown up,
Tribes on the march, planets in motion.
"We are," they said, even as their pages
Were being torn out, or a buzzing flame
Licked away their letters. So much more durable
Than we are, whose frail warmth
Cools down with memory, disperses, perishes.
I imagine the earth when I am no more:
Nothing happens, no loss, it's still a strange pageant,
Women's dresses, dewy lilacs, a song in the valley.
Yet the books will be there on the shelves, well born,
Derived from people, but also from radiance, heights.

Czesław Miłosz

1.   (a)   Outline the ideas expressed by the poet in this poem.
              Support your answer with reference to the text.   (10)

     (b)   Select two images from the poem that you think best convey the poet's ideas.
              Explain your choice.   (10)

OR

2.   Discuss the language used by the poet throughout this poem. Refer closely
     to the text in your answer.   (20)

PRESCRIBED POETRY (50 marks)

Candidates must answer **one** of the following questions (**1 – 4**).

1.   **<u>Emily Dickinson</u>**

"Dickinson's use of an innovative style to explore intense experiences can both intrigue and confuse."

Discuss this statement, supporting your answer with reference to the poetry of Emily Dickinson on your course.

2.   **<u>T. S. Eliot</u>**

"Eliot frequently creates memorable characters and dramatic settings to convey both his search for meaning in life and his sense of disillusionment."

Discuss this statement, supporting your answer with reference to the poetry of T. S. Eliot on your course.

3.   **<u>Elizabeth Bishop</u>**

"Bishop uses highly detailed observation, of people, places and events, to explore unique personal experiences in her poetry."

Discuss this statement, supporting your answer with reference to the poetry of Elizabeth Bishop on your course.

4.   **<u>Paul Durcan</u>**

"Durcan takes a narrative approach to explore a variety of issues in poems of great emotional honesty."

Discuss this statement, supporting your answer with reference to the poetry of Paul Durcan on your course.

Coimisiún na Scrúduithe Stáit
State Examinations Commission

LEAVING CERTIFICATE EXAMINATION, 2015

English – Higher Level – Paper I

Total Marks: 200

Wednesday, 3ʳᵈ June – Morning, 9.30 – 12.20

- This paper is divided into two sections,
  Section I COMPREHENDING and Section II COMPOSING.
- The paper contains **three** texts on the general theme of CHALLENGES.
- Candidates should familiarise themselves with each of the texts before beginning their answers.

- Both sections of this paper (COMPREHENDING and COMPOSING) must be attempted.
- Each section carries 100 marks.

SECTION I – COMPREHENDING

- Two Questions, A and B, follow each text.
- Candidates must answer a Question A on one text and a Question B on a different text. Candidates must answer only one Question A and only one Question B.
- **N.B.** Candidates may NOT answer a Question A and a Question B on the same text.

SECTION II – COMPOSING

- Candidates must write on **one** of the compositions 1 – 7.

TEXT 1

BECAUSE WE CAN, WE MUST

This edited text is based on a speech delivered by U2 front man and well-known humanitarian, Bono, to students graduating from the University of Pennsylvania.

My name is Bono and I am a rock star. I've got a great rock and roll band that normally stands in the back when I'm talking to thousands of people in a football stadium. I never went to college. I studied rock and roll and I grew up in Dublin in the '70s; music was an alarm bell for me; it woke me up to the world. I was seventeen when I first saw the band *The Clash*, and it just sounded like revolution. *The Clash* were like, "This is a public service announcement – with guitars." I was the kid in the crowd who took it at face value. Later I learned that a lot of the rebels were in it for the T-shirt. They'd wear the boots but they wouldn't march. For better or worse that was my education. I came away with a clear sense of the difference music could make in my own life, in other people's lives, if I did my job right.

If members of the faculty are asking what on earth I'm doing here, I think it's a fair question. What *am* I doing here? More to the point: what are *you* doing here? Four years in these historic halls thinking great thoughts and now you're sitting in a stadium better suited for football, listening to an Irish rock star. What are you doing here? For four years you've been buying, trading, and selling everything you've got in this marketplace of ideas. The intellectual hustle. Your pockets are full, even if your parents' pockets are empty, and now you've got to figure out what to spend it on.

Well, the going rate for change is not cheap. Big ideas are expensive. So my question I suppose is: what's the big idea? What's *your* big idea? What are you willing to spend your moral capital, your intellectual capital, your cash, your sweat equity in pursuing outside of the walls of the University of Pennsylvania?

There's a truly great Irish poet; his name is Brendan Kennelly, and he has this epic poem called the *Book of Judas,* and there's a line in that poem that never leaves my mind. It says: "If you want to serve the age, betray it." What does that mean – to betray the age? Well to me, betraying the age means exposing its conceits, its foibles, its phony moral certitudes. It means telling the secrets of the age and facing harsher truths.

Every age has its massive moral blind spots. We might not see them, but our children will. Slavery was one of them and the people who best served that age were the ones who called it as it was – which was ungodly and inhuman. Ben Franklin called it what it was when he became president of the Pennsylvania Abolition Society. There was another one. Segregation. America sees this now but it took a civil rights movement to betray their age.

Fast forward fifty years. What are the ideas right now worth betraying? What are the lies we tell ourselves now? What are the blind spots of our age? What's worth spending your post-Penn lives trying to do or undo? It might be something as simple as our deep down refusal to believe that every human life has equal worth. Could that be it? Each of you will probably have your own answer, but for me that is it. And for me the proving ground has been Africa.

Equality for Africa is a big idea. It's a big expensive idea. Wishing for the end to AIDS and extreme poverty in Africa is like wishing that gravity didn't make things so damn heavy. We can wish it, but what the hell can we do about it? Well, more than we think. We can't fix every problem – corruption, natural calamities are part of the picture here – but the ones we can, we must. The debt burden, unfair trade, sharing our knowledge, the intellectual copyright for lifesaving drugs in a crisis, we can do that. And because we can, we must. Because we can, we must. Amen.

The fact is that this generation – yours, my generation – we're the first generation that can look at poverty and disease, look across the ocean to Africa and say with a straight face, *we can be the first to end this sort of stupid extreme poverty, where in the world of plenty, a child can die for lack of food in its belly.* It might take a while, but we can be that generation that says no to stupid poverty. For the first time in history we have the know-how, we have the cash, we have the lifesaving drugs, but do we have the will? I'm not a hippy; I do not have flowers in my hair; I come from punk rock; *The Clash* wore army boots not Birkenstock sandals. I believe that this generation can do this. In fact I want to hear an argument about why we shouldn't.

I know idealism is not playing on the radio right now, you don't see it on TV; irony is on heavy rotation, the knowingness, the smirk, the tired joke. I've tried them all out but I'll tell you this, outside this campus – and even inside it – idealism is under siege, beset by materialism, narcissism and all the other 'isms' of indifference.

Every era has its defining struggle and the fate of Africa is one of ours. It's not the only one, but in the history books it's easily going to make the top five, what we did or what we did not do. But whether it's this or something else, I hope you'll pick a fight and get in it. Get your boots dirty, get rough, steel your courage, have one last primal scream and go.

You know I used to think the future was solid or fixed, something you inherited like an old building that you move into when the previous generation moves out or gets chased out. But it's not. The future is not fixed, it's fluid. The world is more malleable than you think and it's waiting for you to hammer it into shape. This degree of yours is a blunt instrument. So go forth and build something with it. This is the time for bold measures. This is the country, and you are the generation. Thank you.

This text has been adapted, for the purpose of assessment, without the copyright holder's prior consent.

N.B.   Candidates may NOT answer Question A and Question B on the same text.

Questions A and B carry 50 marks each.

QUESTION A

(i)   Outline, in your own words, three of the challenges Bono issued to students at the University of Pennsylvania when he spoke at their graduation ceremony. Support your answer with reference to the text. (15)

(ii)   Identify, and give your personal response to any two observations made by Bono in the above passage that made an impact on you. Support your answer with reference to the text. (15)

(iii)   Based on what you have read in the extract above, do you agree that Bono is both engaging and inspiring in his address to the graduating students? Support your answer with reference to both the content and style of the extract. (20)

QUESTION B

Your school Principal has decided not to hold any graduation ceremony for the Leaving Certificate Class of 2015. The school's Student Council disagrees with this decision. As Chairperson of the Student Council you have been asked to write a **letter** to the Principal, in which you express the students' dissatisfaction with this decision and make a case for holding a graduation event. Write the letter you would submit to the Principal. (50)

TEXT 2

GHOSTS DON'T SHOW UP ON CCTV

This edited text is based on an article which appeared in the Review Section of *The Guardian* newspaper in July, 2014. In this article, author Joanna Briscoe discusses the challenges faced by writers of ghost literature in an age of reason.

We don't believe in ghosts, so writing ghost literature for a modern readership presents particular challenges. How does one write for an audience that is cynical, yet still wishes to be terrified? What exactly is a ghost, anyway?

We live in an age of reason, a more secular culture than that of those great ghost writers, the Victorians. We rely on the proofs and disproofs of science, psychology and medicine, on the digital recording of much of our lives. We live in brightly illuminated rooms, on streets devoid of the terror of something moving just outside the lamp light. Ghosts don't tend to show up on CCTV cameras and holograms are explicable phantoms. Ghosts should not be visible – at least not in any straightforward way.

While writing my ghost novel, *Touched*, it felt important to me that unexplained presences were not the walking dead, but were just perceived as sounds, scents or misidentifications; at most, they are reflections, or reported sightings or something captured in the split second of a film still. As Roald Dahl boldly claimed: "The best ghost stories don't have ghosts in them." And, as author Susan Hill says: "Less is always more".

The contemporary writer must trade on the power of anticipation, on the unnerving aspects of less obvious settings than candlelit wrecks in fog. I sought brightness for my unease: brilliant green grass and relentless sunshine, so the glimmer in the trees, the hint of eyes in a window, were all the more unexpected. Perfection can be eerie. The power of a ghost story lies in what is feared beneath the surface of the narrative, terrors glimpsed or imagined in the cracks, rather than what leaps out of the shadows.

Form is an issue. There are very few full-length ghost novels because of the difficulties of sustaining suspension of disbelief. Even in ghost writing's heyday, it was the short story – by Dickens, H.P. Lovecraft, Charlotte Riddell – that was the dominant form, while the longer classic of the genre, *The Turn of the Screw*, is only 43,000 words. Readers need to be in a state of tension for the unfathomable to prey on fearful minds, yet this can be maintained by the writer for a limited time without risking nervous exhaustion.

There is a fine balance between the psychological and the spectral. Ghost writing must involve a blurring between reality and madness or projection. The modern ghost writer inherits a tradition of unreliable narrators, vastly ramped up by later psychoanalytic thinking. I found it interesting to subvert this by writing about apparent madness, in a girl who insists on dressing as a shabby Victorian, while the real chaos lies where no one is looking.

Endings can be a problem. It is paramount that narrative demands are satisfied, yet what explanation can there be? Ghost writing is in many ways the opposite of crime or detective fiction, whose worlds are more logical than real life – you find out who did it – whereas the supernatural can have no straightforward point of revelation to work towards. So there is a necessary ambivalence. I firmly believe in tying up narrative strands, so while every human story must be followed to its conclusion, the reader must be left plot-satisfied but intentionally uneasy, the paranormal at play in the margins.

If visions and voices are rationally explained, it's not a ghost story; if they're not, incredulity can set in. If a ghost is a mere psychological delusion, the gleam of the supernatural is dulled. Apparitions cannot be mere symbols, metaphors or projections: the characters, however warped, must experience them as hauntings, the reader on side. The conventions of traditional ghost stories are there to play with, and, for the modern writer, there is pleasure to be had in hidden rooms, with resistant houses and barely heard sounds. Chilling child patterings and mysterious stains are an enticing part of what Henry James called "the strange and sinister embroidered on the very type of the normal and easy".

This is an era conversant with extreme horror

and increasingly successful crime genres, with console games that scatter images of blood on the screen. Yet we still seem to desire less definable hauntings in the form of the gothic, vampiric and ghostly. The truth is an audience can be deeply scared by the very phenomena they don't believe in.

Above all, ghost writing is about atmosphere. The mood and resonance, the sounds, scents and tense awareness that here is a place where anything could happen. What has always appealed to me is the modern gothic, the unsettling and even the unsavoury in literature. It's the glimmer of another presence that lies just outside our normal understanding that intrigues.

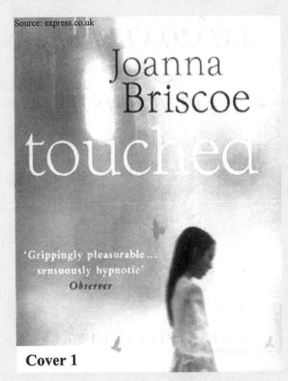

Cover 1

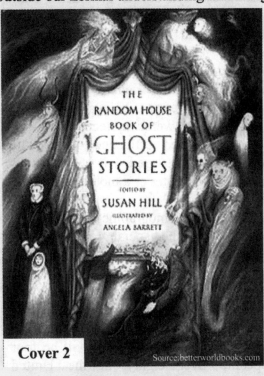

Cover 2

This text has been adapted, for the purpose of assessment, without the copyright holder's prior consent.

N.B. Candidates may NOT answer Question A and Question B on the same text.

Questions A and B carry 50 marks each.

QUESTION A

(i)   Outline, in your own words, three of the challenges facing contemporary writers of ghost literature, identified by Joanna Briscoe in the text above. Support your answer with reference to the text.

(15)

(ii) Based on what you have read in the above extract, do you agree that this article is both an informative and engaging piece of writing? Refer to at least two features of the writer's style in support of your viewpoint.

(15)

(iii) In your opinion, how effectively do the book covers illustrate what Joanna Briscoe has to say about ghost writing in the written text above? Support your answer by detailed reference to both of the book covers and to the written text.

(20)

QUESTION B

The writing group, to which you belong, has decided to develop a website, aimed at aspiring young writers. You have been asked to contribute an article on one of the following genres: detective fiction; travel writing; humour; romance; autobiography; the short story. Write the **article** you would contribute, discussing at least two important characteristics of your chosen genre and offering advice to young people wishing to engage in this type of writing.

(50)

TEXT 3

A LIFE IN TIME

This edited text is based on *Ammonites and Leaping Fish*, a memoir by award-winning novelist, Penelope Lively. In the text she reflects on youth and age and explores the challenges of ageing.

Old age is in the eye of the beholder. I am eighty, so I am old, no question. The extent of the challenge depends on when and where you experience old age. There is anthropological evidence that in a hunter-gatherer society the old are valued simply for experience, their bank of hunter-gatherer knowledge. Things aren't quite like this in a world powered by technology; just as well that increased affluence means that nobody disposes of the aged just because they can't cope with a computer or a mobile phone.

Old age is the new demographic. We are the pioneers, as an established social group, gobbling up benefits and giving grief to government agencies. Before the sixteenth century few people saw fifty, let alone eighty. Scroll back, and average life expectancy diminishes century by century; two thousand years ago, it stood at around twenty-five. By 2030 there will be four million people over eighty in the United Kingdom – out of a population of around sixty million. Suffice it that we are too many. That's one way of looking at it: the administrative point of view, the view perhaps sometimes of the young, who have inherited the world, quite properly, and may occasionally find themselves guilty of ageist sentiments.

I haven't much come up against ageism. There was an occasion, a few years ago, when a teenage granddaughter was advising on the acquisition of a mobile phone and the salesman's enthusiastic attention turned to disdain when he realised that the purchase was not for her but for the old granny, who had no business with any mobile, let alone the latest Nokia. But more usually I find that age has bestowed a kind of comfortable anonymity. We are not especially interesting, by and large – waiting for a bus, walking along the street; younger people are busy sizing up one another, in the way that children in a park will only register other children. We are not exactly invisible but we are not noticed, which I rather like; it leaves me free to do what a novelist does anyway, listen and watch, but with the added spice of feeling a little as though I am some observant time-traveller, on the edge of things, bearing witness to the customs of another age.

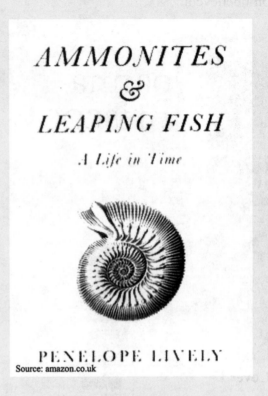

AMMONITES & LEAPING FISH

A Life in Time

PENELOPE LIVELY

Source: amazon.co.uk

Old age is forever stereotyped. Years ago, I was a judge for a national children's writing competition. They had been asked to write about 'grandparents'; in every offering the grandparent was a figure with stick and hearing aid, knitting by the fireside or pottering in the garden. The average grandparent would then have been around sixty, and probably still at work. We are too keen to bundle everyone by category; as a child I used to be maddened by the assumption that I would get along famously with someone just because we were both eight. All that we have in common, we in this new demographic, are our aches and pains and disabilities. For the rest of it, we are the people we always have been – splendidly various, and let us respect that. We do not wish to have assumptions made about our capacities and tastes.

Am I envious of the young? Would I want to be young again? I would like to have back vigour and robust health, but that is not exactly envy. Having known youth, I'm well aware that it has its own traumas, that it is no Elysian progress, that it can be a time of distress and disappointment, that it is exuberant and exciting, but it is no picnic. I don't particularly want to go back there. And in any case I am someone else now.

All of the discussion of how to confront old age focuses on physical and mental activity. Over the last years, I've had surgery and treatment for breast cancer. My sight is dodgy. There is a shoulder problem. As for the rest of my continuing ailments, they seem more or less par for the course for an eighty year old. You get used to it. And that surprises me. Acceptance has set in, somehow, which is just as well, because the alternative – perpetual rage and resentment – would not help matters. The body may decline, may seem a dismal reflection of what went before, but the mind has a healthy continuity. Most people, it seems to me, retain an essential persona, a cast of mind, a trademark footprint. A poet's voice will alter and develop but young Wordsworth, Tennyson, Larkin are not essentially adrift from their later selves. There is this interesting accretion – the varieties of ourselves – and the puzzling thing in old age is to find yourself out there as the culmination of all these, knowing that they are you, but that you are also now this someone else.

I can remember falling in love, being in love; life would have been incomplete without that particular exaltation, but I wouldn't want to go back there. I still love – there is a swathe of people that I love – but I am glad indeed to be done with that consuming, tormenting form of the emotion.

I am as alive to the world as I have ever been – alive to everything I see and hear and feel. Spring was never so vibrant; autumn never so richly gold. People are of abiding interest – observed in the street, overheard on a bus. It is an old accustomed world now, but invested with fresh significance. What we have been still lurks – and even more so within. This old age self is just a top dressing, it seems; early selves are still mutinously present, getting a word in now and then. The day belongs to the young. I wouldn't in the least want to reoccupy the centre stage. I don't remember being any more appreciative of life then than I am now.

This text has been adapted, for the purpose of assessment, without the copyright holder's prior consent.

N.B. Candidates may NOT answer Question A and Question B on the same text.

Questions A and B carry 50 marks each.

QUESTION A

(i)   Outline, in your own words, three of the challenges posed by old age, identified by Penelope Lively in the text above. Support your answer with reference to the text.   (15)

(ii)   Identify, and give your personal response to any two observations the writer makes about young people and youthfulness generally, in the course of the above passage. Support your answer with reference to the text.   (15)

(iii)   Based on what you have read in the above text, do you agree that this extract from Penelope Lively's memoir is both skilfully written and perceptively observed? Support your answer with reference to both the content and style of the extract.   (20)

QUESTION B

Write the **introduction** for a collection of writing (e.g. poems, stories and articles) by young people about older people. In it you should discuss the importance of older people, such as grandparents, in the lives of young people today and the contribution made by older people to society in general.   (50)

SECTION II   COMPOSING   (100 marks)

Write a composition on **any one** of the assignments that appear in **bold print** below.

Each composition carries 100 marks.

The composition assignments are intended to reflect language study in the areas of information, argument, persuasion, narration, and the aesthetic use of language.

1.   TEXTS 1, 2 and 3 deal with the theme of challenges.

      Write a short story in which the main character is transformed when faced with a daunting challenge.

2.   In TEXT 3, Penelope Lively remembers falling in love.

      Write a feature article for a magazine, about the importance of romance in our lives. The article may be light-hearted or serious.

3.   In TEXT 1, Bono talks about some of the defining struggles faced by people through the ages.

      Write a thought-provoking speech, to be delivered at a United Nations Youth Conference, in which you consider some of the causes and possible solutions to what you see as the defining struggles of our age.

4.   In TEXT 2, Joanna Briscoe, writing about fiction, tells us that "Endings can be a problem."

      Write a personal essay about your response to an ending, or endings, in your life that you consider significant.

5.   In TEXT 3, Penelope Lively writes that she sometimes feels like an "observant time-traveller".

      Write a descriptive essay which captures life in Ireland in 2015 from the point of view of an observant time-traveller. The time-traveller may be from the past or from the future.

6.   Bono refers to "... telling the secrets of the age ..." in TEXT 1.

      Write a short story in which a closely guarded secret is gradually revealed.

7.   The writer alludes to "... the digital recording of much of our lives" in TEXT 2.

      Write a discursive essay, in which you discuss the importance of privacy in people's lives and the challenges to privacy in the modern age.

Coimisiún na Scrúduithe Stáit
State Examinations Commission

LEAVING CERTIFICATE EXAMINATION, 2015

English - Higher Level - Paper 2

Total Marks: 200

Thursday, 4ᵗʰ June – Afternoon, 2.00 – 5.20

Candidates must attempt the following:
- **ONE** question from SECTION I – The Single Text
- **ONE** question from SECTION II – The Comparative Study
- **ONE** question on the Unseen Poem from SECTION III – Poetry
- **ONE** question on Prescribed Poetry from SECTION III – Poetry

N.B. Candidates must answer on Shakespearean Drama.
They may do so in SECTION I, the Single Text (*Othello*) or in SECTION II,
The Comparative Study (*Othello, King Lear*).

INDEX OF SINGLE TEXTS

Pride and Prejudice	– *Page 2*
The Great Gatsby	– *Page 2*
Never Let Me Go	– *Page 3*
All My Sons	– *Page 3*
Othello	– *Page 3*

SECTION I   THE SINGLE TEXT   (60 marks)

Candidates must answer **one** question from this section (**A – E**).

A   **PRIDE AND PREJUDICE** – Jane Austen

    (i)   "The relationship between Mr Darcy and Elizabeth Bennet is an attraction of opposites."

       Discuss this view of the relationship between Mr Darcy and Elizabeth Bennet. Support your answer with reference to the novel, *Pride and Prejudice*.

OR

    (ii)   "*Pride and Prejudice* is a novel so concerned with trivial romantic matters that it fails to engage with any substantial issues."

       To what extent do you agree or disagree with this view of the novel? Support your answer with reference to the text.

B   **THE GREAT GATSBY** – F. Scott Fitzgerald

    (i)   "The friendship between Nick Carraway and Jay Gatsby is fascinating because it is both intimate and complex."

       Discuss this view of the friendship between Carraway and Gatsby. Support your answer with reference to the novel, *The Great Gatsby*.

OR

    (ii)   "It is possible to be both attracted to the idealism and repelled by the corruption evident in *The Great Gatsby*."

       To what extent do you agree or disagree with this view? Support your answer with reference to the novel.

C   NEVER LET ME GO – Kazuo Ishiguro

(i)   "Ishiguro, in *Never Let Me Go*, both comforts and disturbs us because so much of human nature is reflected in the lives of the clones."

To what extent do you agree or disagree with this view? Support your answer with reference to the novel.

OR

(ii)   "The steady and relentless erosion of the hopes and dreams of Kathy, Ruth and Tommy contribute to the tragic story in this novel."

Discuss this view of the novel, *Never Let Me Go*, supporting your answer with reference to two of the above characters.

D   ALL MY SONS – Arthur Miller

(i)   "Ann Deever and Kate Keller are admirable because they are brave and honest."

To what extent do you agree or disagree with this view of Ann Deever and Kate Keller? Support your answer with reference to the play, *All My Sons*.

OR

(ii)   "The conflict between self-preservation and social responsibility dominates Miller's play, *All My Sons*."

Discuss this view, supporting your answer with reference to the text.

E   OTHELLO – William Shakespeare

(i)   "Desdemona and Emilia are weak characters who fail to gain our sympathy."

To what extent do you agree or disagree with this view of Desdemona and Emilia? Support your answer with reference to the play, *Othello*.

OR

(ii)   "The values evident in *Othello* have a profound influence on the outcome of the play."

Discuss this view, supporting your answer with reference to at least two of the values evident in the text.

SECTION II   THE COMPARATIVE STUDY   (70 marks)

Candidates must answer **one** question from **either A** – Theme or Issue **or B** – Literary Genre.

In your answer you may not use the text you have answered on in **SECTION I** – The Single Text. All texts used in this section must be prescribed for comparative study for this year's examination.

Please note:
- Questions in this section use the word **text** to refer to all the different kinds of texts available for study on this course, i.e. novel, play, short story, autobiography, biography, travel writing, and film.
- When used, the word **reader** includes viewers of films and theatre audiences.
- When used, the term **literary technique** is taken to include techniques employed by authors, playwrights and directors of films.
- When used, the word **author** or **storyteller** is taken to include playwrights and directors of films.

A   THEME OR ISSUE

1.   "Some texts leave readers with a largely idealistic impression of a theme or issue, while others leave readers with a more realistic or believable impression of the same theme or issue."

     With reference to the above statement, compare the impressions of the same theme or issue you formed when studying **three texts** on your comparative course. Support your answer by reference to the texts.   (70)

OR

2.   "It is possible for a reader to be surprised or shocked (or both) by aspects of a theme or issue encountered in texts."

    (a)   Discuss the extent to which you were surprised or shocked (or both) by aspects of a theme or issue encountered in **one** of the texts you have studied for your comparative course. Support your answer by reference to the text.   (30)

    (b)   Compare the extent to which you were surprised or shocked (or both) by aspects of the same theme or issue encountered in **two other texts** you have studied on your comparative course. Support your answer by reference to the texts.   (40)

B   LITERARY GENRE

1.   "Studying a selection of texts helps to highlight how some authors can make more skilful use of the same literary technique than others."

Choose one literary technique, common to **three texts** on your comparative course, and compare how skilful the different authors are in using this literary technique in these texts. Support your answer by reference to the texts.   (70)

OR

2.   "Compelling storytelling can be achieved in a variety of ways."

(a)   Identify two literary techniques found in **one** text you have studied. Discuss the extent to which these techniques contributed to compelling storytelling in this text.   (30)

(b)   Identify one literary technique, common to **two other texts** on your comparative course. Compare the extent to which this literary technique contributed to compelling storytelling in these texts. You may select one of the literary techniques identified in 2. (a) above or you may choose to use any other literary technique in your answer.   (40)

2015 P2

Candidates must answer **A** – Unseen Poem **and B** – Prescribed Poetry.

A   **UNSEEN POEM** (20 marks)

Read the following poem by Peter Sirr, and answer **either** Question **1 or** Question **2** which follow.

Peter Street

I'd grown almost to love this street,
each time I passed looking up
to pin my father's face to a window, feel myself

held in his gaze. Today there's a building site
where the hospital stood and I stop and stare
stupidly at the empty air, looking for him.

I'd almost pray some ache remain
like a flaw in the structure, something unappeasable
waiting in the fabric, between floors, in some

obstinate, secret room. A crane moves
delicately in the sky, in its own language.
Forget all that, I think as I pass, make it

a marvelous house; music should roam the corridors,
joy readily occur, St Valentine's
stubborn heart comes floating from Whitefriar Street*

to prevail, to undo injury, to lift my father from his bed,
let him climb down the dull red brick, effortlessly,
and run off with his life in his hands.

Peter Sirr

A relic of St Valentine is kept at Our Lady of Mount Carmel Church, Whitefriar St., Dublin

---

By kind permission of the author and The Gallery Press, Loughcrew, Oldcastle, County Meath, Ireland from *Selected Poems* (2004)

1.   (a)   What do you believe is the central message of this poem?
              Support your answer with reference to the poem.   (10)

      (b)   Identify two images that you find interesting in this poem.
              Explain your choices, supporting your answer with reference to the poem.   (10)

OR

2.   Based on your reading of the above poem, identify the emotions expressed by the poet
      and explain how these emotions are conveyed in the poem.   (20)

B   PRESCRIBED POETRY (50 marks)

Candidates must answer **one** of the following questions (**1– 4**).

1.   John Montague

"Montague makes effective use of evocative language to express a profound empathy with others."

Discuss this statement, supporting your answer with reference to the poetry of John Montague on your course.

2.   Robert Frost

"Frost communicates rich insights into human experience using language that is both accessible and appealing."

Discuss this statement, supporting your answer with reference to the poetry of Robert Frost on your course.

3.   Eiléan Ní Chuilleanáin

"Ní Chuilleanáin's demanding subject matter and formidable style can prove challenging."

Discuss this statement, supporting your answer with reference to the poetry of Eiléan Ní Chuilleanáin on your course.

4.   Thomas Hardy

"Hardy's poetry is dominated by bleak imagery which overshadows the comforting reflections found in his work."

Discuss this statement, supporting your answer with reference to the poetry of Thomas Hardy on your course.

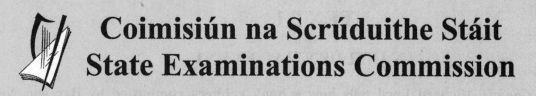

Coimisiún na Scrúduithe Stáit
State Examinations Commission

LEAVING CERTIFICATE EXAMINATION, 2014

English – Higher Level – Paper I

Total Marks: 200

Wednesday, 4th June – Morning, 9.30 – 12.20

- This paper is divided into two sections,
  Section I COMPREHENDING and Section II COMPOSING.
- The paper contains **three** texts on the general theme of INFLUENCE.
- Candidates should familiarise themselves with each of the texts before beginning their answers.

- Both sections of this paper (COMPREHENDING and COMPOSING) must be attempted.
- Each section carries 100 marks.

SECTION I – COMPREHENDING

- Two Questions, A and B, follow each text.
- Candidates must answer a Question A on one text and a Question B on a different text. Candidates must answer only one Question A and only one Question B.
- **N.B.** Candidates may NOT answer a Question A and a Question B on the same text.

SECTION II – COMPOSING

- Candidates must write on **one** of the compositions 1 – 7.

TEXT 1

AN INFLUENTIAL EVENT

In the novel, *Canada*, Richard Ford tells how a bank robbery committed by Bev and Neeva Parsons influenced the lives of their children, Dell and his twin sister, Berner, who were fifteen years old at the time of the crime. In this edited extract Dell remembers his escape to Canada with his mother's friend, Mildred Remlinger.

First, I'll tell about the robbery our parents committed. Then about the murders, which happened later. The robbery is the more important part, since it served to set my and my sister's lives on the courses they eventually followed. Nothing would make complete sense without that being told first.

Our parents were the least likely two people in the world to rob a bank. They weren't strange people, not obviously criminals. No one would've thought they were destined to end up the way they did. They were just regular – although, of course, that kind of thinking became null and void the moment they did rob a bank...

Mildred Remlinger drove up to our house in her battered old brown Ford, came straight up the walk, up the steps and knocked on the front door, behind which I was waiting alone. She came right inside and told me to pack my bag. She asked where my sister Berner was. I told her she'd left the day before. Mildred said we didn't have time to go and look for her. Juvenile officials representing the State of Montana would be coming soon to take us into custody. It was a miracle, she said, they hadn't come already. Then with me in the car seat beside her, Mildred drove us out of Great Falls that late morning of August 30, 1960, and straight north up the 87 highway.

Mildred didn't much speak at first, as Great Falls settled into the landscape behind us. Up on the benchland north and west of the Highwoods, it was nothing but hot yellow wheat and grasshoppers and snakes crossing the highway and the high blue sky, and the Bear's Paw Mountains out ahead, blue and hazy but with bright snow on their peaks. Havre, Montana, was the town farther north. Our father had delivered someone a new Dodge there earlier in the summer. He'd described it as a "desolate place, down in a big hole. The back of beyond". I couldn't imagine why Mildred would be driving

us there. On the map Havre was nearly as far north as you could go in Montana. Canada was just above it. But I felt I was doing what our mother had planned for me.

Mildred was a large square-hipped, authoritative woman, with short black curly hair, snapping small dark eyes, red lipstick, a fleshy neck, and powder on her face that masked a bad complexion, though not very well. She and her car both smelled like cigarettes and chewing gum, and her ashtray was full of lipstick butts and matches and spearmint wrappers, though she hadn't smoked while we were driving.

In Havre, we drove down the hill to the main street and found a sandwich shop. We sat at the counter inside, and I ate cold meat loaf and a soft roll with butter and a pickle and lemonade, and felt better. Mildred smoked while I ate and watched me and cleared her throat a lot and talked. She said she was forty-three, though I'd thought she was sixty or more. She said I should go to sleep in the back seat after lunch, and this was what let me know we weren't just going to Havre that day but were travelling farther on.

From Havre, we drove north, across a wooden railroad viaduct over the tracks and the muddy river and along a narrow highway that angled up the rimrock grade high enough to let me look back to the town, low and dismal and bleak in the baking sunlight. I was farther north than I'd ever been and felt barren and isolated, becoming unreachable. Wherever Berner was, I thought, was better than this.

The land north of Havre was the same as we'd been driving through: dry, unchanging cropland – a sea of golden wheat melting up into the hot unblemished blue sky crossed only by electrical wires. There were very few houses or buildings. Low green hills lay far out ahead in the shimmering distance. It was improbable we were going there, since I speculated those hills would be in Canada, which was all that lay ahead of us.

At a certain point, Mildred took in a deep breath and let it out as if she'd decided something she'd been keeping silent about. She was staring firmly ahead. "I'm taking you to Saskatchewan to live for a little while with my brother, Arthur. It won't have to be this way completely forever. But right now it does. I'm sorry. It's what your mother wants."

"I don't want to do that." I said this with absolute certainty. Mildred's brother. Canada. I felt sure I didn't have to do any of that. I had a say-so.

Mildred drove on for a time without speaking. Finally she said, "Well, if I have to take you back, they'll arrest me for kidnapping you and put me in jail. They're looking for you to put you in an orphanage. You better think on that. I'm trying to save you here." The black road seemed to be my life shooting away from me at a terrible speed, with no one to stop it.

Canada by Richard Ford – book cover

This text has been adapted, for the purpose of assessment, without the author's prior consent.

Used with permission of the author

N.B.   Candidates may NOT answer Question A and Question B on the same text.

Questions A and B carry 50 marks each.

QUESTION A

(i)   From your reading of Text 1 what impression do you form of the landscape in which the extract is set? In your answer you should refer to both the book cover and the written passage above.

(15)

(ii)   The first two paragraphs above are the opening of Richard Ford's novel, *Canada*.
In your view, is this an effective opening? Give reasons for your answer with reference to the first two paragraphs of the text.

(15)

(iii)   Ford's writing is characterised by its engaging narrative, lyrical beauty and concrete realism. Based on your reading from paragraph three onwards of the above extract, to what extent do you think this statement is accurate? Refer to features of Ford's writing style evident in the extract in support of your viewpoint.

(20)

QUESTION B

Imagine that the story of the disappearance of Dell Parsons, outlined in Text 1 above, has captured the public's imagination. You are a reporter with a national radio station. Write the **text of a news report,** on the Dell Parson's story, to be delivered on the station's main evening news bulletin. In your report you should communicate the facts of the case as known (based on Text 1) and further speculate as to Dell's whereabouts and possible developments in the story.

(50)

TEXT 2

CULTURAL INFLUENCES

At an event entitled The Joy of Influence, organised by Andrew O'Hagan, six writers were asked to talk about an art-form, other than literature, that influenced them. This edited text, adapted from *The Guardian* newspaper, is based on the contributions of two writers, Alan Warner and John Lanchester.

1. Scottish novelist, Alan Warner explores the influence of POP MUSIC on his writing.

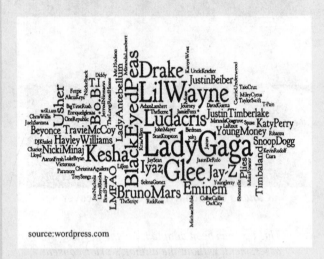

source:wordpress.com

Calibrating how something as ubiquitous as pop music has influenced your writing feels similar to asking, "How has the weather influenced your writing?"

While I love all types of music, pop and rock certainly appear in some of my novels. I would only reference music on the page if it served some narrative function. The carefully indexed lists of song titles in my novel, *Morvern Callar*, enforced Morvern's methodical approach to life. The individual timbres of the songs seemed appropriate to the mood. Morvern is listening to the music of her dead boyfriend on her old Sony Walkman. She is haunted and perplexed by this music, listening objectively but not necessarily with pleasure. So I may not always reference music I necessarily enjoy. It is just what fits the narrative requirements in this world so dressed in song.

I have learned there is real danger listening to music while I'm writing. The moving, dynamic power of great pop songs can soon fool you into believing what you are writing is also dynamic and emotionally powerful.

Pop music functions as this huge repository of personal emotion because it is among these songs

and sounds, on radio and at dances and on television, that our young hearts come alive. All this music continues to live for us as a vital thing, both linking us to our past but able to energise us in the future – and a growing library of new songs is added as life goes along.

While I am aware of this personal emotional heritage, as a writer I have to construct the emotional architecture of my characters – you can't just chuck in a few so-called "popular cultural references" for effect. When I was fifteen and even more daft, I tried to give up rock music and listen only to orchestral – so-called "classical" music. I was always a real sucker for self-improvement (still am) and I thought I could only become a refined writer if I censored aspects of the real world. I did develop a love for Bartók, Stravinsky and Ravel but I kept coming back to rock and pop music. Heavy metal was the real folk music of the small Scottish town I grew up in. All the guys in our town pipe band practised drums and chanter but listened to Deep Purple; it was simply my culture and I became weary of denying it.

Of course some pop music is not popular at all and it doesn't try to be. After punk, bands showed a healthy disregard for audience approval. I was mesmerised by that mocking arrogance and such conviction. I wanted to write like that. It was pop music that helped me decide that great writers could come to me on my own terms alone.

2. Journalist and novelist, John Lanchester reflects on a new art form: VIDEO GAMES.

What's exciting and interesting about video games is their newness. Video games are the first new artistic medium since television. They are more different from television than television was from cinema. They are the newest new thing since the arrival of the movies just over a century ago. That automatically

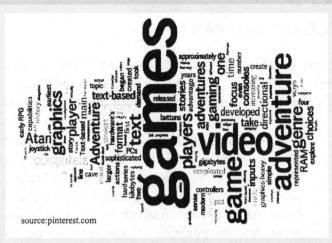

source:pinterest.com

control. Increasingly, it's the case that the player makes the story, makes the game-world. This gives the medium a real kick of intimacy and force. At its best, it can take you inside the world of a character with a force whose only rival – I find to my surprise – is the novel. That wasn't at all what I was expecting.

This takes us to another impact of the new medium, which concerns its effect on older forms. There's a curious link between video games and the novel and it is to do with the experience of being inside a world created by somebody else, but having the freedom to make up your own mind about what you find there. The novel takes you further and deeper inside someone else's head, but the aspect of agency inside video games, the fact that you can make choices that genuinely affect the story, is fascinating and genuinely new.

I'm sure that there is going to be some hybridisation between the two forms: a new beast, slouching towards us. I'm eagerly looking forward to meeting the beautiful mutant.

This text has been adapted, for the purpose of assessment, without the authors' prior consent.

makes them attractive, from the novelist's point of view, as part of the job of the novel is to be interested in the new. The artistic impact of video games goes in two different directions: what is it that this new thing does that's new, and what is it that it does that's old, but done differently? Video games do story and spectacle and there's a particularly distinctive aspect to their sense of progression, of moving through levels and their experimenting with difficulty and frustration and repetition as part of the form.

But the really new thing about video games is the fact that the player in them has agency: she makes decisions, makes choices, has a degree of

N.B. Candidates may NOT answer Question A and Question B on the same text.

Questions A and B carry 50 marks each.

QUESTION A

(i) Outline, in your own words, what either Alan Warner or John Lanchester has to say about his chosen art-form in the above text.   (15)

(ii) Identify two observations from the text that you found thought-provoking: one by Alan Warner about pop-music and one by John Lanchester about video games. Give your personal response to both of these observations. Support your answer with reference to the text.   (15)

(iii) In your opinion, which of the above novelists, Alan Warner or John Lanchester, more effectively conveys his point of view? Explain your answer with reference to features of style evident in both of their contributions.   (20)

QUESTION B

The above text is based on a series of public lectures delivered by various writers on the topic of influence. Young people today are subject to many influences. Write the text of a **talk** you would deliver to your class in which you consider some of the positive and negative influences on young people's lives today and how they respond to these influences.   (50)

TEXT 3
THE INFLUENCE OF THE PAST

Seamus Heaney is best remembered as a poet but he also enjoyed a distinguished career as an academic. This edited text is based on an essay by Heaney entitled *The Sense of the Past*. It appeared in the journal *History Ireland*. In it he reflects on the influence of the past on our lives.

'The Garden Seat' by Thomas Hardy

Its former green is blue and thin,
And its once firm legs sink in and in;
Soon it will break down unaware,
Soon it will break down unaware.

At night when reddest flowers are black
Those who once sat thereon come back;
Quite a row of them sitting there,
Quite a row of them sitting there.

With them the seat does not break down,
Nor winter freeze them, nor floods drown,
For they are as light as upper air,
They are as light as upper air!

Hardy's poem embodies a way of feeling and thinking about the past. It is about the ghost-life that hovers over the furniture of our lives, about the way objects can become temples of the spirit. To an imaginative person, an inherited possession like a garden seat is not just an object, an antique, an item on an inventory. It becomes a point of entry into a common emotional ground of memory and belonging. It can transmit the climate of a lost world and keep alive in us an intimacy with realities that might otherwise have vanished. The more we are surrounded by such objects and are attentive to them, the more richly and connectedly we dwell in our own lives. Our place, our house, our furniture are present then not just as backdrops but become influential and nurturing; our imagination breathes their atmosphere as rewardingly as our lungs breathe the oxygen of the air.

It could even be maintained that objects which have been seasoned by human contact possess a kind of moral force. They insist upon human solidarity and suggest obligations to and covenants with generations who have been silenced. Consider, for example, this passage by the Chilean poet, Pablo Neruda. He is not as concerned as Hardy was with the object as a capsule of the past, but he is testifying nevertheless to the power of the inanimate.

It is well, at certain hours of the day and night, to look closely at the world of objects at rest. Wheels that have crossed long, dusty distances with their mineral and vegetable burdens, sacks from the coal bins, barrels and baskets. From them flow the contacts of man with the earth — the used surfaces of things, the wear that the hands give to things, the air, tragic at times, pathetic at others, of such things — all lend a curious attractiveness to the reality of the world that should not be underprized. (Pablo Neruda).

source: flickr.com

The cupboards we open as toddlers, the shelves we climb up to, the boxes and albums we explore in reserved places in the house, the secret spots we come upon in our earliest solitudes out of doors — it is in such places and at such moments that 'the reality of the world' awakens in us. And it is at such moments that we have our first inkling of 'past-ness'. This is an unconscious process at the time. It has to do with an almost biological need to situate ourselves in our instinctual lives as creatures of the race and of the planet.

In my own case, the top of the dresser in the kitchen of the house where I lived for the first twelve years of my life was like a time machine. This was where all the old nails and screwdrivers and putty and lamp-wicks would end up. When I managed to climb up there, the yellowing newspaper, the bent nails, the dust and stillness and rust all suggested that these objects were living a kind of afterlife and that a previous time was alive in them. They were not just inert rubbish but dormant energies.

The sense of history can also derive from special objects in the everyday surroundings. In our house there was an old double-barrelled pistol, like a duelling piece, fixed on a bracket above a door in the kitchen. It was a completely exotic item in that ordinary world of dressers, churns, buckets, statues and Sacred Heart lamps. It did not belong and it was never explained. Yet when I began to get comics and to read adventure stories, this pistol linked our kitchen to stagecoaches and duels at dawn in the woodlands of great estates. There it perched, unnoticed and ordinary in the eye of the adult, but for me radiant with an eighteenth-century never-never land.

Sensitivity to the past contributes to our lives in a necessary way. It is a fundamental human gift that is potentially as life-enhancing and civilising as our gift for love. Indeed it can be

said without exaggeration that the sense of the past constitutes what the poet William Wordsworth would have called a 'primary law of our nature'.

source: redfin.ie
© Getty/AFP

This text has been adapted, for the purpose of assessment, without the copyright holder's prior consent.

N.B. Candidates may NOT answer Question A and Question B on the same text.

Questions A and B carry 50 marks each.

QUESTION A

(i) Outline, in your own words, three of the reasons given in the above text to support the view that objects from the past are important. (15)

(ii) Identify and give your personal response to any two observations from the above text that made an impact on you. Support your answer with reference to the text. (15)

(iii) 'One of Heaney's gifts as a writer was his ability to make complex and profound ideas accessible to the general reader.' To what extent do you think this statement can be applied to the above passage? Support your answer with reference to features of Heaney's writing style evident in the extract. (20)

QUESTION B

Inspired by Seamus Heaney's essay about the importance of objects from the past, your class has decided to organise an exhibition celebrating the significance of objects from childhood in the lives of well-known people.

Write the **letter** you would send to a well-known person, inviting him or her to contribute an object from his or her childhood and a written explanation regarding its personal significance. In your letter, you should explain the inspiration for the project and include, as an example, a piece you have written about an object from your childhood that is of significance to you. (50)

SECTION II   COMPOSING   (100 marks)

Write a composition on **any one** of the following.

Each composition carries 100 marks.

The composition assignments (in **bold print** below) are intended to reflect language study in the areas of information, argument, persuasion, narration, and the aesthetic use of language.

1.   "It is about the ghost-life that hovers over the furniture of our lives..."   (TEXT 3)

      Write a short story in which a ghostly presence plays a significant part.

2.   TEXTS 1, 2 and 3 are linked by the theme of influence.

      You are representing Ireland in the final of the World Youth Public Speaking Championships. Write a passionate speech in favour of the motion: "Young people should exert their influence by actively engaging with important current issues."

3.   In TEXT 1 we meet the feisty Mildred Remlinger.

      Write a personal essay about your encounters with a variety of interesting or unusual people and the impact they made on you.

4.   "It was a completely exotic item in that ordinary world ... "   (TEXT 3)

      Write a descriptive essay about what you find beautiful or exotic in everyday life.

5.   "How has the weather influenced your writing?"   (TEXT 2)

      Write a feature article for a magazine, which may be light-hearted or serious, about Irish people's obsession with the weather.

6.   In TEXT 1, Dell's future is very uncertain.

      Write a personal essay about one or more moments of uncertainty you have experienced.

7.   **Write a short story for inclusion in a collection of Science Fiction writing inspired by the following quotation from TEXT 2, " ...a new beast, slouching towards us... the beautiful mutant".**

Coimisiún na Scrúduithe Stáit
State Examinations Commission

LEAVING CERTIFICATE EXAMINATION, 2014

English - Higher Level - Paper 2

Total Marks: 200

Thursday, 5th June – Afternoon, 2.00 – 5.20

Candidates must attempt the following:
- **ONE** question from SECTION I – The Single Text
- **ONE** question from SECTION II – The Comparative Study
- **ONE** question on the Unseen Poem from SECTION III – Poetry
- **ONE** question on Prescribed Poetry from SECTION III – Poetry

N.B. Candidates must answer on Shakespearean Drama.
They may do so in SECTION I, the Single Text (*Macbeth*) or in SECTION II,
The Comparative Study (*Macbeth, Othello*).

INDEX OF SINGLE TEXTS

Pride and Prejudice	– *Page 2*
Empire of the Sun	– *Page 2*
Translations	– *Page 3*
Never Let Me Go	– *Page 3*
Macbeth	– *Page 3*

SECTION I THE SINGLE TEXT (60 marks)

Candidates must answer **one** question from this section (**A** – **E**).

A   PRIDE AND PREJUDICE – Jane Austen

   (i)   "Readers can both admire Elizabeth Bennet's character and learn a variety of lessons from her experiences."

       To what extent do you agree with this view? Support your answer with suitable reference to the novel, *Pride and Prejudice.*

OR

   (ii)   "Throughout the novel, *Pride and Prejudice*, Austen uses a variety of techniques to entertain her readers and provide commentary on the society of her day."

       Discuss this view of the novel, supporting your answer with suitable reference to the text.

B   EMPIRE OF THE SUN – J. G. Ballard

   (i)   "Despite his experiences throughout the story, in many ways Jim's character remains unchanged."

       To what extent do you agree or disagree with this view of the character of Jim Graham? Support your answer with suitable reference to Ballard's novel, *Empire of the Sun.*

OR

   (ii)   "In the novel, *Empire of the Sun*, Ballard presents readers with both horror and humanity to create a compelling account of war."

       Discuss this view of the novel, supporting your answer with suitable reference to the text.

C   TRANSLATIONS – Brian Friel

(i)   "Many of the main characters experience conflicting loyalties and learn bitter lessons during the course of the play, *Translations*."

Discuss this view, supporting your answer with suitable reference to at least two main characters in the play.

OR

(ii)   "Friel gives language a central role in *Translations* both as a theme and as a dramatic technique."

Discuss this view, supporting your answer with suitable reference to the play.

D   NEVER LET ME GO – Kazuo Ishiguro

(i)   "Readers of *Never Let Me Go* can have difficulty sympathising with Kathy, Ruth and Tommy because they are too passive and accept their fate without question."

Discuss this view, supporting your answer with suitable reference to at least two of the above characters in the novel.

OR

(ii)   "Ishiguro's novel, *Never Let Me Go*, shocks readers with a relentlessly bleak vision of a morally bankrupt world."

To what extent has this been your experience of reading *Never Let Me Go*? Explain your answer with suitable reference to the text.

E   MACBETH – William Shakespeare

(i)   "Macbeth's relationships with other characters can be seen primarily as power struggles which prove crucial to the outcome of the play."

Discuss the above statement in relation to at least two of Macbeth's relationships with other characters. Support your answer with suitable reference to the play, *Macbeth*.

OR

(ii)   "Throughout the play, *Macbeth*, Shakespeare makes effective use of a variety of dramatic techniques that evoke a wide range of responses from the audience."

Discuss this view with reference to at least two dramatic techniques used by Shakespeare in the play. Support your answer with suitable reference to the text.

SECTION II   THE COMPARATIVE STUDY   (70 marks)

Candidates must answer **one** question from **either A** – The Cultural Context
or B – The General Vision and Viewpoint.

In your answer you may not use the text you have answered on in **SECTION I** – The Single Text.

N.B. The questions use the word **text** to refer to all the different kinds of texts available for study on this course, i.e. novel, play, short story, autobiography, biography, travel writing, and film. The questions use the word **reader** to include viewers of films and theatre audiences.

A   THE CULTURAL CONTEXT

1.   "Various social groups, both large and small, (such as family, friends, organisations or community) reflect the cultural context in texts."

    Compare the extent to which one or more social groups reflect the cultural context in **at least two texts** on your comparative course.   (70)

OR

2.   "The cultural context within a text often dictates the crises or difficulties faced by characters and their responses to these difficulties."

    (a)   Discuss to what extent this statement applies to at least one central character in **one** of the texts you have studied for your comparative course.   (30)

    (b)   Compare the extent to which the above statement is applicable to at least one central character in each of **two other texts** you have studied on your comparative course.   (40)

B THE GENERAL VISION AND VIEWPOINT

1. (a) "The extent to which a reader can relate an aspect of a text to his or her experience of life, helps to shape an understanding of the general vision and viewpoint of that text." —

    Discuss this view in relation to your study of **one** text on your comparative course. (30)

    (b) With reference to the text you referred to in 1. (a) above and **at least one other text** from your comparative course, compare how two other aspects of the texts (excluding the aspect discussed in 1. (a) above) influenced your understanding of the general vision and viewpoint of those texts. (40)

OR

2. "Significant events in texts and the impact they have on readers often help to clarify the general vision and viewpoint of those texts."

    With reference to **three texts** on your comparative course, compare the ways in which at least one significant event in each text, and its impact on you, helped to clarify the general vision and viewpoint of these texts. (70)

SECTION III   POETRY   (70 marks)

Candidates must answer **A** – Unseen Poem **and B** – Prescribed Poetry.

A   **UNSEEN POEM** (20 marks)

Read the following poem by Seamus Heaney from his collection, *Door into the Dark*, and answer **either** Question **1 or** Question **2** which follow.

The Peninsula

When you have nothing more to say, just drive
For a day all round the peninsula.
The sky is tall as over a runway,
The land without marks, so you will not arrive

But pass through, though always skirting landfall.
At dusk, horizons drink down sea and hill,
The ploughed field swallows the whitewashed gable
And you're in the dark again. Now recall

The glazed foreshore and silhouetted log,
That rock where breakers shredded into rags,
The leggy birds stilted on their own legs,
Islands riding themselves out into the fog,

And drive back home, still with nothing to say
Except that now you will uncode all landscapes
By this: things founded clean on their own shapes,
Water and ground in their extremity.

'The Peninsula' from Door into the Dark by Seamus Heaney   *Seamus Heaney*
used by permission of Faber & Faber Ltd.

---

1. (a) In the above poem Seamus Heaney recommends driving "all round the peninsula". Based on your reading of the poem, explain why you think the poet recommends undertaking such a journey. (10)

   (b) Choose two images from the poem that appeal to you and explain your choice. (10)

OR

2. Discuss the effectiveness of the poet's use of language throughout this poem. Your answer should refer closely to the text. (20)

B   PRESCRIBED POETRY (50 marks)

Candidates must answer **one** of the following questions (1– 4).

1.   <u>**William Butler Yeats**</u>

"Yeats uses evocative language to create poetry that includes both personal reflection and public commentary."

Discuss this statement, supporting your answer with reference to both the themes and language found in the poetry of W. B. Yeats on your course.

2.   <u>**Emily Dickinson**</u>

"The dramatic aspects of Dickinson's poetry can both disturb and delight readers."

To what extent do you agree or disagree with the above statement? Support your answer with reference to both the themes and language found in the poetry of Emily Dickinson on your course.

3.   <u>**Philip Larkin**</u>

"Larkin is a perceptive observer of the realities of ordinary life in poems that are sometimes illuminated by images of lyrical beauty."

To what extent do you agree or disagree with the above statement? Support your answer with reference to both the themes and language found in the poetry of Philip Larkin on your course.

4.   <u>**Sylvia Plath**</u>

"Plath makes effective use of language to explore her personal experiences of suffering and to provide occasional glimpses of the redemptive power of love."

Discuss this statement, supporting your answer with reference to both the themes and language found in the poetry of Sylvia Plath on your course.

Coimisiún na Scrúduithe Stáit
State Examinations Commission

LEAVING CERTIFICATE EXAMINATION, 2013

English – Higher Level – Paper I

Total Marks: 200

Wednesday, 5th June – Morning, 9.30 – 12.20

- This paper is divided into two sections,
  Section I COMPREHENDING and Section II COMPOSING.
- The paper contains **three** texts on the general theme of STORY-TELLING.
- Candidates should familiarise themselves with each of the texts before beginning their answers.

- Both sections of this paper (COMPREHENDING and COMPOSING) must be attempted.
- Each section carries 100 marks.

SECTION I – COMPREHENDING

- Two Questions, A and B, follow each text.
- Candidates must answer a Question A on one text and a Question B on a different text. Candidates must answer only one Question A and only one Question B.
- **N.B.** Candidates may NOT answer a Question A and a Question B on the same text.

SECTION II – COMPOSING

- Candidates must write on **one** of the compositions 1 – 7.

TEXT 1

This edited text is based on an article, entitled, *Tune in Next Week – The Curious Staying Power of the Cliff-hanger*. It was written by Emily Nussbaum for *The New Yorker* magazine.

Narrowly defined, a cliff-hanger is a climax cracked in half: the bomb ticks, the screen goes black. A lady wriggles on train tracks – will anyone save her? Italics on a black screen: "To be continued…" More broadly, it's any strong dose of "What happens next?"– the question that hovers in the black space between episodes. In the digital age, that gap is an accordion: it might be a week or eight months; it might arrive at the end of an episode or as a season finale. Cliff-hangers are the point when the audience decides to keep buying. They are sensational in every sense of the word. Historically there's something suspect about a story told in this manner, the way it tugs the customer to the next ledge. Nobody likes needy.

But there is also something to celebrate about the cliff-hanger. It makes visible the storyteller's connection to his audience – like a bridge made out of lightning. Primal and unashamedly manipulative, cliff-hangers are the signature gambit of serial storytelling. They reveal that a story is artificial, then dare you to keep believing. If you trust the creator, you take that dare, and keep going.

Television is just a Johnny-come-lately when it comes to episodic storytelling. The great nineteenth-century novels were famous for their cliff-hangers. Many people associate the form with Charles Dickens, who wrote serial novels so complex, yet so rewarding, that one might even say they resemble the TV show, *The Wire*. Printed episodically in magazines, Dickens' cliff-hangers triggered desperation in his readers and in 1841 fans rioted on the dock of New York Harbour, as they waited for a British ship carrying the next instalment, screaming, "Is little Nell dead?" (Spoiler: she was.)

In Victorian novelist, Thomas Hardy's day, novels were very much like TV. Fiction was the medium decried for leaving "the mind collapsed and imbecile", the half-commercial enterprise that inspired alarmist essays about addiction. Once novels began to be published in blocks, they became art, perhaps in part because the

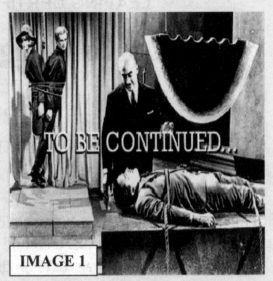

IMAGE 1

author and the reader were held at a more dignified distance. But by then the cliff-hanger – that viral sneak – had jumped into fresh formats. Radio programmes conventionally featured thrill-packed endings. And then there were the movies. The true pioneer of the genre was *The Adventures of Kathlyn*, which arrived in 1913. Each instalment concluded with a titillating disaster, as Kathlyn evaded lions, tigers, leopards, wolves, baboons and elephants (the producer owned a zoo), fled a volcano and subdued her enemies.

In 1980 the first great TV cliff-hanger emerged. Initially, *Dallas*, was a slow-moving soap opera about a family of Texan oil and cattle tycoons. In an episode called "A House Divided" J.R.Ewing, (actor Larry Hagman) was plugged in the gut. The nation had a new catchphrase: "Who shot J.R.?" By the time the resolution aired eight months had elapsed and *Dallas* was a global phenomenon. It became the highest-rated episode in TV history, watched by an estimated three hundred and fifty million people worldwide. The show's success spawned endless imitators: a plane crashing into Wisteria Lane in *Desperate Housewives*, Ross saying "I take thee, Rachel," in *Friends*, the illumination of the Hatch on *Lost*, and so on. In the late nineties, television took a great leap forward. This story could be told in many ways: by focusing on the quality dramas, starting with *The Sopranos*; by emphasising genre myths like

IMAGE 2

Buffy the Vampire Slayer; or by highlighting experimental sitcoms such as *The Office*. The result was one innovation after another: juggled chronologies, the rise of antiheroes and a new breed of challenging, tangled, ambitious serial narrative. In this changing landscape, it's worth acknowledging how cliff-hangers link disparate genres: they echoed through the finales of the smart TV thriller *Homeland*, the exquisite dark comedy *Enlightened* and the delirious melodrama *Revenge*. These shows may have different aims, but each of them uses the gap between episodes in a deliberate manner: they make manipulation a virtue.

Besides, there's another aspect of cliff-hanger history: joy. When done poorly, the cliff-hanger is all about shoddy craftsmanship, the creepy manipulation by a storyteller who has run out of tricks. When done well, however, it can be about much more: surprise, shock, outrage and pleasure – the sort of thing that might send you dancing off the sofa. The cliff-hanger is part of some of the silliest shows on TV; it's also key to understanding many of the greatest ones.

This text has been adapted, for the purpose of assessment, without the author's prior consent.

N.B. Candidates may NOT answer Question A and Question B on the same text.

Questions A and B carry 50 marks each.

QUESTION A

(i) What evidence does the writer offer to suggest that readers or viewers can find cliff-hangers fascinating or alluring? Support your answer with reference to the written text. (15)

(ii) Discuss how effectively each of the visual images (IMAGE 1 and IMAGE 2) helps to develop your understanding of the cliff-hanger as a storytelling device. In your answer refer to both of the visual images that illustrate the text. (15)

(iii) *The New Yorker* has been described as a magazine that informs, entertains and comments. Based on your reading of the written extract above, would you agree with this description? Support your answer with reference to both the content and style of the written text. (20)

QUESTION B

You have been asked to give a talk to your class entitled: *Television and radio in the lives of young people today*. Write the text of **the talk** you would deliver in which you consider the role of television and radio in the lives of young people today. (50)

TEXT 2

This edited text is based on an interview with Irish writer, William Trevor, on *The Art of Fiction*, conducted for the *Paris Review* by Mira Stout.

What is your definition of a short story?

I think it is the art of the glimpse. If the novel is like an intricate Renaissance painting, the short story is the impressionist painting. It *should* be an explosion of truth. Its strength lies in what it leaves out just as much as what it puts in, if not more. It is concerned with the total exclusion of meaninglessness. The novel imitates life, where the short story is bony, and cannot wander. It is essential art.

You have never created a hero. Why is that?

Because I find them dull. Heroes don't belong in short stories. As Frank O'Connor said, "Short stories are about little people", and I agree. I find the un-heroic side of people much richer and more entertaining than black-and-white success.

Time plays a part in your stories – how important is the past?

A huge amount of what I write about is internal, a drifting back into childhood, based on a small event or a moment. By isolating an encounter and then isolating an incident in the past you try to build up an actual life. I think of a short story very much as a portrait. Time is like air; it is there always, changing people, and forming character. Memory also forms character – the way you remember things makes you who you are. People struggle to share a very private side of themselves with other people. It is that great difficulty that I often write about.

I've always wondered how you came to understand a character.

It does seem to me that the only way you can get there is through observation. And what you observe is not quite like just meeting someone on a train, having a conversation and then going away. I mean, really, it's a kind of adding up of people you notice. I think there's something *in* writers of fiction that makes them notice things and store them away all the time. Writers of fiction are collectors of useless information. A face comes back after years and years, as though you've taken a photograph. It is as though you have, for the moment, thought: I know that person very well. You could argue that you have

some extraordinary insight, but actually it's just a very hard-working imagination. It's almost like a stress in you that goes on nibbling and nibbling, gnawing away at you, in a *very* inquisitive way, wanting to know. And of course while all that's happening you're stroking in the colours, putting a line here and a line there, creating something that moves further and further away from the original. The truth emerges, the person who is created is a different person altogether – a person in his or her own right.

William Trevor

You've said that when you start a story, it often begins with a physical event, something you see or overhear which ignites something in you.

Often it does occur like that, but the truth is that stories begin in all kinds of ways. With a remembered schoolteacher, or someone who might later have had something to do with your life, or some unimportant occurrence. You begin to write and in the process of writing it is often the case that whatever it was that started you off gets lost. On other occasions stories simply come out of nowhere. You never discover the source. I remember being on a train and I was perhaps walking down to the bar when I noticed a woman and a boy travelling together. He was in his school uniform and she was clearly in charge of him. I can remember now the fatigue on her face. Afterwards – probably years afterwards – I wrote a story called "Going Home".

Photo of William Trevor by Eamonn McCabe, The Guardian, Saturday 5 September 2009

Do you know how a story is going to end before you write it?

I can see approximately – but only very approximately – how it will be. With a novel I can't even do that. A novel is like a cathedral and you really can't carry in your imagination the form a cathedral is going to take. I like the inkling, the shadow, of a new short story. I like the whole business of establishing its point, for although a story need not have a plot it must have a point.

Do you think that literature has been much diminished by the glare of TV, cinema, video, and by entertainment hunger?

I think there is a danger of that. There's now the pressure of fashion in literature, and I imagine that is something that's demanded by your entertainment-hungry public. Fashion belongs on a coat-hanger. In literature – in any art – it's destructive. Prizes and bestseller lists and fashion tend to *tell* people what to read, and it's discovering what to read for yourself that lends reading half its pleasure. Glamour and glossiness are not what literature is about. Nowadays, books tend to be shovelled into a chat-show wheelbarrow, more talked about than read.

2013 P1

Interview with William Trevor by The Paris Review. Copyright © 1989, The Paris Review, used by permission of The Wylie Agency (UK) Limited.

N.B. Candidates may NOT answer Question A and Question B on the same text.

Questions A and B carry 50 marks each.

QUESTION A

(i) Outline three aspects of William Trevor's approach to story writing, revealed in the above interview. Support your answer with reference to the text. (15)

(ii) William Trevor expresses strong views in his answer to the interviewer's final question. To what extent do you agree with what he has to say? Explain your answer. (15)

(iii) Do you agree that William Trevor's responses to the questions in the interview are rich in language and imagery? Support your answer with reference to the written text. (20)

QUESTION B

Your class has decided to produce a book about "un-heroic" or ordinary people as a fund-raiser for a local charity. Write the **text for the introduction** of this book, in which you explain the purpose of the book and why your class thinks it is important to celebrate ordinary people. (50)

187

TEXT 3

This edited text is based on an article from *The Irish Times* by Belinda McKeon entitled: "New York Stories on a Perfect Platform". It celebrates the hundredth anniversary of the opening of New York's Grand Central Station.

For many New Yorkers, it was the photographs of an evacuated Grand Central Station that drove home the realisation that Hurricane Sandy was on its way. Without people on its marble concourse, the city's huge rail terminal was a place that looked, somehow, lost. It was never meant to be empty. It was designed not just to be full of people but to be given form by people. It was not one of those architectural marvels whose creator secretly wished that visitors would stay away and leave it to its perfection of proportion and line. The vision of Grand Central's chief architect, Whitney Warren, was for a terminal that would be all about the crowd. Turn-of-the-century New York was a human maelstrom, teeming and diverse. Warren sought to offer a more ordered idea of urban existence. What had been an unpredictable stampede elsewhere in the city became, in Warren's carefully engineered spaces, a graceful dance. The passengers wove their way around the concourse, they people-watched from the galleries and they gazed up to the ceiling, arching high overhead, painted with all the stars and signs of the zodiac. It was a seemingly spontaneous choreography.

Unsurprisingly, this daily dance of spectacle and observation has proven irresistible for photographers and film-makers over the years. Perhaps the most iconic images of Grand Central are the black-and-white shots by John Collier. They show the concourse pinioned by great shafts of sunlight. Who wouldn't want to turn a camera on the place? Whether you push in from 42nd Street or trudge up from the grime and ruckus of the subway, the sight of Grand Central's concourse does something to the soul.

And the sounds: the call to the trains, the spry voice of the announcer seeming as though it's addressed to you alone: "Your 4.45 to Poughkeepsie is now on track 102". The inimitable echo: 1,000 footsteps on marble every minute of every day. After all, there are the stories of a city, and there are the stories that a city tells itself about itself, and in many ways Grand Central has been one of those stories. Fiction set there is often the fiction of characters who are unable to see certain realities; who are dazzled by the glow of the things in which they fervently want to believe.

So John Cheever's teenage narrator in *Reunion* (1962) arranges to meet his estranged father here; his young hopes stacked as high as the vaulted ceiling, can only go one way. In another Cheever story, *O City of Broken Dreams* (1948) the Malloy family come to New York in search of fame; as she steps off the train, Alice wonders if the "frosty glitter" of the platform is the dust of trodden diamonds.

Image 1
John Collier's iconic photograph of the concourse of Grand Central Station

In the early Richard Yates' story *A Glutton for Punishment*, a businessman readying for a date uses a "gleaming subterranean dressing room" at Grand Central; washed, shaved and with his suit pressed, he emerges a more polished version of his usual self, but also a little poorer, for in the heady gladness of it all he has tipped the attendant more than he can afford. If there is a poet of Grand Central it must be Yates, whose novels and stories are born out of the very tension between that place's everyday treadmill and its gilded promises.

And in homage to Cheever, Richard Ford's story *Reunions* (2000) is another study in self-

188

delusion at Grand Central, an account of a wrong-headed attempt at reconciliation, during which the narrator allows himself to be unwisely reassured by the "eddying currents" of the crowd. "I had been wrong", he chides himself at the story's end, "about the linkage of moments". Because in Grand Central, we may all of us seem linked for a moment, but who knows really what is going on in any one of those glimpsed lives?

The last time I passed through the terminal was on a Friday in December, going to the Bronx for the funeral of my husband's uncle. As we headed for our track, the arriving trainloads from Connecticut were spilling out on to the concourse, weaving themselves into its choreography, doing their steps of that every-morning dance. It was 9.15 a.m. Hours later, as news too horrific to countenance came out of a Connecticut school, on the train back to Grand Central that evening, a young woman opposite me read something on her phone, and her face twisted with sorrow. Our eyes met and I shook my head – I didn't need a translation – and she shook hers.

In the Biltmore room, an old chalkboard schedule lists the cross-country trains that once arrived at 42nd Street: the Knickerbocker, the Missourian, the 20th Century Limited. Once known as the Kissing Room because of the

many welcomes bestowed here, not least upon returning troops, this space houses little activity now, apart from some shoe-shining and newspaper buying. Still, there's a nook here that is perhaps my favourite of all in Grand Central: the little windowed booth where the dozens of pairs of shoes resoled by Eddie's Shoe Repair sit, in their brown paper bags, all fixed up and ready to go. Ready to echo across that marble again.

This text has been adapted, for the purpose of assessment, without the author's prior consent.

Image 2
The concourse of Grand Central Station

N.B. Candidates may NOT answer Question A and Question B on the same text.

Questions A and B carry 50 marks each.

QUESTION A

(i)   What evidence does the writer offer to suggest that Grand Central Station has gripped people's imaginations since its opening in 1913? Support your answer with reference to the written text.
(15)

(ii) Both the written and visual elements of Text 3 contain many striking images that capture the grandeur and atmosphere of Grand Central Station. Identify three images that you find particularly striking and explain why you find them to be so. The images may be taken solely from the written text or from a combination of the written and visual texts. (15)

(iii) In the above extract, Belinda McKeon effectively communicates both knowledge of, and affection for, Grand Central Station. Discuss this statement with reference to both the content and style of the written text. (20)

QUESTION B

Write **an opinion piece,** for inclusion in a series of newspaper articles entitled: *Must-see Attractions for Tourists*, in which you identify one place or public building in Ireland that, in your opinion, tourists should visit and explain your choice. (50)

SECTION II   COMPOSING   (100 marks)

Write a composition on **any one** of the following.

Each composition carries 100 marks.

The composition assignments (in **bold print** below) are intended to reflect language study in the areas of information, argument, persuasion, narration, and the aesthetic use of language.

1.   In Text 2, William Trevor expresses his views on heroes.

   Write a speech in which you argue for or against the motion, *We live in an un-heroic age.*

2.   "...the storyteller's connection to his audience."   (TEXT 1)

   Write a personal essay in which you explore the storytelling evident in music and song and its impact on you as a listener.

3.   "...they make manipulation a virtue."   (TEXT 1)

   Write a short story in which a central character is either manipulated or is manipulative.

4.   In TEXT 2, William Trevor mentions "the art of the glimpse".

   Write a descriptive essay based on a variety of glimpsed moments.

5.   In TEXT 3, Belinda McKeon refers to the tension between the everyday treadmill and the gilded promises of Grand Central Station.

   Write a personal essay about the tension you find between the everyday treadmill and the gilded promises of life.

6.   "...a more ordered idea of urban existence."   (TEXT 3)

   Write a feature article for a popular magazine in which you discuss the competing attractions of both urban and rural lifestyles.

7.   In TEXT 3, the writer refers to two short stories on the theme of reunion.

   Write a short story about a reunion.

Coimisiún na Scrúduithe Stáit
State Examinations Commission

LEAVING CERTIFICATE EXAMINATION, 2013

English - Higher Level - Paper 2

Total Marks: 200

Thursday, 6 June – Afternoon, 2.00 – 5.20

2013 P2

Candidates must attempt the following :-
- **ONE** question from SECTION I – The Single Text
- **ONE** question from SECTION II – The Comparative Study
- **ONE** question on the Unseen Poem from SECTION III – Poetry
- **ONE** question on Prescribed Poetry from SECTION III – Poetry

N.B. Candidates must answer on Shakespearean Drama.
They may do so in SECTION I, the Single Text (*Macbeth*) or in SECTION II, The Comparative Study (*Macbeth, The Winter's Tale*).

INDEX OF SINGLE TEXTS

Wuthering Heights   – *Page 2*
The Great Gatsby   – *Page 2*
The Grass Is Singing   – *Page 3*
Macbeth   – *Page 3*
Antigone   – *Page 3*

SECTION I

THE SINGLE TEXT (60 marks)

Candidates must answer **one** question from this section (**A – E**).

A **WUTHERING HEIGHTS** – Emily Brontë

(i) In your opinion, to what extent are the values represented by the world of Thrushcross Grange defeated, in Brontë's novel *Wuthering Heights*?

Support your answer with suitable reference to the text.

OR

(ii) "Emily Brontë makes effective use of both Nelly Dean and Mr Lockwood in a variety of ways."

Discuss this statement, supporting your answer with suitable reference to the novel, *Wuthering Heights*.

B **THE GREAT GATSBY** – F. Scott Fitzgerald

(i) "Readers of *The Great Gatsby* are greatly influenced by the narrator, Nick Carraway."

Discuss this statement, supporting your answer with suitable reference to the text.

OR

(ii) "Readers often find aspects of *The Great Gatsby* attractive but ultimately the world of the novel is not admirable."

Discuss this view, supporting your answer with suitable reference to the text.

C   THE GRASS IS SINGING – Doris Lessing

(i)   "Lessing offers a disturbing vision of characters trapped in an unforgiving society."

To what extent do you agree with this view? Support your answer with suitable reference to the novel, *The Grass Is Singing*.

OR

(ii) "Readers can feel both sympathy for and irritation with Mary Turner's character."

Discuss this statement, supporting your answer with suitable reference to the novel, *The Grass Is Singing*.

D   MACBETH – William Shakespeare

(i)   "The variety of significant insights that we gain into Macbeth's mind proves critical in shaping our understanding of his complex character."

Discuss this view, supporting your answer with suitable reference to the play, *Macbeth*.

OR

(ii) "Shakespeare makes effective use of disturbing imagery in the play, *Macbeth*."

Discuss this statement, supporting your answer with suitable reference to the text.

E   ANTIGONE – Sophocles

(i)   "The play *Antigone* offers valuable insights into issues of power and authority."

Discuss this view, supporting your answer with suitable reference to the text.

OR

(ii) "The chorus serves a variety of functions in the play, *Antigone*."

Discuss this statement, supporting your answer with suitable reference to the text.

SECTION II

THE COMPARATIVE STUDY (70 marks)

Candidates must answer **one** question from either **A** – The Cultural Context
or **B** – Theme or Issue

In your answer you may not use the text you have answered on in **SECTION I** – The Single
Text.

N.B. The questions use the word **text** to refer to all the different kinds of texts available for
study on this course, i.e. novel, play, short story, autobiography, biography, travel writing, and
film. The questions use the word **reader** to include viewers of films and theatre audiences.

A   THE CULTURAL CONTEXT

1.   "In any cultural context, deeply embedded values and attitudes can be difficult to
      change."

      Compare the extent to which the above statement is valid in relation to your
      understanding of the cultural context of **at least two texts** on your comparative
      course.   (70)

OR

2.   "The issue of social class is important in shaping our understanding of the cultural
      context of a text."

      (a)   Discuss the importance of social class in shaping your understanding of the
            cultural context of **one** text that you have studied as part of your comparative
            course.   (30)

      (b)   Compare the importance of social class in shaping your understanding of the
            cultural context of **two other texts** that you have studied as part of your
            comparative course.   (40)

B   THEME OR ISSUE

1.   "Studying a theme or issue enables a reader to form both personal and universal reflections on that theme or issue."

Compare both the personal and universal reflections that you formed on a common theme or issue in **two or more texts** from your comparative course.   (70)

OR

2.   "In many texts, a theme or issue may not be resolved to the complete satisfaction of the reader."

(a)   Discuss the extent to which a theme or issue is resolved to your satisfaction in **one** text on your comparative course.   (30)

(b)   Compare the extent to which the same theme or issue (as discussed in (a) above) is resolved to your satisfaction, in **two other texts** on your comparative course.   (40)

SECTION III
POETRY (70 marks)

Candidates must answer **A** – Unseen Poem **and B** – Prescribed Poetry.

A   UNSEEN POEM (20 marks)

Answer **either** Question **1** or Question **2**.

The Fist

The fist clenched round my heart
loosens a little, and I gasp
brightness; but it tightens
again. When have I ever not loved
the pain of love? But this has moved

past love to mania. This has the strong
clench of the madman, this is
gripping the ledge of unreason, before
plunging howling into the abyss.

Hold hard then, heart. This way at least you live.

Derek Walcott

'The Fist' by Derek Walcott from *Collected Poems*, reprinted with permission of Faber & Faber Ltd.

1. (a) Walcott expresses powerful emotions in this poem. Choose one emotion present in the poem and briefly explain how it is conveyed. Make reference to the text in support of your answer.   (10)

    (b) Write a brief personal response to the final line of the poem.

        Hold hard then, heart. This way at least you live.

        Support your answer with reference to the poem.   (10)

OR

2. Discuss the poet's use of language in "The Fist". Your answer should make close reference to the text.   (20)

196

B   PRESCRIBED POETRY (50 marks)

Candidates must answer **one** of the following questions (**1 – 4**).

1.   Elizabeth Bishop

"Bishop's carefully judged use of language aids the reader to uncover the intensity of feeling in her poetry."

To what extent do you agree or disagree with the above statement? Support your answer with reference to the poetry of Elizabeth Bishop on your course.

2.   Gerard Manley Hopkins

"Hopkins' innovative style displays his struggle with what he believes to be fundamental truths."

In your opinion, is this a fair assessment of his poetry? Support your answer with suitable reference to the poetry of Gerard Manley Hopkins on your course.

3.   Derek Mahon

"Mahon uses language and imagery to transform personal observations into universal reflections."

Write your response to this statement with reference to the poems by Derek Mahon on your course.

4.   Sylvia Plath

"Plath's provocative imagery serves to highlight the intense emotions expressed in her poetry."

To what extent do you agree or disagree with this assessment of her poetry? Support your answer with suitable reference to the poetry of Sylvia Plath on your course.

English – Higher Level – Paper I (A)

COMPREHENDING AND COMPOSING

Time Allowed: 2 Hours 50 Minutes

Total Marks: 200

- The paper is divided into two sections,
  Section I COMPREHENDING and Section II COMPOSING.
- This paper contains **three** texts on the general theme of PLACES and TRAVEL.
- Candidates should familiarise themselves with each text before beginning their answers.

- Both sections of the paper (COMPREHENDING and COMPOSING) must be attempted.
- Each section carries 100 marks.

SECTION I COMPREHENDING
- Two questions, A and B, follow each text.
- Candidates must answer a Question A on one text and a Question B on a different text.
  Candidates must answer only one Question A and only one Question B.
- **N.B.** Candidates may NOT answer a Question A and a Question B on the same text.

SECTION II COMPOSING (100 marks)
- Candidates must answer on **one** of the compositions 1–7.

SECTION I

COMPREHENDING (100 MARKS)

TEXT 1

THE WILD AND WONDERFUL WEST

The following extract is taken from a Bord Failte brochure.

1. There is a special quality about the three beautiful counties of Galway, Roscommon and Mayo which is unique in Europe. The welcome is heartwarming; the quality of life, people and landscape are all there for our visitors to share. Each county has its own special attractions and is rich in all that is best in Irish folklore, music and song – you will not be disappointed.

2. The West of Ireland has a wide variety of activities for the visitor. Whether you fish or windsurf, golf or horse-ride, cycle or walk, the environment is traffic-free and breathtakingly beautiful. Delight in the great variety of wild flora and fauna which occupy the unspoilt landscape of Ireland West.

3. The thriving county of Galway has a long association with literary personage. Nobel Prize Winner, W.B. Yeats purchased a Norman Tower called 'Thoor Ballylee' in 1916 which has been restored as a tribute to this great poet. Nearby, Lady Gregory, founder of the Abbey Theatre, often entertained in her Coole Park residence some of Ireland's most famous writers – Shaw, O'Casey and Synge, to name just a few. In fact, an autographed tree remains to tell the tale.

4. The home of Nora Barnacle, wife and inspiration to James Joyce, is open to the public. Located near St. Nicholas Collegiate Church in Galway town, it is said to be Ireland's smallest museum!

5. Galway city is one of the fastest growing cities in Europe. The 'City of Tribes' and the resort of Salthill are set on Galway Bay. This university city has a vibrant atmosphere with plenty to see and do. Visit the impressive Galway Irish Crystal Heritage Centre in Galway, Connemara National Park in Letterfrack and Kylemore Abbey in Kylemore as the county has many places of interest.

6. The county of Mayo provides some of the most important historical and ecclesiastical offerings – Croagh Patrick, Ballintubber Abbey, numerous mediaeval friaries, and of course, the Marian Shrine of Knock. It also sustains numerous wonderful fishing retreats – catch the 'salmon of knowledge' in the River Moy, Lough Conn or Cullin where fighting brown trout will also tow the line. The May fly season is world famous and a week 'on the dap' is never easily forgotten.

7. The county also has a number of visitor centres including Foxford Woollen Mills, the Michael Davitt Museum, Ceide Fields Visitor Centre in North Mayo, Westport House and Knock Folk Museum. Experience island-hopping in Achill and Clare; enjoy lively sessions in Westport and Ballina; participate in any one of the numerous activities which the western terrain presents as it satisfies walker, cyclist, motorist, ornithologist and botanist. The region also has some magnificent golfing challenges including two superb links.

8. Roscommon, towards the very heart of Ireland, gave ancient Ireland its last High King and modern Ireland its first president. West of Castlerea, you will come upon the ancestral home of the O'Conors at Clonalis House. The 45-room mansion was built in 1878. The clan of the O'Conors gave Ireland 11 high kings and Connaught 24 kings. Worth noting on your visit is the exhibited O'Carolan harp. Turlough O'Carolan was the last of the bards and a great harpist. His remains are in the old graveyard of Kilronan, overlooking Lough Meelagh near the village of Keadue. While in this county, visit the Dr. Douglas Hyde Interpretative Centre near Frenchpark, which is dedicated to Ireland's first president and co-founder of the Gaelic League. Other highlights are Strokestown Park House, Gardens and Famine Museum in Strokestown and King House in Boyle.

NB Candidates may NOT answer Question A and Question B on the same text.

Questions A and B carry 50 marks each.

Question A

(i) How does this piece of writing try to persuade tourists to come to the West of Ireland? (30)

(ii) Do the images contribute to the persuasiveness of the message? (10)

(iii) In your view, are the images and text successful in promoting the country? (10)

Question B

Write a short piece (150–200) on your locality (real or imagined) for a website prepared by a local group seeking to attract visitors to the region. (50)

A VIEW OF CHINA

Orville Schell is an American writer. This article appeared in *Granta,* a journal of new writing. The article looks at life in China in the 1980s. In this extract Schell reports on architecture and clothes.

1. Should an archaeologist in the distant future dig up a Chinese high-rise complex from this period, he might be surprised by the unrelieved squareness of the buildings, the poverty of decoration inside and the dull clothing of their denizens. He might well wonder to what cataclysmic event these artistically impoverished people were reacting; what evolutionary imperative had caused such a complete suppression of colour and design during the inter-regnum of Chinese history. For these Chinese buildings are not simply examples of practical minds trying to economise in order to accommodate a people desperate for space; they are a form of extreme anti-design which harkens back to that revolutionary period when any expression of style, architectural or otherwise, was considered dangerously bourgeois. When visiting friends in their cheerless dormitory-style homes, I was often struck by the irony that even the animals in Chinese zoos had more attention paid to the design of their living environment than the average Chinese.

2. Clothing is perhaps the second physical feature noticed by a visitor to a foreign country. During the 'ten lost years' (1966–76), one could look down any long street in China and see nothing but the officially approved colours: blue, khaki and grey for the masses, and dark blue or black for ranking Party officials. Almost everyone wears 'Mao suits', an egalitarian style of dress first introduced by Sun Yatsen after the fall of the last dynasty of 1911. The garb provided is not only a practical unisex style of clothing, but also a shroud to hide all individual distinguishing features. Any change from the standard uniform – a ribbon in the hair, a piece of jewellery, a coloured handkerchief – was considered a dangerous deviation: a clear expression of the kind of individualism the Party feared and wished most to suppress.

3. During the mid-seventies, I often studied carefully the dress of Chinese women for signs of warmth and self-expression. I discovered only one miniscule window in which women felt free to adorn themselves. This was the small triangular space directly under their chins between the lapels of their Mao suits. Here one would sometimes see a pretty button or a brightly coloured piece of blouse peeking out. Otherwise, only small children and minorities like the Tibetans and Mongolians were allowed to dress with colour or flamboyance. It was not surprising that stage and film directors, looking for some romance and brightness for their productions, included roles for minorities to exploit the theatrical value of their costumes. In the explosion of interest in fashion which has marked China these past few years, introducing cosmetic surgery, modelling schools, fashion magazines and fashion shows all across the country, one sees China struggling back towards a notion of sartorial beauty. But more often than not, this notion is imitative of the West. Western wedding gowns are now the style for marriages. Dresses and skirts, trouser-suits, high heels, stockings and even hot pants have taken over women's fashion. Tight pants and T-shirts with inscriptions in English are *de rigeur* for young men. In fact, so popular have blue jeans (called 'cowboy pants') become in China that they featured in a recent Beijing rock and roll song:

Wa wa cowboy pants!
Wa wa cowboy pants!

When my guy wears cowboy pants
He looks so slick and agile.

When my girl wears cowboy pants
She is so sleek and lively.

O why, oh why, oh why
Do cowboy pants cast such a spell over me?

NB Candidates may NOT answer Question A and Question B on the same text.

Questions A and B carry 50 marks each.

Question A

(i)   Select **four** interesting pieces of information about China, in the 1980s, that you found in the text. (20)

(ii)   Select **two** examples where the article moves beyond information. Explain your choices. (30)

Question B

A music magazine invites readers to submit nominations for the song-lyrics that capture the spirit of your generation. Write an email (150–200 words) nominating your choice, giving reasons for your selection. (50)

THE SUBWAY

This is an extract from a long article Paul Theroux wrote on the New York subway.

The subway is New York City's best hope. The streets are impossible, the highways are a failure, there is nowhere to park. The private automobile has no future in this city whatsoever. This is plainest of all to the people who own and use cars in the city; they know, better than anyone, that the car is the last desperate old-fangled flight of a badly-planned transport system. What is amazing is that back in 1904 a group of businessmen solved New York's transport problems for centuries to come. What vision! What enterprise! What an engineering marvel they created in this underground railway! And how amazed they would be to see what it has become, how foul-seeming to the public mind.

The subway is a gift to any connoisseur of superlatives. It has the longest rides of any subway in the world, the biggest stations, the fastest trains, the most track, the most passengers, the most police officers. It also has the filthiest trains, the most bizarre graffiti, the noisiest wheels, the craziest passengers, the wildest crimes. Some New Yorkers have never set foot in the subway; other New Yorkers actually live there, moving from station to station, whining for money, eating yesterday's bagels and sleeping on benches. These 'skells' are not merely down-and-out. Many are insane, chucked out of New York hospitals in the early 1970s when it was decided that long-term care was doing them little good. 'They were resettled in rooms or hotels,' Ruth Cohen, a psychiatric social-worker at Bellevue, told me. 'But many of them can't follow through. They get lost, they wander the streets. They're not violent, suicidal or dangerous enough for Bellevue – this is an acute-care hospital. But these people who wander the subway, once they're on their own they begin to de-compensate.'

Ahm goon cut you up: that woman who threatened to slash me was de-compensating. Here are a few more de-compensating – one is weeping on a wooden bench at Canal Street, another has wild hair and is spitting into a Coke can. One man who is de-compensating in a useful way has a bundle of brooms and is setting forth to sweep the whole of the change area at Grand Central; another is scrubbing the stairs at 14th Street with scraps of paper. They drink, they scream, they gibber like monkeys.

When people say the subway frightens them, they are not being silly or irrational. It is no good saying how cheap or how fast it is. The subway *is* frightening. It is also very easy to get lost on the subway, and the person who is lost in New York City has a serious problem. New Yorkers make it their business to avoid getting lost.

It is the stranger who gets lost. It is the stranger who follows people hurrying into the stair-well: subway entrances are just dark holes in the sidewalk – the stations are below ground. There is nearly always a bus-stop near the subway entrance. People waiting at a bus-stop have a special pitying gaze for people entering the subway. It is sometimes not pity, but fear, bewilderment, curiosity, or fatalism; often they look like miners' wives watching their menfolk going down the pit.

The stranger's sense of disorientation down below is immediate. The station is all tile and iron and dampness; it has bars and turnstiles and steel grates. It has the look of an old prison or a monkey cage. The stranger cannot rely on printed instructions or warnings, and there are few cars out of the six thousand on the system in which the maps have not been torn out. Assuming the stranger has boarded the train, he or she can feel only panic when, searching for a clue to his route, he sees in the mapframe the message *Guzmán-Ladrón, Maricón y Asesino*.

Panic: and so he gets off the train, and then his troubles really begin.

Hey may be in the South Bronx or the upper reaches of Broadway on the Number 1 line, or on any one of a dozen lines that traverse Brooklyn. He gets off the train, which is covered in graffiti, and steps on to a station platform, which is covered in graffiti. It is possible (this is true of many stations) that none of the signs will be legible. Not only will the stranger not know where he is, but the stairways will be splotched and stinking – no *Uptown*, no *Downtown*, no *Exit*. It is also possible that not a single soul will be around, and the most dangerous stations – ask any police officer – are the emptiest.

This the story that most people tell of subway fear. In every detail it is like a nightmare, complete with rats and mice and a tunnel and a low ceiling. It is manifest suffocation, straight out of Poe. Those who tell this story seldom have a crime to repport. They have experienced fear. It is completely understandable – what is worse than being trapped underground? – but it has been a private horror. In most cases, the person will have come to no harm. He will, however, remember his fear on that empty station for the rest of his life.

NB Candidates may NOT answer Question A and Question B on the same text.

Questions A and B carry 50 marks each.

Question A

(i)   What in your view was Paul Theroux's purpose on writing in this article? (20)

(ii)   Identify, in your opinion, the most interesting features of Paul Theroux's style. Explain your choices. (30)

Question B

You are a civil servant. Draw up a seven-point plan, in memo form, for the Minister for Transport, for tackling the problem of Traffic Congestion in our cities. (50)

SECTION II

COMPOSING (100 MARKS)

Write a composition on any **one** of the assignments that appear in **bold print** below.

Each composition carries 100 marks.

The composition assignments are intended to reflect language study in the areas of information, argument, persuasion, narration, and the aesthetic use of language.

1. In TEXT 1, it is argued that the West of Ireland has something to offer every visitor.

   Write an article for the travel supplement of a Sunday newspaper, persuading potential visitors to come to Ireland.

2. In Text 2 it is suggested that the welcome awaiting visitors in the west of Ireland is heart-warming.

   Write a speech for a class discussion in which you try to persuade your classmates that Ireland is or is not a welcoming place.

3. In Text 2, the author refers to the lack of design in the high-rise complexes where many ordinary Chinese citizens live.

   Write an article for your school magazine in which you argue the case for good design in the planning of towns and cities, and the benefits you believe follow good urban design.

4. In TEXT 2, Orville Schell writes about the explosion of interest in fashion in China.

   Write a speech for a school debate on the fashion industry, arguing for or against the idea that the fashion industry is a source of liberation.

5. In TEXT 3, Paul Theroux suggests that the most dangerous subway stations are the emptiest.

   Write a short story set in an empty subway station.

6. In Text 3, Paul Theroux writes about the stranger's sense of disorientation on the New York subway.

   You are a stranger in a foreign place. Write an online blog for a travel site that captures your sense of disorientation.

7. All three texts are about travel and tourism.

   Write a personal essay in which you reflect on the relevance of travel and tourism in our global and interconnected world, in the midst of a growing climate crisis.

LEAVING CERTIFICATE EXAMINATION

English – Higher Level – Paper 2

(SAMPLE PAPER 2 (A))

Time Allowed: 3 Hours 20 Minutes

Total Marks: 200

Candidates must attempt the following:
- **ONE** question from SECTION I – The Single Text
- **ONE** question from SECTION II – The Comparative Study
- **ONE** question on the Unseen Poem from SECTION III – Poetry
- **ONE** question on Prescribed Poetry from SECTION III – Poetry

N.B. Candidates must answer on Shakespearean Drama.

They may do so in SECTION I, The Single Text (*Hamlet*), or in SECTION II, The Comparative Study (*Hamlet*, *Macbeth*).

INDEX OF SINGLE TEXTS

All the Light We Cannot See

The Crucible

Hamlet

Frankenstein

The Picture of Dorian Gray

SECTION I

THE SINGLE TEXT (60 MARKS)

Candidates must answer **one** question from this section (**A–E**).

A **ALL THE LIGHT WE CANNOT SEE** – Anthony Doerr

(i) "For all her intelligence, bravery and resourcefulness, Marie-Laure is like the distressed damsel in a fairy tale, waiting on her prince to rescue her."

To what extent do you agree or disagree with this statement? In your response you should deal with all aspects of the statement, supporting your answer with reference to the text. Develop your answer with reference to Doerr's novel, *All the Light We Cannot See*.

OR

(ii) "At its heart, the world portrayed in *All the Light We Cannot See* is brutal and cruel."

Based on your reading of the novel, to what extent do you agree or disagree with the above statement? Explain your answer, giving reasons for your response. Develop your answer with reference to Anthony Doerr's novel, *All the Light We Cannot See*.

B **THE CRUCIBLE** – Arthur Miller

(i) "The accusations of witchcraft are used by many of the citizens of Salem to settle old scores and animosities."

To what extent do you agree or disagree with this statement? Develop your response with suitable reference to the play, *The Crucible*.

OR

(ii) Why, in your view, does Danforth insist on believing the testimony of Abigail and the other girls? Support your answer with reference to the play.

C   HAMLET – William Shakespeare

(i)   "The imagery and symbols, the supernatural elements and the setting all contribute to the rich complexity of the play."

To what extent do you agree or disagree with this view of the play? Support your answer with suitable reference to Shakespeare's play, *Hamlet*.

OR

(ii)   "Grief and vengeance are important themes in *Hamlet*."

To what extent do you agree or disagree with this statement? Support your answer with reference to Shakespeare's play, *Hamlet*.

D   FRANKENSTEIN – Mary Shelley

(i)   "For all his intelligence, Victor Frankenstein is a morally weak man who brings suffering upon his own head and those he loves."

Based on your reading of Mary Shelley's novel, *Frankenstein*, to what extent do you agree or disagree with this view of Victor Frankenstein? Develop your answer with reference to the novel.

OR

(ii)   "Mary Shelley's *Frankenstein* presents both the nobility and baseness of human beings in their treatment of each other."

To what extent do you agree or disagree with this statement? In your response, you should deal with all aspects of the statement, supporting your answer with reference to the text of the novel.

E   THE PICTURE OF DORIAN GRAY – Oscar Wilde

(i)   "For all his wealth and beauty, Dorian Gray is a manipulative and morally bankrupt individual."

To what extent do you agree or disagree with this view of Dorian Gray? Develop your answer with suitable reference to Oscar Wilde's novel, *The Picture of Dorian Gray*.

OR

(ii)   "Wilde's *The Picture of Dorian Gray* is a celebration of art and the appreciation of beautiful things."

Based on your reading of the novel, to what extent do you agree or disagree with the above statement? Develop your answer with reference to Wilde's *The Picture of Dorian Gray*.

SECTION II

THE COMPARATIVE STUDY (70 MARKS)

Candidates must answer **one** question from **either A** – Literary Genre **or**
B – Theme or Issue.

In your answer you may not use the text you have answered on in **SECTION I** – The Single Text. All texts used in this section must be prescribed for comparative study for this year's examination. Candidates may refer to only one film in the course of their answers.

Please note:
- Questions in this section use the word **text** to refer to all the different kinds of texts available for study on this course.
- When used, the word **reader** includes viewers of films and theatre audiences.
- When used, the term **technique** is understood to include techniques employed by all writers and directors of films.
- When used, the word **author** is understood to include all writers and directors of films.
- When used, the word **character** is understood to refer to both real people and fictional characters in texts.

A   LITERARY GENRE

1.   "Each text creates a unique world for its readers."

Compare the way in which **each of the texts** on your comparative course presents its unique world. Develop your response with reference to your chosen texts. (70)

OR

2.   (a) "Memorable characters and dramatic incidents are the most important features of a good narrative."

Discuss how the author used a memorable character and a dramatic incident to enhance the narrative in **one** text on your comparative course. (30)

(b) Compare the extent to which the authors in the **two other texts** on your comparative course were successful in presenting memorable characters and dramatic incidents. Develop your response with reference to your chosen texts. (40)

B   THEME OR ISSUE

1.   "Our identification (or lack of identification) with a central character can influence our view of the theme or issue of a text."

Compare the extent to which your identification (or lack of identification) with the central character influenced your view of the same theme or issue in **each of the texts** on your comparative study. Develop your response with reference to your chosen texts. (70)

OR

2.   "The experience of the central character is the most important element in establishing the theme or issue of a text."

(a) Discuss the extent to which this statement applies to **one** of the texts you have studied for your comparative course. (30)

(b) Compare the extent to which the experience of the central character helped establish the same theme or issue in the **two other texts** you studied for your comparative course. (40)

SECTION III

POETRY (70 MARKS)

Candidates must answer **A** – Unseen Poem **and B** – Prescribed Poetry.

A   UNSEEN POEM (20 marks)

Answer **either** Question 1 **or** Question 2.

The poem describes the experience of getting lost on a walk in the country.

WALKING IN AUTUMN

We have overshot the wood.
The track has led us beyond trees
to the tarmac edge. Too late now
at dusk to return a different way,
hazarding barbed wire or an unknown bull.
We turn back onto the darkening path.
Pale under-leaves of whitebeam, alder
gleam at our feet like stranded fish
or Hansel's stones.
A wren, unseen, churrs alarm:
Each tree drains to blackness.
Halfway now, we know
By the leaning crab-apple,
Feet crunching into mud
The hard slippery yellow moons.
We hurry without reason
Stumbling over roots and stones.
A night creature lurches, cries out,
Crashes through brambles.
Skin shrinks inside our clothes;
Almost we run
Falling through darkness to the wood's end,
The gate into the sloping field.
Home is light and woodsmoke, voices –
And, our breath caught, not trembling now,
A strange reluctance to enter within doors.

Frances Horovitz

Collected Poems: New Edition (Bloodaxe Books, 2011).
Reproduced with permission of Bloodaxe Books on behalf of the author.

1. (i) Outline as clearly as you can the feelings described in the poem. Make reference to the poem in developing your answer. (10)

    (ii) Select an image or phrase that you think is particularly effective in terms of the feelings or sensations it suggests. Explain your choices. (10)

OR

2. Do you interpret the journey of the poem as an imaginary or symbolic journey, or is it just a description of a walk in the country? Explain your answer. (20)

B   PRESCRIBED POETRY (50 marks)

Candidates must answer **one** of the following questions (**1–4**).

1. **Emily Dickinson**

    "Emily Dickinson's poetry explores extreme states of mind and emotions using language and imagery that fascinate the reader."

    Based on your experience of her poetry, to what extent do you agree or disagree with this statement? Develop your answer with reference to the poetry of Emily Dickinson on your course.

2. **John Donne**

    From your study of the poetry of John Donne, select the poems that, in your opinion, best demonstrate how the poet uses conceit, paradox and startling imagery to explore themes of love and the fear of death.

    Justify your selection and develop your answer with reference to the poetry of John Donne on your course.

3. **Seamus Heaney**

    "While rooted in the local, Heaney's poetry has a universal appeal. This appeal is enhanced by the beauty and simplicity of the language employed in the poems."

    Based on your reading of the poetry of Seamus Heaney, discuss the extent to which you agree or disagree with this statement. Develop your response with reference to the themes, imagery and language of the poems by Heaney on your course.

4. **Sylvia Plath**

    "What emerges in Plath's daring and complex poetry is a portrait of a frail but courageous human being."

    Based on your reading of Plath's poetry, to what extent do you agree or disagree with this statement? Support your answer with reference to the poetry of Sylvia Plath on your course.

LEAVING CERTIFICATE EXAMINATION

English – Higher Level – Paper I

(SAMPLE PAPER 3 (B))

Time Allowed 2 Hours 50 Minutes

Total Marks: 200

- This paper is divided into two sections,
  Section I COMPREHENDING and Section II COMPOSING.
- This paper contains **three** texts on the general theme of RIGHT AND WRONG.
- Candidates should familiarize themselves with each text before beginning their answers.

- Both sections of the paper (COMPREHENDING and COMPOSING) must be attempted.
- Each section carries 100 marks.

SECTION I COMPREHENDING

- Two questions, A and B, follow each text.
- Candidates must answer a Question A on one text and a Question B on a different text. Candidates must answer only one Question A and only one Question B.
- **N.B.** Candidates may NOT answer a Question A and a Question B on the same text.

SECTION II COMPOSING

- Candidates must answer on **one** of the compositions 1–7.

SECTION I

COMPREHENDING (100 MARKS)

TEXT I

RIGHT AND WRONG

Blake Morrison considers the question of right and wrong and the age at which individuals can distinguish one from the other. Morrison reported on the trial of two ten-year-old boys for murder. At the trial, the head teacher of the school where the boys attended suggested that children know right from wrong from the time they first go to school.

Right and wrong, right and wrong. I lie on the bed and think of the four-year-olds who, according to the head teacher, know the difference. I have a four-year-old at home. And if I asked him if it was right to hit a friend, he'd say, no, it's wrong. Why would he say that? Because of the tone of my voice. Because he's picked up enough about parents and teachers to know how to give appropriate answers. Because he goes to nursery school and watches children's television. Because he wants to earn approval. Not because he possesses a mature moral understanding, but because he wants to say the right thing.

He says funny things, this four-year-old of mine, who doesn't know the meaning of the word tomorrow, yet allegedly knows right from wrong. He tells me he wants to marry his friend Charles, and if he can't marry him he wants to marry a Ghostbuster. He asks me if God has a second name, and says he knows how God sees us, it's like Jack and the Beanstalk. He drills a hole in the

sky and looks down. He says he doesn't like going to Granny because one of the trees there talks, and he doesn't like talking trees. He says there are witches in the true world, but not at the bottom of Jonathan's garden. He thinks everything is male or female, including cutlery, crockery, furniture and cars. He says what scares him most in the world is clowns. He watches clouds skimming across the night sky and tells me the moon has a beard, and asks, 'If we say hello to the moon, will he hear us? Will we hear him if he says hello back?'

I have a four-year-old who believes the man in the moon is real – who believes the moon *is* a man. Other four-year-olds have similar beliefs. They think the manikins in shop windows are dead people. They think the sea's there because someone left the tap running. They wonder who the sun belongs to, and whether heaven has a floor, and why people aren't in two all the way up. I know seven-year-olds who believe in the Easter Bunny and the tooth fairy. I know nine-year-olds who believe in Father

Christmas. Long may it live, this belief in magic. More power to *as if*. But don't tell me four-year-olds know the difference between right and wrong.

And eight-year-olds, ten-year-olds? They understand the difference better but can they act on that understanding? Did I? At ten I sole a Ferrari – a Dinky toy belonging to my cousin Richard. It was old and battered, but I thought that, by owning it, some part of Richard – who was bigger, older, more confident – would become part of me: that I could be *him*. I knew I was doing wrong but desire – such a good feeling, which as a child I hadn't learnt to distrust – made it feel right.

'Want doesn't get' my parents used to say, determined not to spoil me. And they were right: want can't get, want can never fulfil its desire. Richard's Ferrari could never have filled my lack. But I thought it would, and so I had taken it. I had moral sense but not moral conviction. How could I have conviction? I was a child.

Rousseau writes of a boy killing a bird *without knowing what he does*. The phrase is reminiscent of Christ's: 'Forgive them, Father, for they know not what they do.' Special pleading from the cross: that people sometimes kill in ignorance, even innocence, and should not be eternally punished for their sin.

The basis of the legal concept, 'incapable of crime', is similar: that before the age of reason, children can't be held responsible. When does the age of reason begin? Every country has its own answer, its own baseline: it's eight in Scotland, ten in England, Wales and Northern Ireland, twelve in Canada, thirteen in Israel, fifteen in Norway, sixteen in Cuba – and in Romania eighteen. The mad arbitrariness. Maybe Rousseau was right or no less wrong than we are, to measure reason in inches rather than years. 'Childhood has its own ways of seeing, thinking and feeling which are proper to it. Nothing is less sensible than to want to substitute ours for theirs, and I would like as little to insist that a ten-year-old be five feet tall as that he possess judgement.'

God knows, adults find it hard enough to act on their knowledge of right and wrong. Can children, whose sense of right and wrong is newer but dimmer, fresher but fuzzier, act with the same clear moral sense? Do they grasp that badly hurting someone is much more wrong than stealing and truanting? Do they have a sense of the awful irreversibility of killing someone? Can death have the same meaning for them as it has for an adult? I submit, your Honour, that the answer to these questions is no, no, no and no.

Extract from *As If* by Blake Morrison, Granta Books.

N.B. Candidates may NOT answer Question A and Question B on the same text.
Question A and B carry 50 marks each.

QUESTION A

(i)   Outline the views of the author on the subject of children's knowledge of right and wrong. (15)

(ii)   What purpose is served by the story of the Red Ferrari? Support your answer with reference to the text. (15)

(iii) Is this an effective piece of writing? Support your answer by reference to the text. (20)

QUESTION B

'By the age of ten, children know the difference between right and wrong.'

Prepare a short speech for a class debate for or against this motion. (50)

THE QUALITY OF MERCY

Nell Mc Cafferty's report from the Dublin District Courts shows the application of the law in practice.

He made his mark on the statement because he's not able to read or write', the guard told District Justice Good in Dublin District Court. 'He's 21 years old and married with two children.'

In the dock sat the defendant, a mild-looking man dressed in his best cheap clothes. He had been caught in the act of breaking into a clothing firm. Convicted and given a suspended sentence. Fingerprints taken had shown he had broken into the same firm the week before, for which offence he was now charged. He had at that time taken some clothes, valued at £44, which he claimed to have subsequently sold in a pub to a stranger.

'Do you know anything about him?' the Justice asked the guard.

'I don't,' said the guard. 'I only came across him on this occasion. I hadn't known him before. Perhaps the solicitor could help.' The solicitor rose to his feet.

'This man and his wife and two young children are living in a flat for which they pay £5.20 a week rent,' he said. 'The only explanation offered by him to me for the commission of this offence is that he was under severe financial strain at this time. He was in receipt of ten pounds a week' unemployment benefit, having stopped work because he had received a bang on the face and was attending hospital.

'He's the sixth eldest in a family of 16 children, Justice. He was 15 when his mother died. From that period on, my client lived in hostels in Dublin and England, where he worked as a labourer.'

'Shortly after they were married and living in Yorkshire, their first child got sick and his wife was worried about it, so they decided to return to Dublin. He works at mending lawnmowers, going round houses and knocking on doors. On days when he gets work he can earn up to five or six pounds a day.'

The Justice wanted to know why the man had broken into the same premises twice.

'I presume he went back a second time because he hadn't been caught the first time,' the solicitor said. He said the man was obviously inexperienced in crime as he hadn't even worn gloves to avoid fingerprints.

'And he went in the same window as the first one he had broken,' said the guard. 'You wouldn't believe the size of it. It was very small. I don't think a child could have gotten in that way.'

'He's very slim,' commented the Justice. He went on to wonder why the man had done these deeds.

'I'd say he was a victim of circumstances. He had no money,' said the guard.

The Justice went on to worry about his claim to have sold the goods in pubs. 'It's an old, old story,' he said. 'It's so old I'm getting sick and tired of it.'

'Well, Mister Solicitor,' said the Justice, 'what do you want of me as regards this man?'

'Well, Justice,' said the solicitor, 'it's not as if he had a long previous record. And he did co-operate with guards. Given his background – his family broken up at an early age, and faring for himself by living in hostels – he has endeavoured to provide for his wife and children.' His wife was in court, he added.

'He couldn't even sign the marriage register,' the Justice snorted.

'That may not have been his fault, given the conditions under which he was reared,' said the solicitor delicately.

'He has no regular occupation to follow,' said the Justice. 'What does he propose to do, assuming I give him a chance?'

'He proposes to continue mending lawn mowers,' said the solicitor. 'Perhaps a Probation Officer could help him?'

The Justice said he was only too happy to put him in the care of a Probation Officer. 'Four people living on that amount of money,' the Justice commented wonderingly.

The Justice decided to impose a six-month suspended sentence and place the man under the care of a Probation Officer. 'I take it his home life is a happy one.'

'Oh it is, Justice. There's no trouble in that line,' said the guard.

'I'm glad to hear that,' said the Justice. 'Well, now, Mr Murphy, the guard has not said anything against you. If anything, he has spoken in your favour, and the solicitor has spoken up for you, and now you have the benefit of a Probation Officer. What more could we do for you?'

Extract from *In the Eyes of the Law* by Nell McCafferty (Abner Stein). Published courtesy of Poolbeg Press.

N.B. Candidates may NOT answer Question A and Question B on the same text.
Question A and B carry 50 marks each.

QUESTION A

(i)   The solicitor gives a brief account of his client's life to the judge. Why, in your opinion, does he include the information he does? (15)

(ii)   Where, in the report, is the attitude of the judge to the defendant most apparent?

        Support your answer with reference to the text. (15)

(iii)   Comment on the appropriateness of the title of the article, 'The Quality of Mercy'. Support your answer with reference to the text. (20)

QUESTION B

'The Quality of Mercy'

Prepare a short talk for early morning radio on the theme of mercy. (50)

IN DETENTION

The following text consists of a visual and a written element. The visual images depict people held in detention. The written text is taken from a report on Newgate Prison written in 1817 by Elizabeth Fry, a Quaker who campaigned for prison reform.

Excerpts from NEWGATE PRISON by Elizabeth Fry

I have just returned from a most melancholy visit to Newgate, where I have been at the request of Elizabeth Fricker [condemned for robbery], previous to her execution tomorrow morning, at eight o'clock. I found her much hurried, distressed and tormented in mind. Her hands cold and covered with something like the perspiration preceding death and in a universal tremor. The women with her said she had been so outrageous before our going that they thought a man must be sent for to manage her. However, after a serious time with her, her troubled soul became calmed. Besides this poor woman there are also six men to be hanged, one of whom has a wife near her confinement, also condemned and six young children. Since the awful report came down he has become quite mad, from horror of mind. A strait waistcoat could not keep him within bounds: he had just bitten the turnkey; I saw the man come out with his hand bleeding, as I passed the cell.

'Excerpts from Newgate Prison' by Elizabeth Fry from *The Faber Book of Reportage* by John Carey, courtesy of Faber and Faber.

N.B. Candidates may NOT answer Question A and Question B on the same text.

Question A and B carry 50 marks each.

QUESTION A

(i)   Taking all the images into account, describe the impact of the visual images upon you. (15)

(ii)   Do you consider Elizabeth Fry's piece to be an effective piece of writing? Explain your answer. (15)

(iii)   If you were invited to add two images to the collection, what images would you suggest? Explain your answer. (20)

QUESTION B

You are one of the people featured in the photographs. Write three or four diary entries that describe your experience. (50)

SECTION II

COMPOSING (100 MARKS)

Write a composition on any **one** of the assignments that appear in **bold print** below.

Each composition carries 100 marks.

The composition assignments are intended to reflect language study in the areas of information, argument, persuasion, narration, and the aesthetic use of language.

1. In TEXT 2, a judge asks a defendant, 'What more could we do for you?'

    Write a short story in which the main character's attempt to help someone who is in trouble leads to unintended consequences.

2. In TEXT 1, Blake Morrison, in thinking about his son's sense of right and wrong, observes that "he says some funny things, this four-year-old of mine".

    Write an article for a school magazine in which you discuss in a serious or a light-hearted way the way in which children understand the world.

3. In TEXT 1, the author writing on the imagination of children, declares, 'Long may it live, this belief in magic.'

    Write a personal essay on the subject of the magic of imagination.

4. In TEXT 2, lack of education, poverty and family circumstances are important in understanding why the defendant is appearing in court charged with theft and breaking and entering.

    Write a speech for a class debate on the motion, 'The law is administered by the rich and punishes the poor.' You can speak for or against the motion.

5. In TEXT 3, Elizabeth Fry paints a shocking picture of a nineteenth century prions.

    Write an article for a popular magazine in which you question the role of prison in Irish society.

6. In TEXT 2, the guard describes the defendant as a victim of circumstances.

    You are the wife of the defendant. Write a series of diary entries in which you reflect on your situation as you and your husband struggle to provide for your children.

7. All the texts deal with issues of justice and right and wrong.

    Write a personal essay in which you consider the most important justice issues which confront face people of your generation.

LEAVING CERTIFICATE EXAMINATION

English – Higher Level – Paper 2

(SAMPLE PAPER 4 (B))

Time Allowed: 3 Hours 20 Minutes

Total Marks: 200

Candidates must attempt the following:
- **ONE** question from SECTION I – The Single Text
- **ONE** question from SECTION II – The Comparative Study
- **ONE** question on the Unseen Poem from SECTION III – Poetry
- **ONE** question on Prescribed Poetry from SECTION III – Poetry

---

N.B. Candidates must answer on Shakespearean Drama.
They may do so in SECTION I, the Single Text (*Hamlet*), or in SECTION II, The Comparative Study (*Hamlet*, *Macbeth*).

INDEX OF SINGLE TEXTS

All the Light We Cannot See

The Crucible

Hamlet

Frankenstein

The Picture of Dorian Gray

SECTION I

THE SINGLE TEXT (60 MARKS)

Candidates must answer **one** question from this section (**A–E**).

A   **ALL THE LIGHT WE CANNOT SEE** – Anthony Doerr

(i)   "Marie-Laure, however much we sympathise with her, is not an heroic character."

Based on your reading of the novel, to what extent do you agree or disagree with the above statement? Explain your answer, giving reasons for your response. Develop your answer with reference to Doerr's novel, *All the Light We Cannot See*.

OR

(ii)   "Resistance, imagination and love are the central themes of *All the Light We Cannot See*."

Based on your reading of the novel, to what extent do you agree or disagree with the above statement? Explain your answer, giving reasons for your response. Develop your answer with reference to Doerr's novel, *All the Light We Cannot See*.

B   **THE CRUCIBLE** – Arthur Miller

(i)   "Discuss the relationship between John and Elizabeth Proctor in the course of the play. Develop your answer with reference to the play, *The Crucible*."

OR

(ii)   "With the exception of Proctor, none of the male characters in the play are admirable."

To what extent do you agree or disagree with this statement? Explain your answer, supporting your argument with suitable reference to the play.

C   HAMLET – William Shakespeare

(i)   "Discuss the relationship between Hamlet and his mother, Gertrude, in the course of the play. Support your answer with reference to the play."

OR

(ii)   "Disease, corruption and death characterise the world of Shakespeare's *Hamlet*."

To what extent do you agree or disagree with this statement? Explain your answer, supporting your argument with suitable reference to the play.

D   FRANKENSTEIN – Mary Shelley

(i)   "Mary Shelley's *Frankenstein* is a chilling exploration of the male desire to control nature and the forces of life and death."

To what extent do you agree or disagree with this statement? Develop your answer with suitable reference to the text of the novel.

OR

(ii)   The creature says that no guilt or misery can be found comparable to his. Do you think this is a fair assessment of his predicament? Develop your answer with suitable reference to the text of the novel.

E   THE PICTURE OF DORIAN GRAY – Oscar Wilde

(i)   Discuss how Wilde's use of language and imagery plays an important part in engaging the reader in the themes explored in the novel. Develop your answer with reference to the text.

OR

(ii)   "What the novel *The Picture of Dorian Gray* reveals is a society obsessed with surface beauty even though it is rotten and corrupt to the core."

Based on your reading of the novel, to what extent do you agree or disagree with this view of Wilde's novel? Explain your answer, giving reasons for your response. Develop your answer with reference to the novel.

SECTION II

THE COMPARATIVE STUDY (70 MARKS)

Candidates must answer **one** question from **either A** – Theme or Issue **or B** – Cultural Context.

In your answer you may not use the text you have answered on in **SECTION I** – The Single Text. All texts used in this section must be prescribed for comparative study for this year's examination. Candidates may refer to only one film in the course of their answers.

Please note:
- Questions in this section use the word **text** to refer to all the different kinds of texts available for study on this course.
- When used, the word **reader** includes viewers of films and theatre audiences.
- When used, the term **technique** is understood to include techniques employed by all writers and directors of films.
- When used, the word **author** is understood to include all writers and directors of films.
- When used, the word **character** is understood to refer to both real people and fictional characters in texts.

A   THEME OR ISSUE

1. "An important theme or issue is best explored through the lives of memorable characters."

Compare the texts you have studied in your comparative course in the light of the above statement. Your discussion should focus on **one character in each of the texts**. Develop your response with reference to your chosen texts. (70)

OR

2. "The treatment of an important theme by the author of a text can affect a reader in a profound way."

(a) Discuss the extent to which you were or were not affected by the treatment of a theme in **one** of the texts on your comparative study. Identify the theme and support your response with reference to the text. (30)

(b) Compare the extent to which you were or were not affected by the treatment of the same theme in the **other two texts** on your comparative study. Develop your response with reference to your chosen texts. (40)

B   CULTURAL CONTEXT

1.   "Class, race or gender can influence a character's prospects of happiness in the cultural context of a text."

   (a) Discuss the extent to which attitudes to class, race or gender impacted on the happiness of a central character in the cultural context in **one** text on your comparative course. You should confine your discussion to **one of the issues**, class, race or gender. Support your answer with reference to your chosen text. (30)

   (b) Compare the extent to which the happiness of a central character, from the **two other** texts on your comparative course, was affected by the attitudes to one of the issues (class, race or gender) in the cultural context in these texts. In response to 1. (b) you may refer to the same or a different issue as that discussed in 1. (a) above. (40)

OR

2.   In relation to **the three** texts on your comparative study course, compare the extent to which the pursuit of individual freedom was tolerated within the cultural context of the world of the text. Develop your response with reference to your chosen texts. (70)

SECTION III

POETRY (70 MARKS)

Candidates must answer **A** – Unseen Poem **and B** – Prescribed Poetry.

A   **UNSEEN POEM** (20 marks)

Answer **either** Question 1 **or** Question 2

The poem records the reaction of a father to the birth of his son. The poem is the final sonnet in a sequence on houses and homes.

Natural Son

Before the spectacled professor snipped
The cord, I heard your birth-cry flood the ward,
And lowered your mother's tortured head, and wept.
The house you'd left would need to be restored.

No worse pain could be borne, to bear the joy
Of seeing you come in a slow dive from the womb,
Pushed from your fluid home, pronounced 'a boy'
You'll never find so well equipped a room.

No house we build could ever hope to satisfy
Every small need, now that you've made this move
To share our loneliness, much as we try
Our vocal skill to wall you round with love.

This day you crave so little, we so much
For you to live, who need our merest touch.

Richard Murphy

From The Price of Stones (Gaber, 1985). Reproduced by permission of Faber & Faber Ltd.

---

1.   (a) Describe the feelings of the father on the birth of his son. Develop your answer with reference to the poem. (10)

   (b) Select an image or phrase that you think is particularly striking. Explain your choice. (10)

OR

2.   Write a personal response to the poem, describing its impact on you. Support your answer with reference to the poem. (20)

SAMPLE P4 (B)

SECTION III (Continued)

B   **PRESCRIBED POETRY** (50 marks)

Candidates must answer **one** of the following questions (**1–4**).

---

1.   **G. M. Hopkins**

"Hopkins's original style expresses both his joy in nature and his religious doubts."

Based on your experience of reading the poetry of G. M. Hopkins, to what extent do you agree or disagree with this statement? Support your answer with reference to the poetry of Hopkins on your course.

2.   **Paula Meehan**

"Whether she is celebrating family or expressing outrage at social injustice, Paula Meehan's poetry is characterised by vivid imagery and her energetic use of language."

To what extent is this your experience of reading the poetry of Paula Meehan? Develop your answer with reference to the poetry of Paula Meehan on your course.

3.   **Eiléan Ní Chuilleanáin**

"Using subtle and mysterious imagery, Ní Chuilleanáin's poetry explores themes of love, family and history."

Discuss the extent to which you agree or disagree with the above statement, developing your answer with reference to the poetry of Eiléan Ní Chuilleanáin on your course.

4.   **W. B. Yeats**

"Passion and detachment compete in Yeats's poetry, as the poet meditates on personal and public matters."

Based on your reading of the poetry of W. B. Yeats, discuss the extent to which you agree or disagree with this statement. Develop your response with reference to the poems by W. B. Yeats on your course.

Edco EXAM PAPERS

The Complete Range for Leaving Certificate!

Exam Extras

> Updated Guide to Better Grades
> Exam Analysis Charts
> Study Planners and lots more...

edcoexampapers.ie

Ireland's No.1 Exam Papers

FREE ONLINE SOLUTIONS
Tutorials & Exam Advice
www.e-xamit.ie
*with selected papers

Available from your Local Bookshop
The Educational Company of Ireland

//:DON'T REPLY/
KEEP THE MESSAGE/
BLOCK THE SENDER/
TELL SOMEONE YOU TRUST://

WWW.WATCHYOURSPACE.IE

Don't Accept Bullying

This Anti-Bullying campaign is supported by the Department of Education and Skills with the co-operation of the Irish Educational Publishers Association.